A MAYOR FOR ALL
THE PEOPLE

Robert C. Holmes

February 12, 2020

A MAYOR FOR ALL THE PEOPLE

Kenneth Gibson's Newark

EDITED BY ROBERT C. HOLMES AND RICHARD W. ROPER

RUTGERS UNIVERSITY PRESS
NEW BRUNSWICK, CAMDEN, AND NEWARK, NEW JERSEY,
AND LONDON

Library of Congress Cataloging-in-Publication Data

Names: Holmes, Robert C., approximately 1944- editor. | Roper, Richard W., editor. | Coleman, Bonnie Watson, writer of foreword.
Title: A mayor for all the people : Kenneth Gibson's Newark
/ edited by Robert C. Holmes and Richard W. Roper.
Other titles: Reflections on the Kenneth A. Gibson era in Newark, 1970–1986
Description: New Brunswick, NJ : Rutgers University Press, [2019] | Includes bibliographical references and index.
Identifiers: LCCN 2018055406 | ISBN 9780813598765 (cloth : alk. paper)
Subjects: LCSH: Gibson, Kenneth A. | Mayors—New Jersey—Newark—Biography. | Newark (N.J.)—Politics and government—20th century. | African American mayors—New Jersey—Newark—Biography. | Newark (N.J.)—Economic conditions—20th century. | Newark (N.J.)—Social conditions—20th century. | Urban renewal—New Jersey—Newark. | Interviews—New Jersey—Newark. | Newark (N.J.)—Biography.
Classification: LCC F144.N653 G53 2019 | DDC 974.9/043092 [B]—dc23
LC record available at https://lccn.loc.gov/2018055406

A British Cataloging-in-Publication record for this book is available from the British Library.

www.rutgersuniversitypress.org

Manufactured in the United States of America

CONTENTS

Foreword by U.S. Representative
Bonnie Watson Coleman   IX
Preface by Robert C. Holmes   XIII

Introduction: How Should We Measure
the Historical Significance of the Kenneth Gibson
Era in Newark?   1
Robert C. Holmes

1   On Being First   41
Mayor David Norman Dinkins
Lieutenant Governor Sheila Oliver
Mayor Patricia Sheehan

2   Navigating Racial Politics   49
Fred Means
Barbara Kukla
Martin Bierbaum
Mayor Sharpe James
State Senator Ronald Rice
Fran Adubato
Sheldon Bross, Esq.
Elizabeth "Liz" Del Tufo
Robert "Bob" Pickett, Esq.
Marie Villani
Steve Adubato Jr.
Harold Hodes
Grizel Ubarry
Junius Williams, Esq.
Charles I. Auffant, Esq.

3   Friends and Family   104
    Elton E. Hill
    Harold Gibson
    Camille Savoca Gibson

4   Trying to Make City Government Work   111
    Rev. James A. Scott
    Diane Johnson
    James "Jack" Krauskopf
    Dennis Cherot
    Phillip Elberg, Esq.
    Robert C. Holmes, Esq.
    Richard W. Roper
    Jerome Harris
    Lawrence "Larry" Hamm
    Vicki Donaldson
    Hubert Williams, Esq.
    Alan Zalkind
    Roger Lowenstein, Esq.

5   An In-Depth Look inside City Government:
    Mayor Gibson's Right-Hand Man   166
    David Dennison

6   Working with the Anchor Institutions   178
    Al Koeppe
    Vincente Perez
    Richard Cammarieri
    Monsignor William Linder
    Saul Fenster
    Zachary "Zach" Yamba
    Gene Vincenti
    Frank Askin, Esq.
    George Hampton

7   Forces beyond Control   208
    Brendan "Dan" O'Flaherty
    Jon Dubin, Esq.

8   Mayor Gibson Reflects   225

    Conclusion: Gibson's Legacy—
    The Man, the Time, and the Place,
    1970–1986   240
    Richard W. Roper

Afterword by Robert C. Holmes   287
Notes on Contributors   291
Index   313

FOREWORD

U.S. Representative Bonnie Watson Coleman

There are moments in life that one never forgets. You will recall with clarity where you were, what you were doing, and how you felt at the time. Some of these moments are private and celebratory, such as the birth of a grandchild or the college graduation of someone dear to you. Others are public and painful, such as the assassinations of Dr. Martin Luther King Jr. and John F. Kennedy. And then there is that third category for a watershed event that marks a historical turning point and has long-term implications for the future. The election of Barack Obama as the forty-fourth president of the United States is a prime example. And from my perspective, the election of Kenneth A. Gibson as the first African American mayor of New Jersey's largest city also falls into that latter category.

Gibson's election in 1970 felt like a victory for the African American community of Newark and beyond. It was a notable win for justice and equality, and it heralded the start of healing in a city that had experienced considerable racial turmoil. His election helped usher in active participation in elective politics by the nation's racial and ethnic minorities. But inspiring as his electoral victory was, Gibson's departure from office sixteen years later was even more so. He left after having served with competence and integrity.

Now, nearly forty years later, as the first African American woman from New Jersey elected to the U.S. Congress, I appreciate the challenge and the pressure Ken Gibson surely faced in his role as "the first." Being first is both a blessing and a curse. In the political realm, your electoral success is an inspiration to your racial group, but as Gibson often said, once elected, you must serve *all* of your constituents—not just those who helped you. Accordingly, you must always be mindful of your responsibility to faithfully represent your total constituency while being respectful of the hopes and dreams of those whose sacrifice made your election possible. This is the delicate balance that every elected official struggles to maintain daily. It is particularly challenging for those of us blessed to be "the first" and is a hallmark of the Ken Gibson story.

There are over thirty-five thousand cities and towns in the United States, and over the course of American history, there have been millions of people elected as mayors. For the most part, these individuals are chosen by the people, serve their time in office, and then simply move on without leaving an indelible mark on history. This scenario applies to all but a handful of elected officials. A good case can be made for Gibson as one of the exceptions.

This book explores the significance of the election and sixteen-year tenure of Gibson as Newark's mayor and the first African American mayor of a major Northeastern city. As the editors point out, the election was undoubtedly a watershed moment in Newark's history. They have assembled an extraordinary collection of reflections by a diverse group of individuals who were asked to comment on the man and the period—described as the "Gibson era"—with very little prompting or guidance. Taken together, these reflections are not just evocative memories of a bygone era. They are also a collective commentary on the effect of that era on current conditions in Newark, the state of New Jersey, and the nation.

There are, for example, myriad references to the spawning of productive and distinguished careers. The city continues to control valuable assets such as the airport, the seaport, and vast watershed lands. Newark Public Radio still operates the region's most prominent public radio station, and some of the state's largest enterprises continue to maintain their corporate headquarters in Newark.

This book can serve as a valuable guide for mayors and other elected officials as to what types of actions and decisions really matter in the long run. Historians and social scientists will find a rich new source of material for their consideration of the Gibson legacy. And anyone with an interest in politics should be curious to see which impressions of those who were there last over time. Readers will find interesting, as I did, a comparison between the Gibson legacy as described by Gibson and the Gibson legacy as depicted in the reflections of this diverse group of contributors.

Kenneth Allen Gibson was reelected in 1974, 1978, and 1982. It is clear from this book that we continue to speak about the man in the present tense. Perhaps that alone provides sufficient proof of his historic significance.

PREFACE

Robert C. Holmes

In 2016, the celebration of Newark's 350th anniversary was punctuated with a recalling of historic and watershed events and periods and the people who made a difference in each case. Watershed events and periods are not necessarily historic. To rise to the level of the historic, an event or period must go beyond its momentary effect and represent a defining or pivotal moment, a turning point, or a major change in what people think or do about something; it must have great and lasting importance, whether that be for good or bad.

There can be little question that the election in 1970 of Kenneth Gibson as the first African American mayor of Newark, New Jersey, and of any major Northeastern city was—at least—a watershed event. The event transitioned Newark from three hundred years of white political leadership and changed how a rapidly growing African American population thought about its position in the city and affected its expectations. Also, it created the potential for generations of people of color to aspire to and reach positions of influence and authority in both the public and private sectors of society. So we agree with Congresswoman Coleman in her foreword when she makes a claim for Mayor Gibson's "historic significance." The questions for us quickly became: What is the nature and depth of the historical impact of the Gibson era? How can we, as former Gibson administration insiders, take advantage of that status without presenting a biased or unrealistically positive portrayal of the man or his impact on the times? Through further exploration, we eventually settled on an approach that would center on the reflections of those people who had an important connection to Newark at the time.

The story behind this book begins with a conversation George Hampton and I had with Ken Gibson in the spring of 2016. Along with my coeditor, Richard Roper, George and I worked in the initial Gibson administration after his election in 1970, and we have stayed in touch as friends of the mayor ever since. At the time of our meeting, two books had recently been released that included significant reference to Gibson's years as mayor and to his legacy. Both books, written by campaign official Robert Curvin and administration-insider Junius Williams, were highly negative in their assessments of the mayor. Still, George and I felt that Gibson was less disheartened by the negative tone of the assessments than he was by the fact that no one had yet written a book that attempted to balance what he failed to accomplish with what, in fact, he did accomplish.

Before we even considered working on a book, George and I agreed that neither of us was interested in an enterprise that would serve only to balance the good with the bad. So we determined to do some further preliminary research; we created two separate platforms to further explore Gibson's legacy. First, we invited a group of African American men to join us in a gathering—with Ken—at the home of Clement Price, noted historian and chairman of the history department at Rutgers University–Newark. Price's home in the Lincoln Park section of Newark has served as a meeting place over the years for various groups seeking to explore issues related to the condition of the African American community. Second, we organized a symposium to explore the Gibson era.

The gathering at Price's house included Richard Roper, Jerome Harris, Harold Lucas, Ralph Grant, Richard Monteith, Dr. Zach Yamba, Dr. Harold Davis, Mark Alexander, Bob Pickett, and authors of books about Mayor Gibson, Dr. Robert Curvin, and Junius Williams. The willing participation of Curvin and Williams signaled to George and me that

The gathering at the home of Clement Price. First row, left to right: Clement Price, Robert (Bob) Curvin, and Kenneth Gibson. Second row, left to right: Richard Monteith, Richard Roper, Zachary Yamba, Jerome Harris, Ralph Grant, Robert Holmes, Mark Alexander, Harold Lucas, and Dr. William Owen. Third row, left to right: Junius Williams, Dr. Harold Davis, George Hampton, and Robert Pickett.

Gibson's historical interest persisted for them despite their mostly negative assessments. At the event, which coincided with the Newark's 350th anniversary, as we went around the room with individual reflections about the man, it became more and more apparent to us that there was a great deal more to be said than had been written. Zach Yamba, former president of Essex County College, described Ken's role in keeping the former Newark Community College in Newark. Mark Alexander, son of the nation's first African American secretary of the army, Clifford Alexander, described childhood memories of conversations at his family's dinner table about the significance of the 1970 election in Newark. Ralph Grant, a former African American member of the Newark municipal council, described Ken's courage and perseverance in confronting a majority-white city council. Inspired by these reflections, the idea of collecting a broad and diverse series of reflections concerning the Gibson era took hold. We thought that, perhaps, we could compile ideas from people who were there at the time as a way of presenting a different kind of story, not a typical history but a kind of quasi-history or tapestry, presented in bits and pieces through the memories of the participants. We hoped that this approach would both satisfy a search for a balanced view of the Gibson era and allow the overall picture to emerge in a way that was not influenced by our personal feelings.

The symposium, held on October 7, 2016, continued the idea of seeking reflections by individuals who had been exposed in some way to the Gibson era. By this time, Richard Roper, who had also played a role in the early days of the Gibson administration, was fully on board as an editor. The panel was moderated by George and included me, New Jersey Lt. Gov. Sheila Oliver, former Newark police director Hubert Williams, and housing consultant Grizel Ubarry. In addition to comments from panelists, comments were also received from audience members. The mayor was present throughout the symposium. Both the participants and the highly interested audience provided copious insights and anecdotes—both positive and negative.

Following the symposium, the team—Richard, George, and I—discussed ways to gather, publish, and promote the various reflections we envisioned. Together, we were struck with the idea that our collected networks could provide access to a unique and diverse collection of important observations. We then gained the support of Rutgers University Press, and here we are.

The reflections contained in this book were not elicited, edited, or organized to point to a particular conclusion about Mayor Kenneth Gibson and his era. We encouraged our contributors to reflect on whatever they wanted and to express it as they wished. Their reflections are edited for clarity and conciseness only. Each individual story is capable of capturing a reader's interest while informing the reader about the period 1970–1986 in the city of Newark. By compiling reminiscences, we believe that we have put together the first truly balanced view of the Gibson years and the Gibson legacy. We hope that the reader experiences some of the same surprise, inspiration, frustration, and understanding that we gained from compiling these reflections. Beyond that, we expect that the story of the Gibson era has important implications for all our cities and our nation as a whole.

The book highlights Gibson's struggle to regain some semblance of Newark's once-prominent status as a Northeastern industrial powerhouse as its private sector contracted, its tax base eroded, middle-income residents—both black and white—abandoned the city, and the poor multiplied. The book concludes by suggesting that as with Barack Obama, America's first African American president, perhaps expectations of what Gibson could accomplish as a leader of a declining Rust-Belt city were unrealistic. Indeed, Gibson's place in history may ultimately be shaped by the simple fact that he was a "first" and possibly by whether his commitment to being "mayor of all the people" of Newark was ever achieved.

We would like to acknowledge the New Jersey Public Policy Research Institute (NJPPRI) for financial support that is consistent with the NJPPRI's mission of raising issues for discussion that are of importance to New Jersey's African American community. We would also like to acknowledge the generous financial support provided by the Fund for New Jersey.

As noted earlier, George Hampton is a principle and invaluable team member without whose great effort the book would not be possible.

Early in the process, we enlisted the help of William Tiersten, our editorial partner, who became a fourth team member as he put in many hours and helped shape our thoughts and writing into the present volume. Thanks to Dirk Van Susteren and Sylvia Tiersten for outside editorial support.

Thanks to my clinical assistant Kaiwan Perez.

We gratefully acknowledge the Celebrate Newark 350th Committee for financial support and for making our project part of the celebration.

Many thanks to the contributors who took time out of their busy lives to provide us with their reflections on what each of them saw as an important time in both their lives and the story of Newark.

We appreciate the support of the New Jersey Black Issues Convention and its chairman, Jerome Harris, for sponsoring the symposium.

Special thanks to George Hawley, Supervising Librarian and Beth Zak-Cohen, Librarian of the Charles F. Cummings New Jersey Information Center, Newark Public Library, for access to their photography collection.

Thanks to the New Jersey Historical Society for its assistance with our research and to the City of Newark archivist, Jose DeSilva.

Thanks, of course, to Lucy Holmes and Marlene Roper.

Finally, thanks to Mayor Kenneth A. Gibson for encouraging us to move forward in the way we saw fit and making himself available without ever attempting to influence our project.

Newark, New Jersey
March 2018

A MAYOR FOR ALL
THE PEOPLE

INTRODUCTION

HOW SHOULD WE MEASURE THE HISTORICAL
SIGNIFICANCE OF THE KENNETH GIBSON ERA IN NEWARK?

Robert C. Holmes

THE GIBSON ERA: A SEA CHANGE?

In his play *The Tempest*, Shakespeare gave us the now commonly used idiom "sea change" to indicate a notable transformation in human affairs.[1] So it seems fair to ask, Did the Gibson era represent a sea change in the affairs of the city of Newark? Did these events change the way people outside of Newark viewed the city? Did Newark residents begin to view their city differently? And more specifically, we ask questions such as: Did the Gibson legacy change hiring practices in Newark? How was the ethnic power structure affected going forward? Were relationships changed among the various power sectors of the city such as the business and academic communities and the state and county governments? And so on.

In *The Tempest*, when Miranda, the daughter of the magician Prospero, first sees her future husband, she famously exclaims, "O brave new world."[2] In the heady first days of African American political power in Newark, residents and observers might have at least hoped for a better and fairer form of government and civic life—that is, a brave new world. So we ask, Was this promise fulfilled? Or did Newark continue on—or reenter—a downward path more comparable to Aldous Huxley's treatment of Shakespeare's

1

famous phrase in his novel—*Brave New World*—about a dystopian future society?³ And what does all this point to for Newark today?

For us to answer any of these questions, we need to recognize that Kenneth Gibson rose to power in Newark at a unique moment in history that allowed him at least the opportunity to shape history. One of the greatest figures of this period, Dr. Martin Luther King Jr., once said in a sermon that "we are not the makers of history; we are made by history."⁴ Given the example of King's own historic importance, clearly it would be a mistake to suggest that his quotation implies the need to passively accept history's dictates. Rather, it suggests to us that King understood that history provided unique opportunities for certain individuals to distinguish themselves by challenging the status quo. This interpretation gains support when we see, in the same sermon, King's reference to Henry Wadsworth Longfellow's precept that men are either hammers or anvils.⁵ Clearly, those who strive to make a difference might turn out to be the hammers that shape the times to come. King's view aligns with that of Gordon S. Wood, a professor at Brown University and the Pulitzer Prize–winning author of *The Radicalism of the American Revolution*, from a piece that ranks the historical importance of individuals in the *Atlantic*.⁶ Professor Wood suggests that undeniably historic people, such as Abraham Lincoln and George Washington, were "peculiar personalities" who were "ideally suited for the moment in which they wielded significant and lasting influence."⁷ Similarly, in the *Atlantic* piece, Professor David Kennedy defines the efforts of "originals" as "laying a foundation for enduring institutions or cultural practices or ways of thinking."⁸

But was Ken Gibson uniquely suited for the challenges of the time, as Professor Wood suggests was the case for Abraham Lincoln at the time of Civil War or George Washington at the time of the nation's struggle for independence? Or is it that historic times inevitably produce historically significant individuals? It may be the case, for example, that Rudy Giuliani, mayor of New York from 1994 to 2001, earned his place among historic figures solely because of his handling of the horrific events that

unfolded on September 11, 2001. We have compiled a group of reflections on the time from people who were in Newark during Gibson's
administration—appointed and elected officials, mayoral aides, activists,
and others who had an important connection to the city. These reflections
will shed some light on the questions raised.

We will look to the reflections to see whether Gibson left any evidence
signaling his lasting impact on specific issues and populations in Newark and whether his impact, for good or ill, can be measured beyond his
own era. As for Gibson's own era, one might have brought to mind the
famous slogan/question of one of Gibson's contemporaries and a fellow
Newarker—namely, New York City mayor Ed Koch: "How am I doing?"
We are clear, as Mayor Koch should have been too, that the answer to this
question depends entirely on to whom it is asked. Progress and social
change are, to a large extent, in the immediate eyes of the beholder but
can also take years, if not generations, to materialize. By pulling together
the memories of many of the people who played key roles in Newark at the
time, we hope to reveal the historic significance of the Gibson era.

A Brief History: Key Figures in Newark's Past

Like other places, the city of Newark's history might be recalled by considering its people.[9] Using this approach, Newark's history begins with
the founding of the city in 1666 by Connecticut Puritans—most notably,
Robert Treat. Names associated with Newark's nineteenth-century industrial growth period include Seth Boyden, the prolific producer of leather
and malleable iron; John Wesley Hyatt, producer of the first commercially
successful plastic celluloid; Dr. Edward Weston, the man who perfected
a process for zinc electroplating; and Thomas Edison, whose inventions
changed people's everyday lives. During the same century, Newark began
its movement toward becoming one of the nation's most important insurance centers, thanks largely to the founding of the Prudential insurance
company by John Fairfield Dryden in 1875.

Thirty-seven years later, Louis Bamberger built the flagship store in Newark, the first link in his famous Bamberger's department store chain. Bamberger contributed further to society and to Newark's history when, through the Bamberger Broadcasting Service, he established the WOR radio station and began operating the station from the sixth floor of the Newark store.

Eleven years after Bamberger built his flagship store in Newark, another commerce leader, Sebastian S. Kresge, catering to the city's upper-middle-class clientele, located his flagship store in the downtown. Kresge saw Newark as a retail hub; he also was interested in the city's potential for other types of commercial development. He started, for example, laying the groundwork for what was much later to become the Gateway Center.[10]

But even more prominent than Kresge in the realm of development were Samuel Lefcourt and Ludwig Mies van der Rohe. In 1960, Mies van der Rohe designed the Pavilion and Colonnade Apartments. Early in the twentieth century, Lefcourt built one of Newark's most iconic buildings, the Raymond Commerce Building. That building today, known as 1180 Raymond Boulevard, is emblematic of Newark's slow but steady renaissance with the return of middle-class residents to the downtown.

Just a few other names naturally associated with the history of Newark include: former New Jersey poet laureate and civil rights activist Amiri Baraka, literary icon Philip Roth, jazz great Sarah Vaughan, and the first president of the public utility later to become PSE&G, Thomas McCarter.

A different kind of historic legacy can be derived as well from the ill that others wrought upon the city. Such individuals might include Abner "Longie" Zwillman, the "Capone of New Jersey"; crime boss Richie "the Boot" Boiardo; drug kingpin Wayne Akbar Pray; and the notorious Campisi crime family.

In the context of Newark's 350-year-plus history, we would, without hesitation, ascribe historic significance to all the aforementioned individuals not because of their fame or the mere fact that they were born or conducted business in Newark but because they left a lasting impression, for good or ill. What place in history is there for Kenneth Gibson, the first African American mayor of Newark and of any major Northeastern city?

KENNETH ALLEN GIBSON—A BRIEF BIO[11]

Who was Kenneth Gibson?

He was born in Enterprise, Alabama, in 1932. He and his parents, Willie and Daisy Gibson, and his younger brother, Harold, moved to Newark in 1940. The move, occasioned by Willie obtaining a job at the Swift packaging plant in nearby Kearny, New Jersey, saw the family settle in Newark's predominantly African American Third Ward, now the city's Central Ward. Ken's parents enrolled the boys in the local public schools. Ken attended Monmouth Street Elementary School, Cleveland Junior High School, and Central High School. Ken graduated from Central High School in 1950 and enrolled that year in Newark College of Engineering (NCE) but dropped out before graduating because of money problems. At age eighteen, he married Ann Mason and began supporting himself and his wife. Like his father, Ken worked at the Swift plant before landing a job with the New Jersey State Highway Department. He reenrolled in NCE as an evening student in September 1952, but his education was again interrupted when, in 1956, he began serving in the U.S. Army, stationed in Hawaii with the Sixty-Fifth Engineer Battalion. Upon his return to Newark in 1958, he resumed classes at NCE and graduated in 1962 with a bachelor's degree in civil engineering.

One of only a few African Americans in the civil engineering field, Ken advanced his career after graduation by becoming the chief engineer for the Newark Housing Authority. He then became, in 1966, the chief structural engineer for the City of Newark, a position he held until 1970, when he became the city's thirty-sixth mayor.

By this point in his life, he was the father of three girls, JoAnn and Cheryl by his first wife, and Joyce, the daughter of Muriel Cook, his second wife.

Like so many African Americans, Gibson gained a new sense of politics during the 1960s. During this period, he was active in several community organizations. He was a member of the Urban League and the NAACP and was widely recognized as a community leader. In 1964, he was selected as an outstanding alumnus by the NCE and also was named as Man of the Year by the Newark Junior Chamber of Commerce. He was drawn into politics through his civil rights activism and by his involvement in campaigns for equal job opportunities.

In 1966, just six weeks before the Newark mayoral election, Gibson entered that race as one of four candidates. His campaign helped raise the political consciousness of the city's black community, while his relatively strong showing—16 percent of the total vote—suggested that the black political leadership had matured. While Gibson's predecessor, Hugh Addonizio, was successful in his reelection bid, the signs of Addonizio's demise were evident in the fact that a runoff was required to achieve that success. Four years later, the black community, composing by that time approximately 50 percent of the city's voters, would assert itself and elect a black man as Addonizio's successor. Gibson, one of seven candidates, won in a runoff.

OUR APPROACH

In looking at the reflections of individuals who played important roles in Newark at the time, we take some cues from three particular efforts at rating a person's historical impact: (1) the 2006 article in the *Atlantic* that asked ten eminent historians to reflect on who are the most influential figures in American history, (2) a 2013 article in which *Time* attempted to identify history's most significant people,[12] and (3) a 1999 study by Penn State University that rated the best and the worst big-city mayors.[13]

Each of the ratings had its own methodology.

The *Atlantic*, for example, instructed historians to interpret "influence loosely," considering a person's impact, for good or ill, both on his or her own era and on the way "we live now."[14] In addition to the aforementioned Professors Wood and Kennedy, the magazine went to Ellen Fitzpatrick, a professor at the University of New Hampshire and author of *History's Memory: Writing America's past, 1880–1980*. Professor Fitzpatrick sees the central question as whether the person's influence "was at once 'long term' and 'fundamental.'"[15] Under this view, Bill Gates would be considered to have less historic significance than John von Neumann "because it was von Neumann's research that helped make computing possible, and so his contribution to the computer was more 'fundamental' than Gates's work."[16] Many of the historians contributing to the *Atlantic* study categorically include "political figures" as poised for significant and lasting influence "precisely because they influence the lives of everybody."[17] Historian Doris Kearns Goodwin, Pulitzer Prize–winning author of *No Ordinary Time: Franklin and Eleanor Roosevelt: The Home Front in World War II*, suggested the key inquiry should be "which figure changed the daily lives of people."[18]

Time decided "to not approach the project the way historians might, through a principled assessment of their individual achievements."[19] *Time* instead "evaluated each person by aggregating millions of traces of opinions into a computational data-centric analysis."[20] *Time* based its analysis on a finding that "historically significant figures leave statistical evidence of their presence behind, if one knows where to look for it."[21]

We look for such evidence of the historic significance of the Gibson years through the unprompted recollections of a diverse group of individuals. Because these individuals were directly involved with or influenced by Mayor Gibson, we do not have to mine the past to the degree that *Time* did in its effort. Thus we take what we believe is a justified shortcut in finding our traces by considering the reflections of individuals who still distinctly recall the Gibson years.

As with the *Atlantic* study, we admit to our bias toward political figures in general. Although big-city mayors may not be history's most famous figures, we argue that an examination of mayors provides fodder for significant historical reflection. Once again, following a lead from *Time*, we are sensitive to the way that historic significance differs from fame or popularity. *Time* notes, for example, that a little-heralded U.S. president like Chester A. Arthur is nonetheless more historically significant than the famous and very popular singer Justin Bieber.[22]

The Penn State study of the best and worst American mayors indicates to us that we may rate mayors against one another through comparisons among those who faced similar challenges. We note again that determining historical significance does not necessarily imply a value judgment as to good or bad. Yet, informed by the Penn State approach, we allow for such a judgment.

Topping *Times*'s list of "best" mayors was Fiorello La Guardia, who served as mayor of New York from 1934 to 1945. The most often-cited element of LaGuardia's tenure that caused contributors to give him top billing was the change he brought about in the perception of ethnic politicians and corrupt politicians as being one and the same.[23] Penn State has as its worst mayor William H. "Big Bill" Thompson of Chicago, who served from 1915 to 1923 and again from 1927 to 1931.[24] The grade was based primarily on Chicago's reputation for corruption at the time. We aren't the first and won't be the last to mention politicians from Chicago and New Jersey in the same breath. Thus we mention number two on the same study's worst-mayors list: Frank Hague, who served as mayor of Jersey City,[25] with which Newark shares a border, from 1917 to 1947.[26] Like Thompson, Hague's historic significance is based primarily on the negative impact his corrupt practices and abuse of power had on the reputation of Jersey City.

THE HISTORICAL MOMENT

Based on the preceding approach, we need to ask whether Mayor Gibson was well suited to the time and place in which he wielded influence. At the time Kenneth Gibson began his political life, there were four powerful historical forces that were shaping Newark's history: (1) the civil rights movement, (2) the creation of severe racial tensions and divisions, (3) mounting frustration among African American residents with rapidly declining living conditions and the rebellion that the frustration engendered, and (4) the establishment of centers of African American power. As Newark both felt the effects of these forces and responded to them in its own particular way, it also had to contend with an increasingly negative image—deserved or not—that was being etched in the public consciousness by powerful public-opinion shapers such as the *New York Times*.

Fred Cook, writing in the *New York Times* in July 1971, one year after Gibson's election as mayor, posited that Newark is a study in the evils, tensions, and frustrations that beset the central cities of America. He offers the following characterization:

> It is a city of 375,000: an estimated 61% Negro, and 11% Puerto Rican. It is a city with an over-all unemployment rate of 14% (25% to 30% among Blacks and Puerto Ricans). Around 25% of those who are employed work only part time, and there are virtually no summer jobs and few programs for the city's 80,000 school children, who now roam the streets. As a result, one of every three Newarkers is getting some form of public assistance. There are, by conservative estimate, 20,000 drug addicts in the city, and only 7% of them are being treated. Newark has the highest crime rate of any city in the nation; the highest percentage of substandard housing; and the highest infant mortality rate. Most of these rates, like crime, are still rising.[27]

There is no dispute that Newark had its share of racial, ethnic, economic, and social challenges at the time of Gibson's election. The effects of suburbanization and racial tensions constrained Newark's ability to meet the needs of its growing poor, minority population. And like other

industrial cities in the North and Midwest, increasing poverty, declining manufacturing activity, an eroding tax base, and a rapidly expanding
social welfare sector defined the position and prospects of this former
industrial powerhouse.

Cook's depiction of Newark, while perhaps overly harsh, would become
the *New York Times*'s and most other media outlets' standard description
of Newark's condition in the years following the 1967 rebellion. Editorialist
and author Robert Curvin writes about his hometown:

> For Newark, perched along the Passaic River and founded in 1666 by
> Puritans from Connecticut, those five days in July 1967 would deep-
> ly change city life and politics. This one piece of history would also
> change how Newark would be perceived by the rest of the nation,
> not only as a city in decline, but one, by all appearances, incapable of
> recovery. In fact, no other American city scarred by racial unrest had
> subsequent reporting about its prospects framed by that unrest as
> much as was the case with Newark. Well into the 21st Century, the
> 1967 Newark uprising would be the lens used by the media in virtu-
> ally all reporting about the city. Ken Gibson, while not the first mayor
> to contend with a city on the ropes, was the first to shoulder the bur-
> den of confronting the challenges of revival under the harsh light of
> not just the nation's leading newspaper, but all aspects of its media.[28]

The Civil Rights Movement[29]

The civil rights movement engendered a major rise in African American
political consciousness, contributed to increasing electoral participation
among African Americans, and produced a new breed of powerful African American leaders who rose to power at this difficult political time.[30]
The movement also brought along the support of a sizable segment of
the white population who supported African American participation
in politics as part of the African American struggle for equal rights in

America.[31] Not coincidentally, the struggle for equal rights occurred at a time when living conditions for inner-city African Americans had reached a historic—and nearly hopeless—low point. *Newsweek* commented on the first generation of African American mayors of major U.S. cities this way: "History has played another cruel joke on the Negroes. The mantle of power now finally within their reach, may no longer be adequate to the problems that come with it."[32]

While America's inner cities were similarly slipping into the condition described in the *Newsweek* article, they did not arrive there on precisely the same path or timetable. Differences can be noted by focusing on cities that elected first-time African American mayors at about the same time as Gibson's election in Newark. Such cities would include Gary, Indiana, where Richard Hatcher was inaugurated in 1967; Cleveland, Ohio, where Carl Stokes was inaugurated in 1968; and Detroit, Michigan, where Coleman Young was inaugurated in 1970.

In each of the four cities, the loss of a large portion of the city's middle-class population, both black and white, left the city vulnerable to economic decline. To be sure, this middle-class and mostly "white" flight from America's inner cities began long before the electability of the cities' first black mayors. After World War II, out-migration increased across American cities, spurred by publicly supported policies and opportunities encouraging relocation to the nation's suburbs for those who were financially able to do so. Such policies and opportunities included the construction of improved highway systems and the GI Bill providing access to college and to low-interest mortgage loans. Further contributing to this situation was action by the Federal Housing Administration—namely, redlining, which is the practice of denying services to a particular group or within a particular geographic area generally based on race or ethnicity. And finally, adding to these factors was a tax structure that favored the construction of new factories in the suburbs over the rehabilitation of old factories in the city. Due to these pressures, Newark and other inner cities were evolving into cities of ethnic ghettos and slums.

Even earlier, the Great Depression brought about a steady flow of man-ufacturers leaving the cities and taking their jobs with them. The flight of the middle class was, on the other hand, not the only factor contribut-ing to urban decline and to the formidable challenges facing select cities' first-time-elected black mayors.

An early 1970s recession combined with two rounds of a gas crisis (1973 and 1979) had a devastating impact on Detroit's primary industry—the manufacture of motor vehicles. As gas prices continued to rise, consumers began to demand smaller, more fuel-efficient vehicles, mostly by foreign automakers. Detroit was also the site of the most costly race-based rebel-lion in U.S. history with the occurrence of the "Twelfth Street Riot" in 1967.

Like Newark and Detroit, Gary was once a thriving industrial hub. In Gary's case, the principal industry involved the production of steel, pri-marily in the mills of U.S. Steel. Again, similar to Newark, an abundance of jobs resulted in Gary becoming an ethnic melting pot. Also, like Newark and Detroit, Gary was deeply affected by the Great Depression. U.S. Steel, for example, dropped its production capacity from 100 percent in 1929 to 15 percent in 1932. Unlike Newark, Gary made a rapid and strong recovery from the devastation wrought by the Great Depression, fueled in large part by the demand for steel brought about by the advent of World War II.

The out-migration that occurred in Newark immediately following the Great Depression was postponed in Gary until 1959 when a 116-day labor strike shut down 90 percent of U.S. Steel's production. This drastic reduc-tion in output opened the door for competition from foreign steel, which had a negligible effect before.

Cleveland weathered the storm of the Great Depression better than Newark, Gary, and Detroit. Early flight from Cleveland was fueled not so much by the loss of manufacturing jobs as by the near-intolerable pres-ence of crime and corruption. Like the other three cities, Cleveland expe-rienced substantial racial tension during the 1960s. Cleveland, similar to Newark and Detroit, was saddled with the scars and reputation associ-ated with race-based rebellion. The city experienced a five-day rebellion in July 1966 among its African American population followed almost one year later by a second rebellion. The former rebellion is referred to as the "Hough Riots"; the latter is referred to as the "Glenville Shootout."

At the least, this difficult period called for leaders who could provide innovative and lasting reform that necessarily would feature African Americans themselves. Activists in the movement for civil rights, who later joined the growing ranks of influential African American leaders and politicians, adopted similar principles in their political platforms. Generally, they promised to reform government in ways that removed government as a contributor to deteriorating living conditions for their African American constituents. They also promised to provide opportunities for young African American professionals to work in their administrations.[33] These promises would establish the primary bases for an assessment of their political success as well as for their legacies.

In Newark, the movement for civil rights took on the mantle of a movement for "black [political] power." Amiri Baraka emerged as the leader of that movement. Baraka began his ascent to the position of leader of Newark's black power movement by convening and controlling a Black Power Conference in Newark in the summer of 1967, immediately following the Newark Rebellion. The conference was chaired by Nathan Wright, an Episcopal minister and an early and prominent advocate of black power, and included the nation's most significant and recognized African American political figures.[34] Baraka later convened a group of local leaders he referred to as the "Black United Front." The Black United Front set as its primary goal the transfer of power from white to black in the 1970 election.

SEVERE RACIAL TENSIONS AND RACIAL DIVISIONS

The nineteenth-century growth spurt in manufacturing and industrialization described earlier brought about a corresponding growth spurt in Newark's population as various ethnic groups seeking work, a better life, or asylum from unstable living environments found a new home in Newark. The earliest immigrants came from Germany and Ireland. Later groups included Italians, Jews, and African Americans resettling from the South. Ethnic groups each occupied a distinct quarter of the city: Italians in the north, Irish in the west, Jews in the south, and African Americans in the center.[35] Severe racial tensions and divisions became a hallmark of life in the city of Newark. By 1940, the year the Gibson family moved from Alabama to Newark, the African American population of the Third Ward—now the Central Ward—had reached 63 percent as compared to just 4 percent thirty years earlier.[36]

While there were measurable improvements in living conditions for African Americans migrating from the white South to Newark, prejudice, discrimination, and overt racism continued to be an everyday part of their lives. One commentator characterized the plight of African Americans in the Third Ward as being treated as "third-class" citizens behind both earlier immigrants, who occupied positions of power in the city, and immigrants arriving about the same time as African Americans from the South. Third-class citizenship included paying excessive rents for substandard housing, being denied the privilege of trying on garments in local department stores, having an unemployment rate double that of white residents, having a median income 58 percent of whites', composing just 10 percent of the police force, having minimal access to union apprenticeships, and attending schools that were becoming more and more segregated. Perhaps the most troubling indicator of third-class citizenship was the unfair and often brutal treatment of African Americans at the hands of the police and the courts.

As Newark approached the now-infamous summer of 1967, racial tension and polarization had peaked. African Americans had reached their limit of tolerance for overt racism while Newark's white residents began to sense the possibility of an uprising encouraged, in their minds, by outside agitators and criminals bent on violence.

Mounting Frustration and Rebellion

In 1949, one of Newark's key historic figures entered the scene: Lou Danzig. As head of the Newark Housing Authority for two decades, Danzig was charged with the agency's policy of so-called urban renewal. During Danzig's tenure, slum clearance was adopted as the key to revitalization. Newark became the American city where the federal government spent the most money for land clearance per capita.[37]

In hindsight, it seems clear that urban renewal resulted in vast negative consequences for Newark and its people. While urban renewal cleared presumptively unsalvageable homes, it also destroyed the small businesses that had served to support the residents of those homes.[38] The housing authority built an extraordinary number of public-housing units, which tended to deteriorate rapidly into unpleasant and unsafe places to live. Another by-product of urban renewal was a vast number of vacant lots for which the city became the owner by default. The result of a policy intended to clear the slums was that the housing authority turned formerly decent places to live into the slums that the housing authority meant to eradicate.[39] The two predominant remaining ethnic populations of Newark—Italian Americans and African Americans—presented a dichotomy fraught with racially charged tension.[40]

In 1962, the beginning of another watershed period in Newark's history, Hugh Addonizio—a former congressman—was elected as Newark's thirty-fifth mayor through his promise to focus on "human needs."[41] Addonizio appealed to both Italian Americans and African Americans—the former because he shared their heritage and the latter because of the pro-civil-rights positions he took in Congress.[42] Furthermore, he promised to end racism in Newark's schools, and he publicly criticized high-rise slums.[43]

It now appears that Mayor Addonizio made little effort to keep the promises he made to Newark's key ethnic populations but rather used his position to promote his own interests and increase his profits.[44] By the time of his reelection campaign in 1966, Addonizio had returned to

Danzig-era slum clearance policies and had angered the African American community by bragging about his success in preventing them from creating an uprising.[45] Then Addonizio attempted the most massive land clearance plan to date—the clearing of 185 acres in the Central Ward to attract the New Jersey College of Medicine and Dentistry to Newark.

To make matters worse, Addonizio also made plans to divest the city of one of its most valuable assets, a thirty-five-thousand-acre watershed reserve.[46] The mayor's plan to deliver the valuable real estate to his friends further affirmed the fact that his personal agenda had been placed ahead of commitments he made to Newark's struggling ethnic groups. The stage was set for both the uprising he had claimed to have avoided and the emergence of Newark's first African American mayor.

CREATION OF CENTERS OF AFRICAN AMERICAN POWER

Gibson's political base was built from the increasing frustration. Several centers of African American power took shape in the city, providing him with a political base. They included the Student Nonviolent Coordinating Committee (SNCC), the Congress of Racial Equality (CORE), the Black Liberation Army, the Newark Area Planning Association (NAPA), and the Committee for a Unified Newark (CFUN). These organizations were headed by a new generation of vibrant African American leaders including Phil Hutchings, Bob Curvin, Albert Osborne (a.k.a. Tony Williams and Hassan Jeru Ahmed), Junius Williams, and Amiri Baraka.

In 1969, Amiri Baraka, through CFUN, took the lead in organizing the African American and Puerto Rican community around a slate of council seats and the mayoralty for the 1970 election. CFUN sponsored the "Black and Puerto Rican Convention," through which participants agreed to support Gibson for mayor. After defeating Addonizio in a runoff election on May 12, 1970, Gibson needed to make good on his campaign claim: "I am the mayor for all the people." His words calmed the fears of some and ruffled the feathers of others. The immense pressure to succeed for "all the people" began as soon as he first took office.

NEWARK'S PARTICULAR PROBLEMS

Once in office, Gibson immediately faced the challenges associated with the effects of "white flight" to the suburbs, including racial tensions, increasing poverty, declining manufacturing activity, an eroding tax base, and an expanding dependency on social welfare among residents who remained. As noted, these challenges were compounded for Mayor Gibson and the city by the relentless depiction of New Jersey's largest city, by the press, elected officials, and others, as a city beyond recovery. Gibson may have further compounded the challenges facing him, when he adopted the slogan "Wherever Cities Are Going, Newark Will Get There First." In 1983, the *New York Times* recalled Gibson's famous slogan and reported simply, "He was wrong."[47] The *Times* article went on to say, "Mayors in places like Austin, Phoenix, Albuquerque and San Jose have little reason to look at Newark and shudder. Even older cities, such as Boston, Baltimore and Chicago, after decades of distress, remain regional and cultural hubs with assets and prospects that Newark lacks."[48] Beyond the underlying perceptible problems he inherited, Mayor Gibson also had the unprecedented task of convincing the outside world that, notwithstanding the negative and hopeless picture painted by the press and others, his city was a reasonable place to live, work, play, and invest.

In the context of determining an individual's historic significance, challenges might alternatively be viewed as opportunities. We again recall the significance that his response to the events occurring on 9/11 had on Mayor Giuliani's place in history. Ken Gibson likewise faced challenges that were unique to his city and to his time in office. Such challenges and events include the longest public-housing rent strike in the nation's history; the longest teachers' strike in the nations' history; struggles surrounding the city's management of its vast watershed land holdings; a riot emanating out of frustrations within the Hispanic community; and the remnants of a culture of corruption, in particular within the police department, that constrained the city's recovery and created a continuing threat of additional uprisings.

THE STELLA WRIGHT RENT STRIKE

Built in 1959, the Stella Windsor Wright (or Stella Wright) Homes were in 1970 one of thirty-two public-housing sites managed by the Newark Housing Authority. The Stella Wright project site, consisting of seven thirteen-story buildings, housed more than 1,100 families.[49] By 1966, it had become apparent that public housing and its complementary urban-renewal program were being used to advance racial segregation in the city. In that year, a New Jersey Advisory Committee determined that 90 percent of tenants in four poorly maintained high-rise public-housing projects in the Central Ward (Felix Fuld Court, Hayes Homes, Stella Wright, and Scudder Homes) were black.[50] At Stella Wright, the numbers were 1,172 black families and 14 white families.[51] By contrast, low-rise—and better maintained—projects on the outskirts of the city bordering the suburbs (e.g., Stephen Crane Village and Bradley Court) had tenant ratios of 90 percent white to 10 percent black.[52] After denying public claims of racism and segregationist practices, Newark Housing Authority Director Lou Danzig explained these racial disparities by simply claiming that "people are more comfortable with their own."[53]

From 1970—the year Ken Gibson was elected—through 1974, the city experienced the longest public-housing rent strike in the nation's history. At times joined by tenants of Columbus Homes, Scudder Homes, and Hayes Homes, the four-year Stella Wright rent strike resulted in scores of residents withholding $6.4 million in rent.[54] Likely fueled by the national movement for civil rights, the Stella Wright rent strike represented a rise in activism among black public-housing tenants who demanded an end to racial disparities in public-housing placements and maintenance and, at the least, equal treatment in the places black public-housing residents resided. A federal court order was required to bring closure to the Stella Wright rent strike. In the end, only modest gains were realized.

By the end of Gibson's tenure as mayor, it had become clear that the Newark Housing Authority, emboldened by federal policies, had determined to abandon high-rise public housing altogether. In spite of the housing authority's attempt—through attrition and reduced maintenance—to reduce the number of families occupying high-rise public-housing buildings, the number of families remaining in these buildings toward the end of Gibson's tenure far exceeded the availability of replacement housing for very low-income families. And despite this problem, in 1984, a public-housing master plan created by the authority called for the demolition of virtually all the existing high-rise public-housing buildings.[55]

How might a mayor who purported to be the mayor for all the people respond to the challenge of losing the city's stock of very-low-income affordable housing, particularly as that segment of the population was growing in proportion to low- or moderate-income residents?

NEWARK TEACHERS' STRIKE(S)

Frustration and discontent, pervasive among Newark residents in the months and years immediately following the 1967 rebellion, were also felt and ultimately expressed by the city's teachers. At the time of the 1970 mayoral election, the Newark Board of Education was an appointed body with appointing authority belonging to the mayor. It would seem then that the mayor could be identified as the person ultimately responsible for the policies and culture of Newark's public education system.

In the early months of 1970, before the election of Gibson, the Newark Teachers Union (NTU) called for a strike by its members. The four-week-long strike was called by NTU President Carol Graves, an African American, even though the union had earlier been served with a comprehensive restraining order. To understand the dynamics of the strike, it is helpful to identify four separate interest groups that ultimately became warring factions in an ongoing struggle to establish a culture for the delivery of public education. There was the interest of the Newark Teachers Union, which was dominated by white teachers; there was the interest of the city's black teachers, most of whom had joined the union, though likely for different reasons than their white counterparts; there was the mayor-appointed board of education; and there were black parents whose interests were often expressed through the voices of black activists.[56]

The NTU complained about wage levels, responsibility for nonteaching duties (such as hall, cafeteria, and playground monitoring), and binding arbitration. Black teachers, who had witnessed or experienced firsthand the pervasive exclusion of blacks from unions in other contexts, were less interested in collective bargaining than in advancing the civil rights campaign.[57] The board of education was interested in improving the quality of public education in Newark or at least in maintaining continuity in the level of performance that had been achieved to date. Black parents and the black community, perceiving the education system as already failing their children, had little sympathy for teachers' demands.[58]

Like so many of the challenges facing Gibson as Newark's first African American mayor, race became a factor in his struggle to get a handle on public education. The lines of racial tension were drawn. On the one hand, striking teachers, who were mainly white, feared outcomes that might follow from a board of education that was black-controlled through appointments made by the city's first black mayor. Transfers or firings might occur with little recourse if binding arbitration remained in force. Meanwhile, black parents and activists argued that teachers living in the suburbs, who were mainly white, could not be expected to have the interests of inner-city black youth as their main concern.

Once again, Ken Gibson was faced with the realization that his commitment to be "the mayor for all the people" might be untenable. No matter what he decided, he would be perceived as favoring one ethnic group over another. Were competing interests for control of the future of Newark public education simply too divergent to manage and control?

The Newark-Pequannock Watershed[59]

Between 1906 and 1918, the City of Newark purchased thirty-five thousand acres of land situated in parts of three New Jersey counties—Morris, Passaic, and Sussex—and parts of six municipalities: West Milford Township, Hardyston Township, Jefferson Township, Kinnelon Borough, Vernon Township, and Rockaway Township. The aggressive land acquisition was a response to nineteenth-century water problems related to Newark's reliance on its water supply from the Morris Canal and the Passaic River. Prior to the advent of the new water supply system, Newark had suffered from outbreaks of typhoid and cholera.

Unlike the standard tax-exemption policy for municipally owned lands, a statutory provision that imposes local property-tax liability on municipally owned watershed lands was added to the laws of the state of New Jersey in 1910. Thus the City of Newark was faced with a tax liability on its thirty-five-thousand-acre watershed land holdings.

So who and what does this law protect? Most likely, it derived from a concern over the sovereignty and fiscal well-being of rural communities whose lands were being acquired by powerful urban communities with an insatiable demand for clean water to combat diseases and to support an expanding industrial base. Over the years—and despite tax appeals—the tax bite on Newark's watershed lands continued to rise significantly. Newark's watershed tax payments rose, for example, by more than 300 percent from 1965 to 1975, at the same time the city was facing racial discord, economic misfortune, and civil unrest.

The suburban watershed communities were concerned with their own problems. And one was the need—or at least the desire—for tax revenue.

To the extent that watershed communities did not develop an alternative ratable base, they were drawn into a dilemma: they attempted to assess watershed lands as property with intrinsic development potential in order to justify the substantial taxation of those lands, but simultaneously they treated the same lands for planning and zoning purposes as lands unsuited for development of any kind. This problem was compounded in 1975 by a New Jersey Supreme Court ruling mandating that all of New Jersey's developing communities withdraw from a practice of exclusionary zoning in favor of accepting a fair share of its regional affordable-housing demand. The landmark decision is commonly referred to as the *Mount Laurel* case. As usual, these competing interests would pit largely white suburbanites against largely minority urban dwellers. So the question arises, Could Gibson further the interests of his city while fending off the wrath of the city's suburban neighbors when it came to taxing?

THE PUERTO RICAN RIOT OF 1974

In September 1974, the Puerto Rican community took a turn at rebelling against their living conditions that had become, if not unbearable, at least unacceptable. At the time, unemployment among Puerto Ricans in Newark ranged between 25 percent and 27 percent, their school drop-out rate was 42 percent, and the Puerto Rican community had no representation on the Newark City Council.[60] It is noteworthy that the incident sparking the Puerto Rican Riots involved an incident between the police and the Puerto Rican community, which is reminiscent of the incident sparking the more publicized rebellion of 1967 and virtually all 1960s rebellions in the nation's inner cities. County police patrolling in Branch Brook Park came upon a dice game involving a group of Puerto Rican men who were otherwise participating in a family day outing in the park with an estimated six thousand people in attendance. When the police disrupted the dice game more aggressively than onlookers believed was necessary, several young men began attacking the police with rocks, bottles, and beer cans. This reaction caused the police to become even more aggressive, as they rode their horses into a crowd, injuring a number of people, including a four-year-old.

Having quickly arrived on the scene, Gibson invited representatives from the crowd to walk with him to city hall to discuss the incident. That meeting resulted in an agreement that the mayor would meet the next day with leaders from the Puerto Rican community to discuss a broader range of grievances. Expecting to meet with an older, established group of Puerto Rican leaders, Gibson was instead confronted with a group of young Puerto Ricans, including Sigfredo Carrion, head of the Puerto Rican Socialist Party, and Ramon Rivera, former head of the Young Lords in Newark, a group that patterned itself after the Black Panther Party.

To make matters even worse, the younger Puerto Rican negotiating team included Amiri Baraka, who was no longer a friend of the Gibson administration. A sizable crowd assembled outside of city hall as a show of support for the group negotiating with the mayor.

When it became apparent to the crowd outside city hall that negotiations were not producing gains for their community, some returned home; others stayed behind and began what was to become known as the Puerto Rican Riots of 1974. On that day, city hall was bombarded with rocks and bottles. The police retaliated, leaving one man dead from blows to his head. That evening, stores were burned and looted in Puerto Rican neighborhoods, and another man was shot to death. Rioting and looting continued in Puerto Rican neighborhoods for three days.

Clearly, an assessment of how Mayor Gibson handled this difficult challenge will depend on who is asked to respond. The reflections will offer voices from several perspectives in the hope of presenting a broad and balanced view.

ELIMINATING THE REMNANTS OF CORRUPTION

Even as he was faced with these difficult and often deteriorating problems, the new mayor would need to find a way to undo the city's well-earned reputation for entrenched corruption. Such a reputation discouraged "good" people from wanting to live, work, play, or invest in the city and further gave county and state legislators a ready-made excuse to deny the city their support. In addition to the fact that a poor image imposed major constraints on the city's ability to move forward, political corruption undermined performance in the delivery of critical city services. One commentator points out, for example, that "the mayor [Addonizio] used Newark's 'big government' to profit himself and his supporters to the detriment of the overall welfare of the city and the Black population in particular."[61] Another commentator points out Addonizio's appointment of a crony to the board of education who had no relevant credentials for the position over a far more qualified black candidate who was a certified public accountant with an extensive educational background.[62] In addition, Gibson, early in his first term in office, had to deal with the reality that virtually every city contract had been inflated by 10 percent to factor in kickbacks.[63]

By 1970, the City of Newark had a well-established and well-known reputation for corruption. By some accounts, political corruption in the city had become a "tradition." This brings to mind the activities of Longie Zwillman in the Old Third Ward, the activities of Richie "the Boot" Boiardo in the North Ward, corrupt activities of the Campisi Family centered primarily in the West Ward, and the citywide drug dealing of Wayne "Akbar" Pray.[64] While in office, Gibson was himself indicted and acquitted for the crime of providing a no-show job to a former city councilman. Just three weeks after Gibson took office, Hugh Addonizio was found guilty on thirty-three counts of extortion and one charge of conspiracy.

For members of the black community, political corruption was most immediately felt through the actions of the police. In addition, there was in the black community an unwavering perception that police routinely used excessive force and otherwise abused their power. Indeed, it was the belief that a black taxi driver had been abused by white police officers outside of the Fourth Police Precinct that set in motion the infamous Newark Rebellion of 1967, which put Newark on front pages across the country.

There can be little doubt that the police were principal instrumentalities of political corruption. It has been reported, for example, that the Campisi Family sponsored a fund-raising party for Addonizio during the 1970 election campaign. According to an account of the party, Dominick Spina, the police director, was invited to be the guest speaker.[65]

It would follow then that a newly elected mayor in Newark seeking to reverse the city's reputation for corruption might begin by overhauling the police department and discouraging abusive practices. He might also seek ways to improve relations between the police and the communities they are charged with protecting and serving. Just how did Mayor Gibson address police issues and to what degree did he succeed?

Trying to Make Newark Work: Not the Province of the Mayor Alone

Of course, just as the relative success or failure of the United States can never be attributed to the president alone, a big-city mayor may not be held solely responsible for his city's fate. The particular form of government, the power of other anchor institutions, and the relationship between the city and the county and state are all complexities with which any mayor has to contend. Newark's form of government, it turned out, sometimes worked to the mayor's advantage and sometimes did not.

In 1953, the city voters moved the city from a commission form of government to a mayor-council form of government.[66] Under this latter form, Newark has a municipal council consisting of nine members, five of whom are elected by wards and four at-large. All elected officials in Newark, including the mayor, are elected on a nonpartisan basis for four-year terms.

With the authority to appoint heads of all municipal departments, the mayor of Newark has considerably more than ceremonial powers. This influence is constrained to some extent by the power of the municipal council to concur with the mayor's major appointments and the ability to review and approve, disapprove, or amend municipal budgets as presented to the council by the mayor.

NONGOVERNMENTAL ORGANIZATIONS

At any level, it would be naïve to believe that all the needs of any constituency can be satisfied by government alone. With the inducement of tax benefits, our country recognizes and encourages nongovernmental organizations (NGOs) to play their part in satisfying citizens', sometime seemingly insatiable, needs. Newark throughout its history has been rich with such organizations. One such group of NGOs is commonly referred to as Community Development Corporations (CDCs). Founded in 1968, by the time of Gibson's election in 1970, the New Community Corporation (NCC) was becoming one of the most active and powerful CDCs in terms of delivering community services to the residents of Newark. The stated mission of the NCC is "to help inner-city residents improve the quality of their lives to reflect individual God-given dignity and personal achievement."[67]

It is the opinion of some that the NCC—and other similar organizations—is tantamount to a parallel institution to the city government, as they offer an array of cradle-to-grave services such as day care, senior citizen care, housing, and job training.[68] The NCC has been recognized as having filled in with services where city government was ineffective or even dysfunctional.

OTHER ANCHOR INSTITUTIONS

In addition to the CDCs, other institutions in Newark held power that was largely independent of the mayor's office. Often referred to as "anchor institutions," these power sectors operating within the city included, among others, major corporations; county, state, and federal offices; and public and private institutions of higher education. This latter category includes Rutgers University–Newark, the University of Medicine and Dentistry of New Jersey (now part of Rutgers University), New Jersey Institute of Technology, Seton Hall Law School, and Essex County College.

A look at one of the universities can give us an idea of just how independently these anchor institutions can operate. Among a city's primary tools for controlling its growth and destiny is the power of land-use control exercised through a master plan enforced by the city's planning and zoning boards. In 1971, Rutgers University filed an action in the superior court seeking a declaration that the university was not subject to Piscataway Township's zoning ordinances.[69] The case ultimately reached the Supreme Court of New Jersey. The supreme court held that "in enacting statutes respecting Rutgers University, [the] legislature intended that the growth and development of the University, as a public university for all of the people of the state, was not to be thwarted or restricted by local land use regulations and that it is immune therefrom."[70] The effects of this decision extended to Newark, as the Rutgers–Newark campus is unconstrained by the city's planning and zoning boards.

SOME PRELIMINARY ASSESSMENTS OF MAYOR GIBSON

Before we get to the reflections, it seems fair to mention the tone of the few existing attempts to evaluate Kenneth Gibson's mayoralty. These assessments—often offered by some of the same key leaders who formed Newark's new centers of African American power—were generally not good. We give voice to these negative opinions at the same time we hope to place them in a broader, more inclusive, and ultimately, fairer context. In Shakespeare's *Julius Caesar*, Mark Antony notes, "The evil that men do lives after them; the good is often interred with their bones. So let it be with Caesar."[71] Many scholars seem to have adopted the position "so let it be with Gibson." As the rest of his speech and the history play reveals, Antony had much more on his mind than simply laying Caesar to rest. As Antony begged the audience to "lend me your ears," we ask our readers to consider the broader reflections offered in this book before judging Mayor Gibson. It seems only reasonable to consider the extraordinarily difficult moment in time in which Gibson emerged on the scene. It was also a moment in which other African American mayors were coming to power in American cities, and of course, the larger context always shifted with changes in state and local government.

Leaving aside what many historians describe as Amiri Baraka's "unrealistic visions of black power," other much less nationalistic Gibson supporters soon after the 1970 election were similarly disillusioned with Gibson's administrative and political style. Having set forth three elements of Gibson's promise as a reform candidate, Robert Curvin, for example, provides several examples and testimonials to support the legitimacy of this disappointment. It would seem reasonable to posit that the successful achievement of an ambitious reform platform would qualify as historic. Similarly, negative implications associated with the abandonment of certain elements of the platform—or the stark failure to achieve certain elements of the platform—might equally qualify as historic, if those implications can be traced and measured and even if there appear to be sound reasons for the abandonment or failure.

Curvin's version of the principal elements of Gibson's reform platform includes improving government, reforming bureaucracies, and ensuring that young black professionals are given an opportunity to work in Newark's government and related agencies. Curvin summarizes his belief that Gibson quickly abandoned his reform movement by saying, "Gibson changed from an arguably good government public service type to a calculating politician, wheeling both on the local and national levels. The Gibson administration began to look more like the one it had replaced."[72] Curvin offers examples to support his claim. He reports that Harold Hodes, a former Addonizio appointee, became an aide to Gibson and that Donald Malafonte, Addonizio's principal aide, was retained by Gibson as a consultant for the Model Cities Program. Curvin further supports his claim by offering quotes from two of Gibson's key advisors, Gus Heningburg and Dennis Sullivan. Heningburg is quoted as saying, "He simply lacked certain skills a mayor needs, such as knowing how to work with business leaders." Sullivan reports, "When I got back (he returned after a year spent studying at Oxford after working on the Gibson campaign) everything had changed. The people who had talked about changing government and making it work for the citizens were gone. The sharp operators from Addonizio's administration were now on staff or close to the mayor, and they were pretty much calling the shots."[73]

Curvin summarizes the Gibson years this way: "On the basis of the three important characteristics of effective mayoral leadership, Gibson might fairly receive an okay for management. However, on the matters of vision and integrity, he failed."[74] Even as concerns management, Curvin characterizes Gibson's style as a continuation of the old practice of patronage politics: "Trading for a job or position with little or no regard for the concerns or conditions of the poorer citizens of the city."[75]

Junius Williams describes the advent of a new black political class as "unfortunately taking greater pleasure in imitating its White predecessors in office than in pursuing a more radical goal of seeking inclusion of more people at the table: younger leaders; people with different backgrounds with new ideas for community development; people heretofore left out of the leadership development process; and people who were leaders in confrontation politics."[76]

The negative opinions are increasingly harsh, and they don't end there. Following an evaluation based on twenty-four criteria, a January 1975 article in Harper's Magazine ranked Newark as the worst city in America.[77] The report was referenced by former mayor Sharpe James in the 1986 mayoral campaign. Harper's found Newark among the worst cities in nineteen out of twenty-four criteria and "dead last in nine of them."[78] In addition to his reference to the Harper's Magazine report, James reminded voters in 1986 that Newark faced a $40-million budget deficit, that the city led the nation in auto thefts, and that the city was crime ridden. Disappointed that the mayor had focused on the downtown district and not the neighborhoods, Amiri Baraka labeled the mayor a neocolonialist.[79] A broadly expressed theme was that Gibson was a political lightweight, not nearly experienced or savvy enough to handle the monstrous challenges that faced him.

It will be interesting to see how the diverse and knowledgeable group of contributors of the reflections that follow rate Gibson in terms of his management style, his competence, and his adherence to campaign promises.

COMPARING GIBSON TO OTHER FIRST-TIME AFRICAN AMERICAN MAYORS

Ken Gibson stepped into the mayoralty with no prior political experience. While it is true that he had been active in several community-based organizations, he had not held a position in which his leadership skills had been tested. In fact, his only political experience had come through his failed 1966 run for mayor.[80] These facts are in stark contrast to the experience of Coleman Young, Richard Hatcher, and Carl Stokes, first-time-elected African American mayors in Detroit, Michigan; Gary, Indiana; and Cleveland, Ohio, respectively, and figures with whom Gibson is often compared and contrasted. At the time of his election, Coleman Young had previously served as a delegate to Michigan's Constitutional Convention. He was also elected to the state senate.

Their leadership experience and style differed in other ways. Unlike Gibson, both Young and Hatcher rejected an integrationist style for their mayoral administrations; both had been strongly affected by the black power movement. Hatcher, before becoming the mayor, had served as a deputy prosecutor for Lake County, Michigan, and was later elected to Gary's city council.

Prior to his election as mayor of Cleveland, Stokes served as an assistant prosecutor and as a three-term member of the Ohio House of Representatives. He was in line to become a U.S. congressman but deferred to his

brother Louis Stokes. Carl Stokes needed to do little to establish his position as the "mayor for all the people," being the only one among the three
mayors described earlier—Gibson, Young, and Hatcher—who was elected
by a majority-white electorate.

WORKING WITH STATE AND FEDERAL GOVERNMENTS

In his first term, Mayor Gibson may be seen as the victim of unsympa-
thetic regimes in Washington and Trenton. In the first several years of the
Gibson administration, Republican Richard Nixon was the president and
Republican William Cahill was the governor. While neither was openly
hostile to the administration of the first African American mayor of a
major Northeastern city, who was a Democrat, neither went out of his way
to be helpful. Federal and state financial support was not easily secured,
and what was obtained was far less than was needed for Gibson's struggling city. In his first year in office, Gibson was able to attract the relatively
small sum of $50 million in federal support.

Gibson was quoted by Fred Cook of the *Times* as saying about federal aid, "I'm afraid that amounts we manage to spring loose will be small
compared to our needs. We will probably have to cut down on staff and
change the way of doing things even to provide the basic services the city
has now. Next year, if we are still in the same situation, we will simply have
to cut back staff, and this means we will have to cut services—the number
of times you collect the garbage and clean the streets. I think this is going
to happen before we get more money."[81]

Gibson's second term in office benefitted from the election of a Democrat to the White House and another to the governor's office in New Jersey. With the election of Jimmy Carter as president in 1976, federal funds
flowing into Newark steadily increased. In Trenton, the enactment of
the personal income tax, orchestrated by Democratic Governor Brendan Byrne, increased state funding of public schools; implementation of
a state-sponsored "payment in lieu of taxes" program provided financial

assistance to municipalities hosting state facilities by offsetting some of the costs associated with providing local services to such facilities. This infusion of additional state and federal funds to Newark was, however, not enough to staunch the loss of tax ratables, as businesses and middle-class residents continued leaving the city.

Gibson's election as president of the U.S. Conference of Mayors in 1976 helped propel him to reelection in 1978, as his national prominence made him a local celebrity. Many Newarkers were proud of the fact that their mayor was at the helm of a major national organization that helped define the federal policy agenda for cities throughout the country. But not all Newarkers were impressed. The voices of disaffection were getting louder as conditions in the city, especially in its neighborhoods, did not show much, if any, meaningful improvement. In the 1982 race, Junius Williams, Gibson's 1970 campaign manager and a former member of his administration who Gibson had fired ten years earlier, ran against him. Earl Harris, the first black president of the Newark City Council, also entered the race supported by former Gibson loyalists. Williams had the backing of community activists who felt Gibson was too comfortable with the city's white power structure and had done little to improve quality-of-life conditions for Newark's black and brown residents.

In what was regarded as an interesting development, a fourth candidate, Joseph Frisina, an Italian and Newark's tax assessor, also entered the race. Many thought Gibson encouraged, possibly even sponsored, Frisina in the hope of limiting Harris's vote total among white voters. At the time of the election, both Gibson and Harris were under federal indictment for awarding no-show jobs, a fact that contributed to the *New York Times*'s endorsement of Williams. Gibson, who defeated Harris in a runoff, was returned to office for a fourth term. Frisina placed third in the election, and Williams came in last.

To many, Gibson's final years in office were an exercise in muddling through. The city's residents were dispirited and seemed to lack an interest in what city hall was doing. By the time his fourth term ended, in 1986, the city's unemployment rate had risen to 50 percent, its population had continued to decline, it had no movie theaters and only one supermarket, and only two-thirds of its high school students were graduating. It would, of course, be unfair to ascribe Newark's continuing plight after sixteen years in office on Ken Gibson alone. On the other hand, it might be fair to say that his leadership had been unsuccessful in meeting the expectations of the city's black and brown residents. The reflections will no doubt shed some light on this matter.

EVALUATING MAYOR GIBSON'S HISTORICAL IMPORTANCE

As the first African American mayor of Newark—and of any major Northeastern city—it is indisputable that Ken Gibson is an "original." On the other hand, it seems reasonable to question whether, similar to Mayor Fiorello Laguardia, Gibson changed perceptions regarding ethnic politicians. Laguardia was able to remove the perception of Italians as being predictably associated with the underworld. The hope for Gibson, as a reform candidate, was that he would provide a governmental vehicle for black and Hispanic residents of Newark to advance the quality of their lives. This was, after all, the promise and purpose of the Black and Puerto Rican Convention, orchestrated by one of Gibson's principal supporters, Amiri Baraka, and the platform that made Gibson electable.

Was Kenneth Allen Gibson the right man for the position of chief executive officer at one of the lowest points in Newark's history? There were, to be sure, other notable African American figures on the scene at the time with either or both a strong interest in the job and notably deeper credentials. Such figures included Oliver Lofton, Harry Wheeler, and George Richardson. Lofton, a prominent attorney who had served on the Governor's Select Commission on Civil Disorder[82]—although discussed as a potential candidate—expressed no interest in the office. Wheeler, on the other hand, remained an active candidate for mayor until his withdrawal from contention just two days before the general election. After the election, a prominent local community leader was heard to say, "Harry Wheeler should have been the mayor."[83] Like Gibson, Wheeler had no political experience in an elected office. Unlike Gibson, Wheeler was born and raised in Newark and distinguished himself as an exceptional urban strategist and emerging politico. His credentials in these regards include, among others, being instrumental in the election of Newark's first African American councilman in 1954, serving as chairman of the 1968 convention called by Amiri Baraka to fill two vacancies on the city council, serving as head of the Committee Against Negro and Puerto Rican Removal, being invited by Baraka to join a group of emerging politicos called the "United Brothers," and serving as a community representative on the team assembled by Governor Hughes to negotiate the settlement of the medical-school fight that had been a contributing cause of the 1967 rebellion. Also, unlike Gibson, Wheeler was considered by most to be charismatic, outgoing, and an eloquent speaker.

George Richardson had prior political experience having served in the New Jersey General Assembly. It is ironic that Richardson encouraged Gibson to run for mayor in 1966, presumably as a stalking horse for Richardson's own intention to run in 1970. While Gibson was able to win the 1970 election in a runoff against the incumbent, Hugh Addonizio, Richardson was able to garner a mere two thousand votes.

And now the question arises, Did Gibson lay the foundation for enduring institutions and cultural practices or ways of thinking? Maybe. Sharpe James, the man who defeated him in 1986 and succeeded him as mayor, often claimed, "Ken mixed the mortar, and I began to lay the bricks for a new Newark."

If he was mixing the mortar, not much was achieved in the economic development sphere, at least not during his first term. The delivery of social services saw more substantial growth, primarily in the area of improved health services. He lost the support of many activists by 1974, though he won reelection that year. The Latino community had for the most part turned against him, believing that he had done little to address the concerns of

Puerto Ricans. The black and Latino coalition formed to bring about the election of a black mayoral candidate in 1970 no longer existed, and Gibson was blamed for the dissipation.

Given the enormity of the challenges that Gibson faced, just how much progress might have been expected? Even those who rate him most harshly acknowledge the daunting scale and scope of the problems that would have challenged any leader. And despite the negative assessments from detractors, many of those unhappy with his tenure still acknowledge significant achievements.

Was there a sea change?

That's for the readers of the reflections to decide.

In the pages that follow, those who played key roles in Newark from 1970 to 1986 present facts and share their opinions, so now it is up to readers to judge the mayor's place in history.

NOTES

1. William Shakespeare, *The Tempest*, act 1, scene 2, in *No Fear Shakespeare: The Tempest*, ed. John Crowther (Charlotte, N.C.: Spark, 2003), 188.

2. Shakespeare, *Tempest*, act 5, scene 1, in *No Fear Shakespeare*, 48–49.

3. Aldous Huxley, *Brave New World* (New York: Harper and Brothers, 1932).

4. Martin Luther King Jr., *Strength to Love (Minneapolis, Minn.: Fortress Press, 2010)*, 13.

5. King, *Strength to Love*, 13–14.

6. See Ross Douthat, "They Made America," *Atlantic*, December 2006, 1–18.

7. Douthat, "They Made America," 6. Professor Wood also included figures such as Duke Ellington and Louis Armstrong, "who could embody a hugely collaborative industry, art form, or cultural change."

8. Douthat, 6. Professor Kennedy omitted most athletes, icons, and celebrities because entertainment is "highly evanescent" and most entertainers tend to "leave no lasting legacy."

9. The editor's understanding of Newark's history comes from numerous sources, including Brad R. Tuttle, *How Newark Became Newark: The Rise, Fall, and Rebirth of an American City* (New Brunswick, N.J.: Rutgers University Press, 2009); Robert Curvin, *Inside Newark: Decline, Rebellion, and the Search for Transformation* (New Brunswick,

N.J.: Rutgers University Press, 2014); Sharpe James, *Political Prisoner* (Newark, N.J.: Nutany, 2013); Mara S. Sidney, *Urban Slums Report: The Case of Newark, U.S.A.* (Newark, N.J.: Department of Political Science, Rutgers University, 2003); David Levitus, "Planning Slum Clearance and the Road to Crisis in Newark," *Newark Metro*, accessed June 23, 2016, http://newarkmetro.rmutgers.edu/essays/display.php?id=173; Junius Williams, *Unfinished Agenda: Urban Politics in the Era of Black Power* (Berkeley, Calif.: North Atlantic, 2014); Julia Rabig, *The Fixers: Devolution, Development, and Civil Society in Newark, 1960–1990* (Chicago: University of Chicago Press, 2016); Mark Krasovic, *The Newark Frontier* (Chicago: University of Chicago Press, 2013); *Wikipedia*, s.v. "History of Newark, New Jersey," accessed February 8, 2016, https://en .wikipedia.org/wiki/History_of_Newark,_New_Jersey.

10. The Gateway Center is a mixed-use commercial complex consisting of four office towers adjacent to Newark's Penn Station. In addition to office space, the complex includes retail space, restaurants, and a Hilton Hotel. Towers one and two were opened in 1972, tower three was opened in 1986, and tower four was opened in 1988. Two other towers were planned but never built. One controversial aspect of the complex was the inclusion of overhead pedestrian walkways connecting the towers to each other and to the hotel as well as to other adjacent buildings. For some, the walkways represented a deliberate—and inappropriate—way to allow occupants and visitors to avoid making contact with local streets, thereby depriving local merchants of any benefits that might have come from a significantly increased daytime population.

11. Gibson's biography was derived from a number of sources, including personal interviews with Ken Gibson; "Gibson, Kenneth Allen 1932–," Encyclopedia .com, accessed May, 30, 2019, https://www.encyclopedia.com/education/news -wires-white-papers-and-books/gibson-kenneth-allen-1932; "Kenneth A. Gibson," *Wikipedia*, accessed January, 28, 2016, https://en.wikipedia.org/wiki/Kenneth _A._Gibson; and Bunthay Cheam, "The Black Past: Remembered and Recorded," April 5, 2007, http://www.blackpast.org/aah/Gibson-kenneth-1931.

12. See Steven Skiena and Charles B. Wood, "Who's Biggest? The 100 Most Significant Figures in History," *Time*, December 10, 2013.

13. See Melvin G. Holli, *The American Mayor: The Best and Worst Big-City Leaders* (University Park: Penn State University Press, 1999).

14. Douthat, "They Made America," 2. The exercise sought to encourage creativity and to leave the work of definition to the historians.

15. Douthat, 5.

16. Douthat, 5. Von Neumann did not make the final list of the top one hundred.

17. Douthat, 7. Professor H. W. Brands, a professor at the University of Texas and the author of *The Money Men: Capitalism, Democracy, and the Hundred Years'*

War over the American Dollar, took the lead with this position. University of Notre Dame professor Mark Noll, author of *America's God: From Jonathan Edwards to Abraham Lincoln,* generally agreed with Professor Brands on this point but suggested that "this was a reflection of how history is taught—as a political narrative or as a reaction against political narrative."

18. Douthat, 6.

19. Skiena and Wood, "Who's Biggest?," 1.

20. Skiena and Wood, 1. *Time* integrated a diverse set of measurements about each individual's reputation into a single consensus value.

21. Skiena and Wood, 1.

22. Skiena and Wood, 1. Bieber was assigned the rank of 8,633rd.

23. Holli, *American Mayor,* 4.

24. Holli, 8.

25. Holli, 8.

26. Holli, 8.

27. Fred Cook, "Mayor Kenneth Gibson Says—'Wherever Central Cities Are Going, Newark Is Going to Get There First," *New York Times,* July 25, 1971.

28. See, for example, Kate King, "Shootings in Newark Surge," *Wall Street Journal,* August 21, 2015, https://www.wsj.com/articles/shootings-in-newark-surge -1439945824. See also "Baraka Blasts Article Detailing Newark Shootings Surge as 'Incomplete,' 'Skewed,'" https://www.nj.com/essex/2015/08/baraka_blasts_article _on_newark_shootings_surge_as.html.

29. To the extent that the phrase the "civil rights movement" connotes an effort to bring the nation's African American population within the realm of full citizenship, the movement could be said to have begun in the early nineteenth century (or earlier). For example, the slave trade was banned in the United States in 1808. Nat Turner staged a historic slave rebellion in 1831. President Abraham Lincoln moved the Emancipation Proclamation to fruition in 1863. And the Thirteenth Amendment to the U.S. Constitution was adopted by Congress in 1865. For purposes of this volume, the American civil rights movement as it affected the life and political career of Ken Gibson can be described as occurring between 1955—the date of Rosa Park's heroic refusal to take a seat in the back of a Montgomery, Alabama, bus—and 1968, the date of the assassination of Martin Luther King Jr.

30. See, for example, "Street Fight," *Black Mayors: Newark in Context,* PBS premiere, July 5, 2005.

31. "Street Fight."

32. "The Black Mayors: How Are They Doing?," *Newsweek,* August 3, 1970. This first generation of African American mayors would include Richard G. Hatcher, elected mayor of Gary, Indiana, in 1966; Carl Stokes, elected mayor of Cleveland,

Ohio, in 1967; and Coleman Young, elected mayor of Detroit in 1973. See appendix A for a statistical comparison of Newark and these three American cities that elected African American mayors for the first time between 1966 and 1973.

33. See, for example, Curvin, *Inside Newark*, 177.

34. At the time of Nathan Wright's death in 2005, the *New York Times* reported that Dr. Wright's greatest fame came in 1967, "when he was chairman of the National Conference on Black Power in Newark." Douglass Martin, Nathan Wright's obituary, *New York Times*, February 24, 2005. In a book review of one of Dr. Wright's eighteen books, the *Times* reported that the conference "sounded the first prolonged blast in the Black power campaign." Anthony Lukas, "Ready to Riot," *New York Times Book Review*, 1968.

35. See David Levitus, "Planning, Slum Clearance and the Road to Crisis in Newark," *Newark Metro*, accessed June 23, 2016, http://www.newarkmetro.rutgers.edu/display.php?id=173, 2.

36. Tuttle, *How Newark Became Newark*, 149.

37. Levitus, "Planning," 3.

38. Levitus, 3. See also "Street Fight."

39. Levitus, "Planning," 4.

40. See Curvin, *Inside Newark*, 151.

41. Levitus, "Planning," 4.

42. Levitus, 4.

43. Levitus, 4.

44. Levitus, 4; and Curvin, *Inside Newark*, 21.

45. Levitus, *Planning*, 5.

46. See Gibson lawsuit in Curvin, *Inside Newark*, 252.

47. Paula Span, "Newark's Failing Dream," *New York Times Magazine*, October 2, 1983, 1.

48. Span, "Newark's Failing Dream," 1.

49. See Curvin, *Inside Newark*, 36.

50. See Tuttle, *How Newark Became Newark*, 141; see also Curvin, *Inside Newark*, 36.

51. See Curvin, *Inside Newark*, 36.

52. Tuttle, *How Newark Became Newark*, 141.

53. Tuttle, 141.

54. Joseph F. Sullivan, "Rent-Strike-Plagued Stella Wright to Be Shut By Newark Housing Unit," February 6, 1974, https://www.nytimes.com/1974/02/06/archives/rentstrikeplagued-stella-wright-to-be-shut-by-newark-housing-unit.html.

55. See "Memorandum of Law in Support of Plaintiff's Motion for a Temporary Restraining Order and Preliminary Injunction," Newark Coalition For Low Income Housing et al., Plaintiffs v. Newark Redevelopment and Housing Authority, and

Jack F. Kemp, secretary of the United States Department of Housing and Urban Development, Defendants, 4.

56. A comprehensive account of the Newark teacher strikes can be found in Steve Golin, *The Newark Teacher Strikes: Hopes on the Line* (New Brunswick, N.J.: Rutgers University Press, 2002); also see a review of the Golin book by Lois Werner entitled "Class, Gender, and Race in the Newark Teacher Strikes," *New Politics* 9, no. 2 (Winter 2003): 1–8.

57. Werner, "Class, Gender, and Race," 2.

58. Werner, 2.

59. The editor served as executive director of the Newark Watershed Conservation and Development Corporation from 1979 to 1987 and is, as a result, personally familiar with the facts contained in this section.

60. Curvin, *Inside Newark*, 175.

61. See Levitus, *Planning*, 4.

62. Tuttle, *How Newark Became Newark*, 157.

63. See Tuttle, *How Newark Became* Newark, 175.

64. See Curvin, *Inside Newark*, 25–27, 40–44, and 178–179.

65. See Curvin, 26.

66. Optional Municipal Charter Law ("Faulkner Act"), NJSA 40:69A-1, et seq. plan C.

67. Taken from the New Community Corporation's website at https://www .newcommunity.org/about/ on November 1, 2017.

68. See, for example, Mara S. Sidney, *Urban Slums Report*.

69. Rutgers University v. Piluso, 113 N.J. Super. 65 (1971), 272 and 573; 60 N.J. 142 (1972).

70. Rutgers University v. Piluso.

71. William Shakespeare, *Julius Caesar*, act 3, scene 2, in *No Fear Shakespeare: Julius Caesar* (Charlotte, N.C.: Spark, 2003), 4.

72. Curvin, *Inside Newark*, 178.

73. Curvin, 178.

74. Curvin, 183.

75. Curvin, 5.

76. Junius Williams, *Unfinished Agenda*, 2.

77. "A History of Newark, New Jersey," *Wikipedia*, accessed November 17, 2015, https://en.wikipedia.org/wiki/History_of_Newark,_New_Jersey.

78. "History of Newark."

79. "Kenneth A. Gibson."

80. In 2008, Professor John Balz, in the Department of Political Science at the University of Chicago, conducted a detailed study to measure the value of prior

political experience in predicting greatness for elected officials—in particular, the president of the United States. The Balz study concluded that "overall there is no evidence that political experience improved the chances of extraordinary presidential performance and some weaker evidence that certain political positions, most notably membership in the U.S. Congress, lead to poorer performance." See John Balz, "Presidential Greatness and Political Experience," Department of Political Science, University of Chicago, June 6, 2008.

81. Cook, "Mayor Gibson Says."

82. Also known as the "Lilley Commission."

83. My own recollection.

CHAPTER 1

ON BEING FIRST

As U.S. representative Bonnie Coleman detailed in her foreword, when—like Kenneth Gibson—one is the first African American to achieve a certain high political office, that person must consider the need to represent all their constituents.

In 1990, David Dinkins became the first African
American to serve as mayor of New York City.

Mayor David Norman Dinkins

When I reflect on Ken Gibson's election as the first African American mayor of Newark, indeed, as the first African American mayor of a major city in the Northeast, I recall contrasting emotions of pride and promise and of concern and apprehension. Twenty years after he took office, I was elected New York City's first African American mayor, and to this day, it saddens me that I remain the only African American who ever held that office.

In 1976, Gibson also became the first African American president of the U.S. Conference of Mayors, which I was proud to join in 1990. While each of us may have felt confident about our individual readiness for the challenges of our city's highest elected office, uncertainty about the readiness of our electorate's support always loomed large. Like Ken before me, I embraced the principal role of serving as a mayor for all people, not just those who were supporters. And in that regard, I owe a debt of gratitude to Ken for delivering a sixteen-year example as he served all residents of a dynamic American city. His tenure, occurring during a period of political maturation in America, gave us all hope.

As I think back to the resources available to me as New York City's mayor, I have an even greater appreciation for Mayor Gibson's accomplishments. Newark was a city with far fewer such resources while also having a reputation for corruption. It was still reeling from the ravages of the 1967 rebellion and still struggling through violent outbreaks, the result of extreme racial divisions. Most remarkably, Ken Gibson started his career as a political novice, having never held any publicly elected position before 1970. Additionally, his civil-engineering background was considered less-than-ideal preparation for the role of mayor of any major U.S. city. However, the citizens of Newark were looking for a fresh approach and kept him in office for four terms until 1986.

The likelihood of a mayoral candidate's success in office usually rests on his or her commitment to improving the lives of constituents. That's the key to an enviable legacy. Ken Gibson, as a private citizen, was committed to the people of his community before he became mayor. He maintained that commitment throughout his mayoral career while setting an example for others who were to become politically involved.

So many of us now stand on his shoulders. Indeed, he is one of Newark's most significant historic figures.

Newark native Sheila Oliver was New Jersey's first African American woman to serve as the Speaker of the New Jersey General Assembly. In 2017, she became New Jersey's first African American lieutenant governor.

LIEUTENANT GOVERNOR SHEILA OLIVER

As a high school student during the late 1960s, I participated in citywide student boycotts led by Larry Hamm, who later became known as Adimu Chunga. Donald Payne, who later was elected the first black congressman representing the Tenth Congressional District, was an active supporter of

Newark's black youth during this period. Through his work at the Newark YMCA, Payne helped establish black fraternities and sororities that were effective engines of energy that advanced the boycotts. The network of fraternities and sororities, based at schools throughout the city, propelled many of the students into the streets.

At that exciting time, as Newark was becoming a black majority city, my family developed a close working relationship with many of its key black political actors. Men and women such as Honey Ward, the leader of the Central Ward Democratic Committee; Shirley Rutherford and her husband, Clarence Coggins, a fabled community organizer; my uncle Alvin Oliver; and Willie Brown, who would later become an assemblyman, were all movers and shakers in forging a new Newark. These were some of the people who shaped me politically. Some were radical for their time, some were socialists, and others were simply moved by the philosophy of "black power." This was, after all, the time in which black power became a topic in the public square.

I left Newark in 1970 to attend Lincoln University, a historically black institution in Pennsylvania. While there, I participated in the excitement unfolding in Newark through the college's academic program that allowed students to spend the month of January working on projects that enhanced their college experiences. I chose to work in Newark and, because of my family's connections with city hall, I was able to obtain an internship in Mayor Gibson's office in 1971. I did research and analyzed issues such as housing development, zoning, and land-use planning. I was also involved in the contentious discussions about the proposed construction of Kawaida Towers, a low-income housing project sponsored by social activist Imamu Amiri Baraka, which was to be built in the heart of the Italian community in Newark's North Ward. That project ultimately was not built.

After completing my undergraduate education, I attended Columbia University and obtained a master's degree in planning and public affairs. My first job after graduate school was at Lincoln University, where I served for two years as the director of cooperative education. I then returned to Newark and worked briefly for Catholic Community Services before joining the Gibson administration. There I worked in the Office of Youth Services and Special Projects in the Mayor's Office of Employment and Training (MOET), headed by Harry Wheeler. Harry had been a candidate for mayor in 1970 and a Gibson opponent but withdrew from the race and supported Gibson, who promptly hired Wheeler after the election.

Working for Harry was an amazing but exhausting experience. He promoted me to head the Office of Youth Services, and I worked my tail off. We had to come into the office on Saturday mornings—Harry would provide breakfast and lunch—and we worked until three or four in the afternoon. I got to know and work with Mary Willis, Harry's hard-charging, dedicated, capable sister, and with Mary Darden, another strong, capable black woman. These women were mentors. They understood the system and knew how to work it to the community's advantage. Darden and I became Harry's federal grant writers, and we trained the rest of his staff on federal program rules and regulations. Harry spent much time on the road, traveling to cities such as Detroit and Chicago, helping black mayors prepare their personnel to effectively implement federal regulatory procedures under the Comprehensive Employment and Training Act (CETA) and other antipoverty programs then available. These programs were instrumental in creating the black middle class in cities where the programs existed. The programs provided jobs that were federally subsidized and that provided professional, managerial employment opportunities. This represented something new, exciting, and critically important to minority communities across the country. Its importance was in no small way tied to the belief that the programs facilitated black self-determination in social service delivery.

This experiment in black participation in local government service delivery, however, was not to last. Federal officials soon began to tighten the rules governing how funds could be used and managed. This development was a direct response to pressure from local government officials who felt community-oriented local programs were being used to incubate potential political opponents. In response to heightened federal oversight, Darden and I had to redouble our efforts to ensure that all federal rules and regulations were being strictly adhered to—at the risk of losing increasingly scarce funds. We helped our people meet record-keeping, monitoring, and placement requirements, which was no easy task. Thankfully, Harry was a master at negotiating with federal officials and mollifying their concerns about what we were doing. His command of detail, with the assistance of Dan O'Flaherty, his right-hand man (now a Columbia University professor of economics), was astounding.

I left city hall in 1980 to become the director of the Leaguers, a major community empowerment organization founded by Mary Burch, the wife of a prominent African American physician. Mrs. Burch was the driving force behind the organization, which sought to equip black youngsters with the social, educational, and cultural skills needed to successfully navigate in a majority-white society. That experience too was thrilling. I loved the organization, and I loved Mary Burch. She was a grand lady.

Looking back on that period in my life and the life of Newark, I would say that those of us in city government worked very hard; we felt we were on a mission, a mission of community service. We were determined to make the most of the opportunities that were beginning to come our way and that benefited the people we cared about.

Ken, the engineer who became Newark's first African American mayor, was our inspiration, our leader. His quiet, laid-back style was deceptive, for it in some ways masked his accomplishments. I believe that style contributed greatly to his early effectiveness. He was, above all, dedicated to his city.

At about the time that Kenneth Gibson was elected the first African American mayor of Newark, Pat Sheehan was elected as the first woman mayor of New Brunswick. Sheehan draws some interesting parallels between the obstacles facing first-timers in any high office. Of course, like every barrier breaker, she was faced with not only the struggles of being first but also the particularly difficult problems of the place and time in which she was elected.

MAYOR PATRICIA SHEEHAN

Reflections about what it means to be a "first" in government brings back bittersweet memories. Being a first is an honor but also a responsibility, not only for your own success but also for those who might follow you. In my case, I was the first female mayor of New Brunswick, New Jersey, from 1967 to 1974. In 1974, I became the first woman to become the commissioner of the New Jersey Department of Community Affairs. In this latter regard, I find a level of satisfaction in the fact that another woman, Ann Klein, had previously been appointed by the governor to serve as commissioner of the New Jersey Department of Institutions and Agencies. This meant to me that I had not simply filled the "woman's slot" in the governor's cabinet.

Like Ken Gibson, I understand the challenges associated with taking charge of a city in such a degree of decline that residents took to the streets in rebellion. I understand and appreciate, of course, the difference in scale between Newark and New Brunswick in terms of those challenges and, in particular, the need to remove the damage to the reputation, image, and appeal of our cities postrebellion.

A source of strength for me—and I suspect for Ken Gibson and others in our unique position—was my access to professional organizations. Most important among such organizations for me was the U.S. Conference of Mayors and the New Jersey League of Municipalities. Within both of these organizations, support was responsive to my office, not my particular political party, my gender, or my personal connections.

It was in meetings of the Conference of Mayors and the League of Municipalities that I met, worked with, and learned from Ken Gibson. My immediate impression of Ken was that he put the well-being of his city and its residents ahead of any personal agenda. I learned from him the importance of being willing to listen, even to those who had previously been denied access to the positions we held, and creating a strong team. I also learned from him that seeking and receiving assistance for our cities was not a sign of weakness but a recognition and understanding of the fact that the declining condition of our cities was the result of strong external forces that led to an erosion of the tax base and the fostering of growth and development in the suburbs. I recall, for example, that veterans were unable to take advantage of VA-insured mortgages in New Brunswick because the housing stock was too old. The highway trust funds were for new roads and not for repairs of roads and related infrastructure needed by New Jersey's older cities. With new roads came better access to the suburbs and the flight out of cities by financially able residents. How much more impactful must these "unintended" consequences of public policies have been on a city the size of Newark?

I believe that Ken would agree with me that the creation of the Department of Community Affairs in the State of New Jersey, under the leadership of Governor Richard Hughes and with its extraordinary initial commissioner, Paul Ylvisaker, was an important milestone for the recovery of New Jersey's cities. For the first time, New Jersey municipalities had a voice in Trenton that was able, willing, and prepared to provide assistance for such things as the development of new housing, the creation of safe and clean streets, professional training for municipal employees, inspection programs, and interlocal government agreements for shared services, to mention just a few examples. Mayors like me and Ken Gibson for once felt that we had some level of control over the challenges we faced and the solutions we sought.

I certainly like to believe that I have been a positive factor in the progress that has been made by women seeking positions of authority in appointed and elected public offices. There was no rule book for me or other women who were "firsts." We had to ignore the slurs (real or presumed); we had to be willing to speak our piece and hold our ground. We had to ignore unfounded rumors and miscommunications, the ever-present hazards of the job. No doubt, Ken Gibson, as the first African American mayor of Newark and of any major Northeastern city, faced even greater challenges in his effort to restore his city to a place with broad-based appeal. His reputation for being quiet and laid-back belies the fact that in his interactions with others, he at all times remained steadfast in his resolve to improve his city and bring a better quality of life to its residents. The exciting place I see Newark today, its leadership, and the path it appears to be on into the future must unquestionably be attributed in large measure to the pioneering efforts of Mayor Kenneth Gibson.

CHAPTER 2

NAVIGATING RACIAL POLITICS

Mayor Gibson famously declared that he would be the "mayor for all the people." This was much easier said than done. The Newark he inherited from the corrupt administration of Italian American Hugh Addonizio suffered from the deep racial divides that had spurred the tragic rebellion of 1967.

Fred Means, who eventually became a member of the Newark School Board, describes the racial struggles of African Americans that led him—and many contemporaries—to join the civil rights movement. He gives us a sense of the atmosphere from which black political power began to emerge.

FRED MEANS

I was born in South Carolina during a time when most Negroes worked as farmers, as other opportunities were rare. My father and mother, however, worked as servants in Saratoga Springs, New York, in the summer and St. Petersburg, Florida, in the winter while sending money home to South Carolina to support my grandmother and me. During those first nine years of my life, I knew that I was loved. Although I did not fully grasp the meaning of the segregation, discrimination, and separation that so completely consumed our lives, I did know that whites and blacks were not treated the same. And folks around me said that that was not right.

When my grandmother died, my family and I became a part of that Great Migration of blacks to the North. We went to Saratoga, where I first experienced cold weather and snow. We moved from Saratoga to Philadelphia, Pennsylvania, to East Orange, New Jersey, and finally, we settled on Sherman Avenue in Newark. I graduated from Miller Street School and South Side High School. Growing up in Newark during the 1940s and 1950s, I experienced discrimination and de facto segregation. Negroes could not go to Olympic Park in Irvington, Dreamland skating rink in Elizabeth, Palisades Park on the Hudson River, or most New Jersey beaches. I resented not being able to do everything that my white school-mates were able to do. Were we not all human beings? Perhaps it was then that the seeds for fighting this evil entered my psyche.

In 1951, I was denied admission to Rutgers, the State University of New Jersey. However, I was accepted at Howard University and New York University. I chose NYU, where the cost was $25 per credit, a great deal of money for a poor black family. For two years, I and everybody else in my family worked to keep me at NYU. All the time, the military draft board chased me for service. When we ran out of money, I told the army that I was ready to cancel my deferment and serve.

Wake-Up Call

After four weeks of basic training at Camp Pickett, Virginia, I and three black recruits, two from New Jersey and one from Texas, who had been given weekend passes, decided one day to get dinner following the bus ride to Blackstone, Virginia, I noted a restaurant above the bus station, but the recruit from Texas expressed concern. Since I insisted we go, the two others agreed to enter and sit down. Noticing the waitress continuing to ignore us, I called to her. She approached, saying, "I'm sorry, but I can't serve y'all here. . . . Y'all can go around the back." I was stunned with the irony of the situation. We were in the uniform of our country, preparing to fight for our country, and were being refused food in this common restau-rant housed atop a common public bus station. This was one of the events that strengthened my determination to fight against the de facto and de jure discrimination in America. What would be my role in confronting such evils? This is the question that each generation must ask, even now. What is your role today?

After the army, I returned to NYU with the economically lifesaving GI Bill, which enabled me to complete my bachelor of science degree. But seeking a job revealed another pattern of discrimination. Being denied employment in several New Jersey suburban school districts, I finally obtained a teaching position at PS 621 in New York City, which at the time was the only school for emotionally disturbed girls in the country. Bill Payne, Bob Curvin, and others tell similar personal stories of earning college degrees and facing serious job discrimination during the early 1960s.

In 1960, I obtained my second teaching position, this time in the Newark public school system. The Newark Board of Education presented a different form of discrimination. Regular teachers were required to pass the National Teacher Examination, a requirement above the state's requirement. Some Negro teachers and others were unable to pass the exam. They were hired as substitutes and assigned to regular classes but were paid $1,500 or more less than the regular teachers. This was a situation that the Organization of Negro Educators (ONE) confronted later.

In 1961, I visited the Bridge Club on Washington Street, where my father served as a bartender. The Bridge Club and the Owl Club were places where many of the upwardly mobile citizens met to discuss civic, social, and political matters. I overheard a group of black and white people at a corner table talking about taking direct action to confront the discrimination that they observed and experienced in the Newark area. Among the group were Bob Curvin, Richard Proctor, Gail Lissex, Willard Geller, Delora Jones, and Charles Tuller. This was my introduction to the Newark-Essex chapter of the national organization the Congress of Racial Equality (CORE). They were meeting at the Bridge Club because pastors of local black churches were afraid to permit these "agitators" to meet in their churches. Soon, the Rev. Homer J. Tucker, pastor of the Mt. Zion Baptist Church on Broadway in Newark, where I was a member, agreed to allow CORE to meet there.

In 2015, Bob Curvin and I, with the support of former CORE members and others, placed a plaque at Mt. Zion memorializing the prophetic pastor and the church. Eventually, CORE was able to rent an office at 136 West Market Street. I remember many nights standing on a soapbox in front of that office, addressing people gathered around seeking information and advice on ways to navigate the racist system. During the summer, we invited local children to come to the CORE office for tutoring.

CORE was formed to abolish discrimination based on color, race, religion, or national origin, stressing nonviolent direct-action methods. This was the same strategy for change employed by Dr. Martin Luther King Jr., who was inspired by India's Mahatma Gandhi. James Farmer, a proponent of nonviolence and direct action, was one of the founders of CORE at the University of Chicago. In 1961, Mr. Farmer became CORE's national director, and almost immediately the organization stepped into the vanguard of the American civil rights movement by leading "freedom rider" pilgrimages into the South.

In Newark/Essex, CORE was at the forefront of the struggle against discrimination in issues of employment, housing, education, and police-community relations. Perhaps the chapter's most successful effort was in obtaining more-equal employment. Beginning in the summer of 1961, CORE conducted a massive demonstration against White Castle, where young Negroes loved to eat but were refused work. I remember picketing at the one on Elizabeth Avenue as a summer thunderstorm approached. I heard the counter server say that the storm will scatter the protesters. The rain, thunder, and lightning exploded with a vengeance. The feeling of "we shall not be moved" rose up in all of us in the line. When I finally returned home, I could wring the water from my clothes, even my underwear. It was that level of resolve and determination that characterized the participants in all our demonstrations.

In his book *Inside Newark*, Bob Curvin describes in detail the struggle that CORE had confronting the endemic problems of discrimination in companies in the Newark area. Some of the many companies that CORE called out were Pabst Brewery, Hoffman-La Roche, Western Electric, New Jersey Bell Telephone, and Sears. I remember picketing Sears on Elizabeth Avenue with my preteen sons, Vincent and Marc, carrying signs protesting the lack of Negro employees. An unusual number of pictures by a photographer unknown to us were taken, and I later found it strange that my Allstate auto insurance was not renewed for any explainable reason. Indeed, in the struggle, for every action, there is a reaction.

One of the most successful victories of CORE was with New Jersey Bell Telephone, which agreed to hire Walter Chambers, a black Newarker, as an executive. One of Walt's first responsibilities was to establish a training program on civil rights for the firm's management employees. Among his many successes, Walt led Bell to finance a documentary film aimed at minority high school students across the nation regarding the challenges and responsibilities involved in preparing for a job. This and other fights, such as the struggle with unions to hire minorities in the building of the new Barringer High School in Newark, led to the formation of the Business and Industrial Coordinating Committee—a civil rights / community / business / labor partnership comprising the major leaders from those sectors who met monthly to discuss and act on pressing concerns.

In the summer of 1965, CORE conducted a major march from Lincoln Park to Military Park, where a rally of several hundred people called for a police review board. News accounts indicated that both James Farmer, national director, and Fred Means, local chapter chair, spoke passionately about police beatings and the killing of Negro men, such as the shooting in the back of Lester Long by policeman Martinez in North Newark. Although Mayor Addonizio refused the demands of CORE, police brutality was cited by the governor's "Lilley Commission" as one of the causes of the 1967 rebellion and remains an issue in America some fifty years later.

However, CORE as an organization soon began to change. The call for "black power" by Stokely Carmichael caused CORE, a highly integrated organization, to examine its fundamental goal of integrating into the current system through nonviolence. The new thrust in the movement called for structural change via separation and more self-determination. Floyd McKissick's replacement of James Farmer as chair represented CORE's move in the direction of militant black separatism. When, in 1968, McKissick left CORE to form "Soul City," in North Carolina, Wilfred Ossery from California briefly became chair. However, Roy Innis, with his crew from Harlem, New York, assumed leadership of the organization and moved its focus from civil rights to black nationalism. His supporters changed the constitution to ban white members. He and his son Niger then moved the organization to the extreme right, later supporting the Tea Party and condemning the Black Lives Matter movement. According to an interview given by James Farmer in 1993, "CORE has no functioning chapters; it holds no conventions, no elections, no meetings, sets no policies, has no social programs and does no fund-raising. In my opinion, CORE is fraudulent." James Farmer's and even Floyd McKissick's visions of CORE were no more.

Turmoil in Education

Rapid population changes in Newark presented serious challenges to the city and to its education system. According to Newark Board of Education figures, in 1950, the black student population was approximately 25 percent. In 1961, it had grown to 55 percent. The black student population doubled between 1950 and 1960 and increased another 30 percent between 1960 and 1973. During that same period, the Spanish-surname school population grew from about 9 percent to 16 percent. As late as 1967, there was one black vice principal and there were no black principals in Newark. Many black teachers were hired as substitutes and paid lower salaries without equal benefits; they were fired in June and rehired in September. The money saved by the board was used as a contingency fund.

To confront these inequities and concerns about the quality of education, Negro teachers came together and formed the Organization of Negro Educators (ONE). I served as the founding president.

Representing ONE, I often addressed the board of education about issues of great concern to us. As reported in the *Newark Evening News* on February 27, 1968, I was to address the board about changing the status of permanent substitute teachers to that of regular teachers. In support of that demand, some one hundred substitute teachers marched peacefully in front of the board building. ONE won that battle.

Political cronyism was a major problem. Mayor Addonizio used the school system to pay off his political supporters. The position of secretary to the board of education became available, and the opening allowed the mayor to pay off a friend. This position was the second most important in the system after superintendent. As a result, the mayor proposed the appointment of Irish councilman James Callahan, a high school graduate, over Wilbur Parker, the state's first black CPA. ONE and most community organizations opposed the mayor's decision to put politics over qualifications. As reported in the *Newark Star Ledger* on June 29, 1967, a group of twenty members of ONE met with the mayor in his office to ask that he stop playing politics with the board of education and see that Negroes were given a fair opportunity in hiring at all levels of the school system. But it was to no avail: the mayor simply told the group that politics was a part of the education system.

The issue of Parker versus Callahan festered and was cited as another cause of the 1967 rebellion.

ONE was an organization of teachers concerned about not only themselves but also the quality of education. We realized that to improve education for black and brown children, we would have to improve other elements in the city. In fact, ONE became a civil rights organization. ONE joined with the Bronze Shields, the black police organization, to play an annual basketball game to raise funds to support scholarships for black students. We launched a monthly meeting to discuss critical issues affecting the black community. Out of our meetings and workshops, we began to develop a philosophy that I described in an article that appeared in the

New Jersey Education Association (NJEA) Review in May 1969, titled "The Black Agenda." To meet the needs of children, I proposed four basic functions that Newark schools should perform:

1. Help children establish positive images of themselves so that they see themselves as worthy human beings with hope of succeeding in life.
2. Help students gain strong basic skills with which to function in society.
3. Help identify, develop, and project black heritage and culture as positive and place it in a world perspective.
4. Help students face, adapt to, cope with, understand, and change our racist society.

Helping Gibson

Of course, ONE joined with other community groups in 1970 to help Ken Gibson become the city's first black mayor. Many of us had already been with Ken when he challenged Addonizio unsuccessfully in 1966.

Among the first challenges that faced the new mayor was a disastrous eleven-week teachers' strike called by the Newark Teachers Union (NTU). Earlier, ONE competed unsuccessfully in an election with NTU to be the bargaining agent for teachers with the board of education. ONE teachers joined with community people to keep the schools open during the strike. ONE saw the NTU applying a labor-union model, which meant getting as much money and power for the workers as possible with minimal effort. NTU won the contract, but we believed what may have been good for teachers was not good for Newark's children.

In 1973, Mayor Gibson appointed me to a three-year term as a member of the Newark Board of Education. It turned out to be one of the most frustrating experiences of my life. After my first nine months on the board, I wrote and read at the public board meeting on March 26, 1974, a paper I called "The View from This Side of the Microphone." I asked the question of other board members, "How do you see your role as a board member?"

I wrestled with the question of how to best deal with education in a city where the school board was as concerned about political patronage as it was about schooling.

Unfortunately, I was on the four side of five-to-four votes on many issues. Clearly, this was a frustrating experience for Helen Fullilove, Vickie Donaldson, and George Branch, the other three with whom I voted on many losing issues.

In 1975, I completed my EdD at Rutgers and accepted a position at Jersey City State College. Reflecting back on all things, I have concluded that I probably was naive and too expectant of more rapid change. Looking in the mirror, however, I will not trade that bright-eyed optimism of my youth for a more calloused or cynical approach.

If the young lose optimism, change will be impossible. Our very society will wallow in a pessimism that accepts the status quo. As far back as 1857, Frederick Douglas told us, "Power concedes nothing without a demand."

Barbara Kukla, a white reporter and editor for one of New Jersey's largest newspapers, the *Newark Star Ledger*, sets the scene at the time of Gibson's first electoral victory and goes on to offer a brief assessment of the mayor's tenure.

BARBARA KUKLA

I grew up in North Arlington, New Jersey, and came to Newark when I was hired by the *Newark Star Ledger*. This was shortly after the 1967 Newark Rebellion. I was the only woman news reporter working at the paper at that time.

I remember the excitement in the city the night Ken's victory was declared; it was huge. I recall a mass of people marching down Elizabeth Avenue in celebration, many of whom were en route to parties throughout the city. I managed to attend three of the all-night parties.

The excitement, however, could not hide the fact that Ken had inherited a city facing huge challenges. Newark had been losing population for several decades and was losing its economic base. Middle-class residents and their tax dollars were leaving in large numbers; most were white, but middle-class blacks were also abandoning the city. The pace of population loss picked up considerably after the rebellion. The nearby suburbs were the principal beneficiaries of migration from Newark, especially Livingston, West Orange, the Caldwells, Belleville, Nutley, and Verona, where whites migrated, and East Orange and Irvington, where blacks relocated. Major businesses were also moving from Newark. Retail and commercial enterprises, however, were moving to the outer suburbs, places like Roseland and municipalities in Morris and Union Counties. Prudential, one of the oldest and most important businesses in the city, was threatening to relocate. The fear of economic devastation these losses foretold forced the city to make financial concessions to many companies in order to keep them. The impact on the city's financial health was substantial, and the effects remain visible today.

———

Ken brought quiet leadership to the city. Indeed, he was one of the most unobtrusive persons I had ever met. He also was thoughtful. He approached the city's challenges with an attitude of slow but consistent determination.

Many in the white community feared that a black mayor would not respond to their needs and, consequently, white movement out of the city continued apace. Tony Imperiale, a major voice in the heavily Italian North Ward was a constant critic of Gibson. Imperiale's influence, however, was counterbalanced by Ken's alliance with Steve Adubato, another prominent North Ward resident. Adubato sought, through his relationship with Ken, to ensure that the Italian community had access to city hall. Imperiale's election to the state legislature, however, gave him a platform to raise the level of his criticism of Gibson. But even there his voice was muted by the election of another Adubato, Mike, Steve's brother, to the state legislature around the same time.

Aside from confronting the economic decline and racial tension, Ken faced many internal challenges, with which his administration had mixed results. I think an example of this involved the board of education. When he came to office, Newark Board of Education members were appointed by the mayor. The black community, therefore, expected the mayor to use his appointive power to diversify the board's membership, making it more reflective of the city's racial makeup—white, black, and Hispanic. It also was expected that more blacks would be hired by the school system, blacks would get access to contracts offered by the board, and the city's public schools serving black students would see improvement.

Gibson tried to meet these expectations and made progress in some areas but not to the satisfaction of many city voters. He achieved success in making racially diverse appointments and sought in various ways to impose his will on board actions. In this regard, he required new appointees to sign resignation letters as they assumed office. I recall Carl Dawson, an aide to Mayor Gibson who the mayor appointed to the school board and who orchestrated his election as board president, reading board member Brenda Grier's letter of resignation after she failed to support the mayor's candidate for school superintendent. Grier said that she had not actually resigned. Carl replied that she should take that up with the appointing authority.

Gibson ultimately lost control of the school board when city residents voted to replace the appointed board with an elected one.

Martin Bierbaum, who was an urban-studies teacher at Rutgers–Newark and wrote a column for *New Jersey Reporter* magazine, reflects back on an opportunity he had to interview the mayor at the end of his long administration. He analyzes Gibson's qualities as mayor in the context of the time and the place he served.

MARTIN BIERBAUM

In May 1986, a few weeks after Mayor Kenneth Gibson lost the election to Council President Sharpe James and a month before Gibson would have to step down, the mayor agreed to meet with me for an interview in his office. The mayor was about to move on, but to just where remained unclear. His electoral defeat reportedly came as a surprise to him.

At the time, I was directing an urban-studies program in the evening college at Rutgers–Newark. Most of my students were adults working full-time. A number were local community activists. Local law enforcement members were also well represented. My classes had become weekly debriefs on Newark's current events. Classes hotly debated issues related to Kawaida Towers, Stella Wright, the Newark Teachers Union, community-police relations, and various urban reinvestment strategies. The Gibson administration's steps in meeting these challenges were part of classroom conversations.

I simultaneously penned a regular column aptly labeled "Letter from Newark" for the *New Jersey Reporter* magazine. An interview with the mayor after sixteen years in office seemed especially timely.

More than thirty years have passed since Mayor Gibson and I sat alone in his office for a couple of hours talking about his experiences as Newark's first African American mayor. Although memories tend to fade, I still remember walking up city hall's steps and recalling my whereabouts shortly after the mayor was first elected in 1970.

For the summer of 1970, I signed on to work for the Southern Rural Research Project, based in Selma, Alabama. Most of my work involved preparing petitioners to testify before the U.S. District Court in Tuscaloosa to try to recover their voting rights. However, as the end of summer neared, I also became involved in facilitating small group workshops for high school students in preparation to integrate Selma High School in the fall.

Climbing those city-hall steps, I recalled the boost my credibility received in the South at the mere mention that I was from Newark. The outcome of Newark's recent mayoral election provided the buzz, even among young people in southern Alabama. Many knew Ken Gibson by name, and more than I expected knew that he was born in nearby Enterprise, Alabama.

A few students also talked about Amiri Baraka. They were drawn to his brand of black nationalism, which was gaining popularity as the civil rights movement splintered in different directions. H. Rap Brown and Stokely Carmichael had been organizing in neighboring counties. Their exploits grew in the retelling. Students talked with me about the way that Newark might become a cultural "promised land" under Baraka's tutelage, now to be enhanced by the government access provided by Ken Gibson as Newark's mayor. Some even talked about moving to Newark once they finished high school. I didn't want to dampen their enthusiasm, but I was certain that the Newark I knew, despite the election's recent results, could not live up to their youthful idealistic expectations.

As federal government changes began to occur under the Nixon administration to weaken civil rights and urban programs, the civil rights movement seemed to be moving into its next phase. Carl Stokes became the mayor of Cleveland, Ohio, in 1967. Richard Hatcher was elected mayor in Gary, Indiana, a year later. Despite the violent protests that erupted in the wake of the assassination of Dr. Martin Luther King Jr. in April of that year, election campaigns in cities with sizable African American populations seemed to be the movement's next logical stage.

Ken Gibson followed Mayors Stokes and Hatcher in 1970 after his unsuccessful initial run in 1966. Mayors Maynard Jackson in Atlanta and Tom Bradley in Los Angeles would continue this trend in 1973. Yet it was still unclear whether these local ballot-box victories were signs of social progress or just hollow prizes as the long list of urban ills mounted and the federal government began to apply the brakes on social programs.

Kenneth Gibson's political path also seemed uncertain. Just what did the Gibson victory mean for Newark? To what extent would the mayor's ambitions transcend the city? Faced initially with a hostile transition, the mayor nevertheless reached out to the city's business community, which was still unsure where to turn in the wake of Newark's 1967 rebellion. He also began building bridges to Trenton, first to Republican Governor William Cahill and later to Governor Brendan Byrne's Democratic administration. Gibson learned quickly that Newark lacked essential resources to go it alone.

He drew from a national talent pool in an effort to gather the expertise he believed the city required to place it in recovery from the earlier social turmoil and accelerated white flight. In addition, despite bitter criticism and especially in light of the tense transition his administration underwent, Gibson carefully selected members of the discredited former city administration to join his own. He recognized the value of deep knowledge of the local political terrain.

As I ascended those city-hall steps, I wondered if Ken Gibson fit the mold that had been cast for the period's African American politicians. Think Jesse Jackson! Think Al Sharpton! Gibson's personal predilections led in dissimilar directions. He seemed to be a different kind of politician, maybe even a nonpolitician, marching to his own drummer. He appeared more modest than flamboyant; he exuded a quiet competence.

That he started out as a political reformer was hardly surprising. Following on the heels of the disgraced Addonizio administration, it would have been difficult to imagine any successor doing otherwise. He was not a demonstrator or disruptor but a bridge builder and problem solver. There were occasional forays beyond Newark's boundaries, but for the most part, he seemed so Newark-focused. He appeared interested in just doing his job rather than moving on to the next one, so atypical of so many politicians.

Some questioned whether Ken Gibson's demeanor would interfere with how he would fare in the city's rough-and-tumble political world, which was tainted by rumors of corruption and Mob ties. Carl Stokes, who campaigned for Gibson during Gibson's unsuccessful 1966 mayoral bid, reportedly questioned whether the mayoral hopeful was "built for this business." Yet given Ken Gibson's persistence, he significantly outdistanced the Cleveland mayor's political longevity. Stokes, like so many others, underestimated Ken Gibson's tenacity.

Gibson's training as an engineer may have reinforced misimpressions. His vision was modest and methodical, not bold. He placed his "to-do" lists with notes on three-by-five cards. For him, local governance was about budgets, personnel, and the effective and efficient delivery of services. His approach was practical. He set priorities and thought through the feasible alternatives to achieve goals. He would never be a cheerleader like his rival Sharpe James was to become.

Ken Gibson's motto, one the media seized upon, was "Wherever American cities are going, Newark will get there first." The saying seemed to fit. It showed he cared. Despite his two gubernatorial runs and ascendancy to the top of the U.S. Conference of Mayors, Newark was Gibson's home. He was a part of Newark as much as Newark was a part of him.

His family moved from Enterprise to Newark when he was just eight years old. He was a product of the Newark school system, a graduate of Central High School. For college, he only moved next door to the Newark College of Engineering (NCE), now the New Jersey Institute of Technology (NJIT). He worked while going to school, taking eleven years to obtain his degree.

His formative professional experiences were as a government engineer operating within the inherent constraints of state and local government bureaucracies. He had never been an outspoken civil rights advocate or a political candidate. He left such trailblazing to others. His civic activities were limited—his most important being vice president of the city's anti-poverty agency.

Yet the young Gibson was a quick study. He learned about the ways that government had to operate, without drama, between elections. He knew the difference between mindless campaign rhetoric and words that actually addressed government's institutional imperatives.

Still, in that interview in city hall, he admitted to being unprepared.

My first question to the mayor after he welcomed me into his office was, essentially, "What do you know now that you did not know when first elected?" His response was surprising. I expected him to tell me that his engineering background helped him do his job as mayor. After all, his demeanor, his analytical approach, and even the way he dressed suggested engineer—a good background for the job.

In fact, he thought that engineering had inadequately prepared him to be mayor. It was too precise. The problems tackled by engineers were too well-defined. Managing a city like Newark could not be engineered. Relationships among federal, state, and municipal governments were constantly shifting. Resources were too often in short supply. Political support often proved unreliable, while attacks from critics could come any time.

As mayor, Ken Gibson also shared an important lesson learned. He told me that he had to be flexible, especially as alliances shifted and issues changed. Solutions often needed to be refashioned. He learned that few, if any, solutions to Newark's problems could be addressed within a single mayoral term.

I asked the mayor what he considered to be his greatest success and his greatest failure. As to his greatest success, he cited improvements to the city's health-care system. He mentioned improvements in maternity and infant mortality and tuberculosis rates.

He rejected the notion that he had a "greatest failure" but instead reframed the question as his "greatest frustration." In the reframing, he conveyed an incident in Branch Brook Park in which he failed to quell a fight involving Hispanic youths that resulted in a needless loss of life.

The mayor understood both the opportunities and constraints inherent to his office. "It is a good job, a rewarding job," he said, avoiding any hint of resignation or complaint. He said that he was wary of all-powerful chief executives who could operate free of checks and balances.

He said that checks on power do not mean a mayor can't make a difference. He talked about making a difference in the way that the garbage was picked up and the ways that police and fire protection were provided: "You can't solve all the problems, but you can make a difference."

We touched upon race and the difficulties he had in dealing with black nationalism as personified by Amiri Baraka. We also talked about his white ethnic opposition that emanated mainly from the Italian community as personified by Anthony Imperiale. There were also challenges from the Hispanic community.

How did he manage to survive?

His response was a judicious one. He said that his goal was to be the mayor of all of Newark's people. Despite the remark, I suspected that Baraka's charges of "neocolonialism" early in his administration must have pained him.

Ken Gibson remained optimistic. He noted that important changes had already occurred. He thought that the role of race in local politics had diminished: "It is no longer a novelty for a black man to be elected mayor of a major American city. That is a changed situation. That is a good thing." He hoped to see black governors as well.

I asked the mayor to respond to criticisms that I had heard about him and his administration having recently grown too removed, too isolated, maybe even aloof. He was perceived as too easygoing. Others believed that Newark needed a bolder vision, one that he seemed incapable of providing. Perhaps, after sixteen years, he was tired.

Gibson admitted that he may not have matched the stereotypical gregarious, outgoing politician, but that did not mean that he was not up to the job. He said that the people of Newark elected him to manage the city's affairs and not to run a circus.

Finally, we talked about local government corruption. His response? He warned that corruption did not come suddenly. He also mentioned it was not just public officials seeking to enhance their income who were to blame but also a flawed civic culture with a public that too often seeks special treatment.

If there was an advertisement for the position of Newark mayor in 1970, it might have called for a decision maker who understood Newark's politics and government operations while guaranteeing a modicum of stability and order in a world spinning toward chaos and violence. Ken Gibson was that man. In retrospect, he seemed to be the right man in the right place at the right time.

Did Ken Gibson think about the inspiration he provided to those high school kids I met in Alabama in 1970? By the end of his fourth term, it was doubtful that he ever viewed himself as the leader of any social movement. He asked to be Newark's mayor for four terms. In that role, he served as a personal rebuttal to the malignant myths of white supremacy and black inferiority. That was the inspiration he provided to those high school students I met in Selma, Alabama.

As mayor, Ken Gibson brought a rare set of personal qualities and professional skills to the office. In addition to his government experience that he gained over the years, he exhibited a basic decency, an ability to listen and learn, and an affability that helped him build meaningful working relationships. These were obvious strengths. Yet given the city's often unforgiving politics, some viewed his strengths as weaknesses. Frequently clashing and at times irreconcilable interests were bound to lead to disappointment by those who wanted more. Where to direct those frustrations but at the person in charge for the past sixteen years—at Mayor Ken Gibson?

Sharpe James defeated Kenneth Gibson and replaced him as mayor in 1986. He describes the racially charged electoral politics of the time and offers an assessment of Gibson's strengths and weaknesses.

Mayor Sharpe James

Ken Gibson wore Newark on his sleeves and was dedicated to making Newark better, increasing the number of black elected officials, improving education for our children, and creating economic growth in an urban environment. He was a man for all the people—offering a warm smile, a firm handshake, and advice when sought or needed. He never forgot where he came from, but he worked hard at building a consensus around issues. He was my leader and friend before I ran against him, and we became even closer after I ran against him and after he graciously offered to help me hit the ground running. He is still my mayor. In speeches, I have said, "Ken Gibson mixed the mortar for sixteen years, and I followed by laying the bricks for a better and more prosperous Newark." We both loved Newark.

As political figures, Ken and I are both products of the Black and Puerto Rican Convention, which took place over three days in November 1969, at Clinton Place Junior High School (later renamed University High School). I remember attorney Raymond A. Brown delivering a keynote address and touching on the need for black unity in the 1970 elections. "Blacks, Puerto Ricans, and white people of goodwill must work together toward the achievement of intelligent and progressive city government," he declared.

Gibson had the backing of social activist Amiri Baraka, who organized the convention and had established the New Ark Fund to raise money for the Gibson campaign. But Gibson also had a formidable white campaign director, Daniel Armet, and was able to attract the support of national black political and entertainment figures.

At age thirty-eight, Gibson had a quiet demeanor. He was an engineer with a turn-the-other-cheek, nonthreatening personality. Gibson was someone with whom the white establishment could feel comfortable. Ken was inclined to avoid offending people.

This trait was evident throughout the campaign and into his first term as mayor. For example, during the campaign, Ken conducted himself in such a manner as to not offend anyone supporting other candidates. This included at times appearing to run independent of the slate while the rest of us always acted as a team. This independent approach to the campaign often included separate fund-raising, a behavior that irked other members of the slate.

Similarly, once elected, Ken took an independent approach to the exercise of his newly gained political power. While key advisors, such as political organizer and social activist Bob Curvin, believed that the mayor would share the power of his office in designing plans for running the city, they faced a rude awakening. Once in office, Ken soundly reminded them that he was in charge, saying, "I got elected, not you." This is not to say that Ken did not look to others for advice. In this regard, he sought counsel and advice both during the transition period and well into his administration from Gus Heningburg, the president of the Greater Newark Urban Coalition. Gus, who served as the transition team leader, was highly intelligent, strictly business oriented, well liked, and an extraordinary consensus maker.

Gibson's famous election theme, "Wherever American Cities Are Going, Newark Will Get There First," would come back to haunt him. While Newark appeared to residents to remain at the starting line, other troubled American cities—Cleveland, Seattle, and Atlanta—were beginning to improve dramatically. The failed promise of the campaign allowed others with mayoral aspirations to emerge, the most prominent among them another African American, Earl Harris, one of the three members of the seven-member Community Choice Team who ran successfully for city-council seats in 1970. A racially divided city council with a six-to-three advantage for white councilmen was more threatening to Ken's political agenda and aspirations than to Earl's.

The racial division within the city council during Gibson's early years in office manifested itself in numerous and varied ways. There was the bitter fight over the naming of a police director. Then there was the fight over Baraka's plan to construct a high-rise residential building known as Kawaida Towers in the Italian American North Ward. And perhaps most infuriating to the black community was the gun incident involving city councilman Anthony Carrino. Together with North Ward vigilante, Anthony Imperiale, Carrino stormed into the mayor's office after having been denied access during a dispute. The incident involved breaking down the mayor's door and exposing a loaded revolver. The black community, responding to the threat against the mayor, argued that the intruders should have been shot by city-hall security guards. The guards' reluctance to act made Gibson seem weak in the eyes of his supporters.

There were also times when Gibson found himself alone against a racially mixed opposition within the council. I recall, for example, Ken supporting a revaluation of the city's residential and commercial property-tax laws while five members of the council—including myself—refused to support the plan, insisting that Newark residents were already over-burdened with taxes and decreasing services. We took the position that we would risk going to jail rather than submit to what we considered an unjust burden on residents. This and other examples of Gibson's fights with the city council occurred even after he was able to push for the election of other African Americans on the council.

On the other hand, I can also recall times when I found myself alone in my support of a position taken by Ken. For example, I came under fire from other council members for not supporting them in their request for higher pay and more perks. In most instances, one thought of the mayor as the CEO of the city, as opposed to the position taken by other members of the council, led by Earl Harris, that the city council was meant to run the city.

By 1982, Gibson was losing popularity. He found himself facing large numbers of homeowners who refused to pay their property taxes, which left him with mounting budget problems. Both he and Earl Harris faced criminal charges for allegedly providing a no-show job to former city councilman Michael Bontempo. In addition, Gibson faced a harsh fight over the issue of privatization of city services; his personally preferred housing-authority director, Daniel Blue, was a visible failure; his operation was a cesspool for patronage; and there were too many abandoned properties in the city, with the result being a shrinking tax base. By 1986, Newark faced a $40-million budget deficit; the city was crime ridden, led the nation in auto thefts, and was rated one of the worst cities in America by *Harper's Magazine.*

Having watched and learned from Ken Gibson as he fought the good fight, often against a hostile city council, I decided the city needed a "Sharpe Change." I defeated Gibson in his bid for reelection in 1986, though to this day, I believe that I was able to lay bricks only after Ken had mixed the mortar.

NOTE

Source: Taken in part from my book *Political Prisoner: A Memoir by Sharpe James* (Newark, N.J.: Nutany, 2013).

State Senator Ronald Rice, like many of his contemporaries, was swept up in the dynamic possibilities for a Newark that might be headed by a member of its majority-black population.

State Senator Ronald Rice

I returned to Newark from Marine Corps service in Vietnam in 1970 in the midst of the mayoral campaign. Initially, I had been asked to consider working on behalf of Harry Wheeler, a Newark school teacher who was another black candidate seeking the mayor's office. I ultimately decided to work for Ken Gibson in light of his endorsement by the Black and Puerto Rican Convention, a convening that sought to unite the two minority communities behind one minority candidate.

Once in office, Ken did something for me that I'll always remember: he was instrumental in my struggle to become a Newark police officer. I passed the police exam in 1972, one of approximately 1,100 candidates who took it, but was told that because I wore eyeglasses, I was ineligible to serve. It was an insult that the Newark Police Department wouldn't hire me. I took the position that if I could serve as a combat-reconnaissance marine in Vietnam wearing military-issued eyeglasses, I surely should be able to serve as a police officer in Newark wearing them. I told the police interviewer as much, but his position was that because I did not have twenty-twenty eyesight, I could not be hired as a police officer. The civil-service rules, I concluded, had to be changed.

I appealed my case, with Ken Gibson's support, to the New Jersey Civil Service Commission. Mayor Gibson asked his director of the Newark Human Rights Commission, Daniel Blue, to work with me in fighting the state to change the civil-service rules. I won the appeal in a short period of time. The new rule that came into effect because of my appeal was that one could become a police officer if one's vision could be corrected to twenty-thirty vision. Sharpe James, a city councilman at the time, also supported my application. I became a police officer, and the more-stringent twenty-twenty-eyesight provision was never again applied.

Ken also helped me get elected to the city council in 1982. I defeated Michael P. (Mickey) Bottone, who it was said could not be beaten. While Ken did not personally endorse me, he allowed several of his associates to assist in my campaign. Elton Hill, who was the president of the KAGCA (Kenneth Allen Gibson Civic Association) and the mayor's political field general, had a good friend, Waymon Jessie, work with me as my campaign manager. Waymon was able to bring other field soldiers from the KAGCA to work with us—behind the scenes—helping with the campaign's mechanics. I was elected to office and became the first black councilman to represent the city's West Ward.

Though he supported me in the election, Ken and I didn't always agree, for I wanted to push harder for more and better services for the people of my ward. Councilpeople always want more for their constituents, and I felt that the other wards were given better treatment than mine. The South Ward was the most favored because it was—and still is—home to most of the city's black elected and appointed officials. The North Ward had Steve Adubato as its advocate, someone Ken's administration worked hard to keep happy. The East Ward was home to the city's substantial and politically influential Portuguese population. The Central Ward, on the other hand, although it had a powerful Democratic chair by the name of "Honey" Ward, tended to get shortchanged. I was not going to let that happen in the West Ward. And it didn't.

I'm proud that as councilman, I was able to secure funds to start the citywide Pop Warner League. I got the council members to agree to put $50,000 in the municipal budget for the kids, but Ken took the money out of the budget. It infuriated me because it was for our children. The following budget year, I put the $50,000 in the budget again, and this time, Gibson approved it. I was able to keep it in the budget from that point on during my sixteen years as councilman. Now the Newark Pop Warner Citywide Football League has existed for thirty years. There is still a line item in the city's budget for the program, but unfortunately, the amount is not enough.

I guess my biggest criticism of Ken relates to the extent to which he, along with other black, white, and Latino officials in Newark, aided Steve Adubato in building the political organization that he was able to create at the expense of taxpayers, in general, and black folks, in particular. I didn't believe Ken needed Adubato's North Ward to be successful in his efforts, whether at election time or in his dealings with the council. Ken, however, was of the opposite view. He was particularly concerned about limiting the influence of Tony Imperiale, a North Ward rabble-rouser, and felt that Steve was key to containing him. That appears to have been the initial rationale for the support Steve received from Gibson's administration. In my view, that support enabled Steve, over time, to build a political power base that took advantage of senior and disabled citizens, disenfranchised voters via voter fraud, and achieved statewide significance in the process.

Ken also sought to attend to matters of statewide importance. He and Rev. S. Howard Woodson, the first black speaker of the New Jersey Assembly, should be given credit for attempting to establish a statewide black political platform. I, frankly, don't think the effort was taken seriously by white political bosses and observers, largely because in the late 1970s, there were too few black elected officials to make building a sustainable black political organization a realistic possibility. But the fact that they realized the need to marshal the political power of the black community spoke to their growing political sophistication. Today, I think such an effort would be much more likely to succeed.

When Ken ran unsuccessfully—twice—to become the governor of New Jersey, he had my strong support. He was unable to achieve the goal, but I respected his effort. So did other urban politicians and a few white activists throughout the state. Urban mayors throughout the country, especially black mayors, looked to Ken as their leader. He was seen as a force for positive change in Newark and in urban America generally. Yes, we disagreed in some instances, and the disagreements were intense, but in the final analysis, we were able to work together to advance the interests of the residents of Newark and other cities. I believe Ken deserves accolades for the path he blazed.

Overall, I'm inclined to view Ken's tenure in office as a success. Yes, in the latter years, exhaustion set in as the search for needed resources became more and more difficult. He slowed down. After sixteen years in office, he hardly fought for reelection in 1986.

Yet he was, above all, a survivor. And Ken still advises us and helps us shape good policy by making those of us who listen think before we act. He's our hero.

Fran Adubato is the wife of Steve Adubato Sr., who was and is a powerful political figure in Newark's predominantly Italian American North Ward. He established the North Ward Center to meet various social needs of his constituents.

FRAN ADUBATO

I can with enthusiasm and sincerity describe the relationship between Ken Gibson and my husband, Steve, and me as very special. And it has been so for many years. Just saying this in my predominantly Italian American community is to relegate myself to outsider status. At times, the relationship exposed me and my family to name-calling and even threats of violence.

The relationship began at the time of the 1970 mayoral election. Ken Gibson, an African American, challenged incumbent Hugh Addonizio, an Italian American. Even though Addonizio was under indictment for corruption and ties to the "Mob," he was considered by virtually every voter in the Italian North Ward as the only acceptable choice. My husband, Steve, disagreed. Having only recently gained control of the Democratic Party in our district, Steve vigorously supported Ken in the election.

I can vividly recall confronting Steve and reminding him that his political choices were putting our children at risk. We were all at risk. During the latter days of the 1970 campaign, I felt it necessary to send my three children away from the house to stay with relatives in a nearby town. On election night, my Uncle Frank, who was a sergeant on the Newark police force, stood guard for us on our front porch with a shotgun. I can also recall the rioting that took place at Thomm's Restaurant that night, where Addonizio's election headquarters was located. There were large crowds of angry people and television cameras to record the event. On the other hand, when the election results came in, I can honestly say that I shared Steve's excitement and satisfaction with the results.

After the election, I remember thinking to myself, How will this new mayor ever be able to bring together such a racially divided city? I don't think he ever really captured full admiration or respect from the Italian American North Ward. He certainly never carried the ward in any of his subsequent bids for reelection. I did find that Ken made an earnest effort to be the mayor of all the people. He never appeared to hold the lack of voter support against residents of the North Ward when it came to the distribution of city services. With hindsight, I can see that Ken did manage to calm the waters. And he was certainly helpful to Steve in his efforts to serve the residents of the North Ward—a population that was changing quite dramatically in terms of ethnic makeup.

Soon after the 1970 election, Ken, as well as others in his administration, assisted Steve in his effort to establish the now well-known North Ward Center. I recall the time the center was nearly totally destroyed by fire. Ken made sure that Newark's fire department, with its director, John Caulfield, was swiftly deployed. The center's application for funding from the Ford Foundation was also greatly enhanced by support from Ken. I cannot think of any occasion when a request for help from Ken or members of his administration was denied.

In the end, I suppose it is a mutual love of Newark that created and continues to sustain the warm relationship between Ken Gibson and the Adubato family.

Newark attorney Sheldon Bross traces the formation of his
attitude toward race from his upbringing as a Jewish American
in a predominantly Italian American section of Newark.

SHELDON BROSS, ESQ.

Being asked to reflect on my long relationship with the city of Newark most immediately brings back memories of racial divides and racial tension. I am now eighty years old. My earliest memories regarding race relations go back to the 1940s and 1950s. My Orthodox Jewish parents had fled Poland around 1910, married in 1932, and established a home in Newark. Our home was not in the Weequahic section of the city, well-known as a Jewish settlement. We lived on South Seventeenth Street. We were renters, not homeowners.

It is difficult for me to talk about my early recollections about race relations. This is due to the fact that my family was, unfortunately (as I see it now), typical among white people across the nation at the time: black people were considered inferior and not to be interacted with socially. I have tried to reconcile these early memories with my Jewish religion. That has not worked. Unfortunately, when it came to race, there did not appear to be any moral standard or standard for fairness built into our religious precepts. The best I have been able to do in terms of understanding the treatment of black people at the time—at least as far as my family was concerned—is to accept that people feel better about themselves when they can view others as less than they.

That said, there is a bright side to my recollections about race and race relations in Newark during my youth. Hiring blacks in the white retail sector was practically nonexistent. To some extent, Jewish merchants represented an exception to this exclusionary practice, including my father, who hired a gentleman named Randolph to work in our family business of peddling bananas on Prince Street. In the work context, Randolph was treated fairly and respectfully. There was just no social intercourse to follow.

There were no black students in my grammar school on South Seventeenth Street. My earliest recollection of black classmates derives from my years at Madison Junior High School. I at last began to discover that black students were not unlike me. We were all early teenagers, confused and struggling to grow up. I vividly recall a class outing to city hall with my all-time favorite teacher, Ms. Rous. We were allowed to sit in on a meeting of the Newark Municipal Council. What I recall most from the visit is watching Irvine Turner fall asleep during an important discussion. I still had no black person to counter the negative images instilled in me as a child. The thought of a black person becoming the mayor of the city was in the realm of the impossible. Even as I moved on to Weequahic High School, where I encountered more black students—and even called some of them my friends—there was still no serious social interaction between the races. Also, there were no black teachers to admire and respect.

By the time I entered Rutgers University, my views about race were changing dramatically. I met Bob Curvin and Donald Payne, both of whom belied all my earlier impressions of blacks. Then, in law school, at Rutgers–Newark, I had the extraordinary experience of taking a course with brilliant and loveable Clarence Clyde Ferguson. Professor Ferguson, my first black instructor at any level, went on to become a professor at Harvard Law School, a prominent scholar, and a U.S. ambassador.

By 1970, when Ken Gibson was elected the first African American mayor of Newark and of any major Northeastern city, I had fully turned around with respect to my attitude about race. Ken represented all that was excellent in a person. He was an engineer. He was highly intelligent and articulate. He represented a refreshing change from his corrupt predecessor.

I believe that much of my behavior as an adult, whether consciously or unconsciously, has been influenced by my desire to atone for my participation in practices related to race relations that I now view as offensive. The process of atonement began with my marriage to a woman who was raised in a family environment that was dramatically different from mine. My wife's Italian mother and stepfather instilled in her the principles of justice and equality for all people. Together, my wife and I instilled similar values in our children.

I take pride—and perhaps assuage additional guilt—by telling the story of my sister-in-law adopting a three-year-old black girl then living in the "projects" in New Brunswick. That girl went on to attend Dartmouth College, where she received a medical degree. Her diploma was handed to her by Bill Clinton. She is like a daughter, and although she lives in Jacksonville, we vacation together annually.

During the Gibson years, I was a practicing attorney in downtown Newark. In that capacity, I represented countless black clients, including a lawyer named Maurice Strickland, who later became my law partner. It was Maurice who introduced me to Ken Gibson. As best I can recall, my law firm was the only integrated law firm in the city. As much as I despised some of the statements made by Louis Farrakhan about Jews, I also represented a Black Muslim mosque, which I continue to represent today. When Ken was scheduled to marry Camille, the couple decided to avoid unwanted publicity by having a quiet ceremony the week before the publicly announced date. I served as best man, and my wife served as maid of honor.

For more than thirty years, Ken and a group of us Newark old-timers spent Friday morning laughing at breakfast at Chamblee's. I regard Ken Gibson as a bright light in the history of Newark and in my life.

Liz Del Tufo, despite undergoing a terrifying experience because she planned
to sell her house to African Americans, decided to stay in Newark.

ELIZABETH "LIZ" DEL TUFO

When I look back on memories of Newark, I think first about the condition of the city just after the 1967 rebellion. The city that Ken Gibson
inherited as the first African American mayor in 1970 was a city renowned
for break-ins, purse snatchings, and auto thefts. These crimes and others,
while relegated primarily to the downtown, still produced an overall feeling of distress throughout the city. In addition to an inordinate amount
of crime, Newark also had an inordinate number of fires, many of which
were suspicious in terms of origin.

I arrived in Newark in 1960, when I married former New Jersey superior court judge Raymond Del Tufo. Raymond and I settled in the city's
Italian American North Ward in a lovely house where I still reside. I vividly
remember the night the rebellion started. The well-known activist lawyer
(he had represented the Chicago Seven) Len Weinglass was visiting Raymond and me that evening. The conversation actually had turned to the
possibility of an uprising in the city based on eroding living conditions
among a large segment of Newark's population. Still, we were surprised
when soon after Len left, he called to advise us that a riot had begun in
the city.

While I am not sure I understood all of the tension that ultimately led to
violence, I soon was given a firsthand taste of some of the bitterness that
existed in the city. When Raymond died in 1970, I considered moving from
Newark. Toward that end, I put the house up for sale. The house was VA-
approved. A lovely African American couple offered to buy it. The husband was an army veteran. Not long after word got out that I was about to
sell to an African American family, the house was firebombed and badly
damaged. That ended the planned sale. For those who remember the
period, the firebombing of my house occurred at the time of the highly

controversial and racially charged plan by Amiri Baraka to construct a
residential complex in the North Ward known as Kawaida Towers.

Should I continue plans to leave, or should I stay? Somehow, the firebombing inspired me to stay and confront the ills that had produced such
a horrific display of racism. I repaired my house and dedicated myself to
improving the city. I was fortunate in the fact that Steve Adubato Sr. had
created anchor institutions that kept our area of the city stable and fundamentally safe. What I remember about the years immediately following the rebellion and the early days of the Gibson years is the esprit de
corps that existed among many of the city's most prominent and powerful
people, many from either the corporate or arts world.

My earliest hint of Ken Gibson's approach toward governing came
when he said that his job was "to make sure the garbage gets picked up."
No doubt his words were meant to suggest that his first priority was to
keep the city going and to restore at least some degree of normalcy. Ken
seemed more comfortable with the workaday aspects of the job, though I
admit, at the time, we thought that he should have been more of an obvious promoter, more of a cheerleader for Newark.

My own efforts to improve Newark were varied, and Ken embraced
some of my activities, while others he did not. At worst, Ken assumed a
neutral posture toward initiatives that he couldn't fully embrace. One
such disagreement was over my cofounding of the Newark Preservation
and Landmarks Committee. Focused initially on the lovely brownstone
townhouses on James Street, the committee sought to and did secure state
and national historic preservation designations for such structures, plus
parks, public art, and historic districts. I am to this day uncertain why Ken
disapproved of the committee's efforts. I can only speculate that he viewed
our efforts as contributing to elitism and the potential for gentrification
at a time when he was keenly focused on the immediate needs of those
remaining in the city following dramatic declines in the city's population.

Ken also disapproved of the creation of a historic preservation commission in the city. Perhaps, looking back, Ken would now recognize that

a number of projects critical to Newark's slow emergence from the ravages of the rebellion would not have been possible without the availability of historic tax credits facilitated by the efforts of our commission.

Finally, Ken showed little support for my efforts to help remake Newark as a center for arts and culture. I had initially worked on these initiatives as the first director of cultural affairs for the county of Essex. I continued my efforts when I left the county by cofounding the Newark Arts Council. Still—though Ken was not enthusiastic about our efforts—he did nothing to block them.

One of my favorite activities in Newark has been to give guided tours of the city—tours that continue to this day. Nothing makes me happier than hearing someone at the end of a tour say, "I will never think of Newark the same way again."

These tours were an information highway of sorts, with me disclosing details about the city while also gathering up information. During one event, for example, I met Mrs. Lou Danzig, whose husband had been roundly criticized back in the day for creating large clusters of public housing in Newark. The criticism was centered on the fact that most of the public housing was located in areas that once had single-family homes. There also were complaints that the housing would produce concentrations of poverty and crime. Mrs. Danzig insisted that her husband never intended or expected such negative outcomes associated with his urban renewal and public-housing initiatives.

For the record, I am not critical of public housing; I believe that it represents an important housing option for poor people.

Overall, I am at times amazed that Newark has recovered as well as it has from those days of the rebellion. For this, we can thank a host of private citizens and public officials, chief among them being the mayor during those difficult years.

Ken Gibson, I believe, was the right man for the job at the time he was elected. The city needed his calm demeanor and his relaxed governing style, which allowed other creative folks in the city to try out their ideas for improving the city's image. By 1986, I confess, I had become attracted to the cheerleading style of Sharpe James, yet I credit Ken for bringing stability to the city when we desperately needed it.

Robert "Bob" Pickett gives us a sense of the possibilities in Newark for a young African American lawyer who became involved in politics in the late 1960s.

ROBERT "BOB" PICKETT, ESQ.

I was a young twenty-year-old in 1968, a pivotal year in the history of this nation. It was only three years after President Lyndon B. Johnson signed the historic Civil Rights Act into law. It was just one year removed from the racial unrest and uprising that tore through and rocked Newark, leaving some twenty-six people dead and 1,100 injured and costing approximately $10 million dollars in property damage. The year 1968 was also when we lost both Martin Luther King Jr. and Robert F. Kennedy through assassination. It was the year I returned to Newark as a young staffer for the vice president of the United States, Hubert H. Humphrey, as he sought the Democratic nomination for president. My assignment with Humphrey was to help develop strategies to marshal the "youth" vote and to plan for his campaign trips to urban communities.

As part of an advance team, I would head to locations ahead of the vice president, and it was during just such an event in Newark that I first met Kenneth A. Gibson and a number of key Newark political folks.

I wound up introducing Gibson to Vice President Humphrey. Gibson at the time was contemplating a run for mayor. He seemed focused, serious, and, oddly for a politician, shy and humble. I instantly felt that in one capacity or another, he could help the city of my youth. Gibson's roots in the state of New Jersey and in Newark were not especially deep. Like many African Americans, his family came north from the Deep South during what is commonly called the Great Migration to escape the entrenched racism in the Southern states. He worked as an engineer for the New Jersey

Highway Department from 1950 to 1960. He was the chief engineer for the Newark Housing Authority from 1960 to 1966 and chief structural engineer for Newark from 1966 to 1970. With the help of such political luminaries and activists as Amiri Baraka, Donald Tucker, and the United Brothers group, Gibson was picked to run for mayor in 1970 during the historic Black and Puerto Rican Convention. Gibson was elected in a tough and racially charged runoff general election, defeating incumbent mayor Addonizio.

When I returned home from law school in 1972 to work for the largest law firm in New Jersey, McCarter and English, I was only the second African American attorney hired by the firm. During my stint at McCarter and English, I worked with and represented numerous community groups and prominent activists, including Amiri Baraka, Gus Heningburg, and Councilman Donald Tucker. It was during this period that Gibson recognized my passion for social justice and the law. As a result, the mayor recommended me for the position of general counsel for the Newark Board of Education, which at the time was in complete disarray administratively and legally. In this capacity, I had a unique opportunity to observe firsthand Gibson's leadership and management style as he interacted with his top aides and the public.

What I found was a mayor who sincerely listened to their concerns. He was low-key yet meticulous in his development of public policy. He was a tireless boss as he managed his talented young city-hall staff. I saw him deal with old-school Newark politicians respectfully yet firmly. Mayor Gibson embraced the opportunity to help many of us who went away to college, maybe to graduate school or law school, who then came back to "our" city as the next generation of leadership.

Revitalizing downtown, working to create safe and affordable housing, improving services, facilitating job growth, and repairing a troubled education system were among his goals. Gibson was pivotal in cultivating the city's health services and reducing high rates of tuberculosis and infant mortality. Because the overall quality of life improved for Newark residents, Gibson was reelected three times.

The Great Migration dramatically changed the demographics of Newark. The flood of new people and the later loss of industry resulted in rising unemployment and chronic poverty. Life in the city was grim, but when it was most needed, Gibson brought hope.

He was a man of the people who, unlike many city politicians of the past, genuinely cared about the residents of Newark. Perhaps just as important, he laid a foundation for African American leadership throughout America. In 1979, he was awarded the Senator John Heinz Award for "the greatest level of public service by a public official." It was a little-known award, but honoring Gibson with it spoke volumes.

We are now, in America, at an interesting crossroads in our political and social spheres. I see many parallels with 1968 as we face the need to fight for justice and equality. Now, when many of our gains are being challenged, it's important to remember the inspired governance of Newark's first African American mayor.

Marie Villani took over her husband's seat on the powerful
Newark City Council and, despite serious personal risk, formed
and maintained an alliance with Mayor Gibson.

Marie Villani

I first joined the Newark City Council in 1972 to complete the final year of my husband Ralph Villani's third term as a councilman elected at-large. The council offered the seat to me as a courtesy, since I had no previous political experience or, for that matter, any previous interest in politics. I hadn't even been involved in any of Ralph's campaigns. Ralph had been a mainstay on the council: in addition to serving three terms, he was the council president from 1962 to 1970. I was elected to a council seat of my own in 1973, and I served five terms until 1993. I served for virtually all of Ken Gibson's sixteen years as mayor.

Prior to the time that I joined the council, my life and my personal interests were focused on our home in the North Ward and my career in fashion and design. I still have fond memories of the elegant fashion shows I hosted at places like the Plaza Hotel in Manhattan. Once I thought I could make a difference and help bring the city back from the ravages of the 1967 rebellion, I abandoned my fashion and design career for politics. Something important remained with me, however, from my days involved in the arts and culture. In that world, I learned to accept people for their talent without regard for race or creed. For me, diversity was a normal, healthy, and desirable part of professional life. That guiding principle spilled over into my political career, and, sad to say, it was the source of harsh reprisals from my own Italian neighbors in the North Ward.

I was born in Newark in 1921 to first-generation Italian immigrants. Like many others at my age, ninety-five, I certainly do have memory lapses, but I vividly remember how racially divided Newark was in 1970 when Ken took office as our first African American mayor. The racial division was apparent not only in the neighborhoods but within the ranks of the city council. There were five white councilmen (actually four white council-men and one white councilwoman) and four black councilmen. Votes on most matters were cast strictly along this racial divide.

I became the fifth vote on issues of importance to Ken and to the black council minority. Being the fifth vote to help Ken move his agenda caused my life to be a living hell. One such vote that immediately comes to mind was the vote on Ken's choice of an African American for police director. There were four yes votes from the black councilmen, four no votes from the white councilmen, and a deciding yes vote from me. Such votes made me feel extremely lonely on the council as well as in my neighborhood. My voting brought the wrath of members of the Italian community. There were times when I was afraid to go home, and there were times when I cried myself to sleep.

The most vicious and hurtful act was the killing of our family dog. The pet was killed and left on our doorstep as a warning. I found this particu-larly painful and frightening when I had to explain its possible implica-tions to my children. Other actions against me included having my car tires slashed and the windows in our home broken. There was also the time my house was robbed of almost everything of value, including furniture. It made little or no difference if I reported these crimes to the police (by which I mean the local precinct). There was, in fact, a police officer living right next door with whom I had virtually no contact. I was not inclined to create publicity about these incidents outside of my local community.

I was a woman alone. I seldom discussed my principles or political agenda with my white colleagues on the city council. I had very few white friends, yet I always enjoyed comfortable margins of victory in my elections thanks to enormous support from the black community. I can remember campaign events where Ken's mother would tell the audience that there was no other choice but to vote for Marie Villani.

My political objective was simply to do the right thing. I firmly believe that my long life in good health is my reward for sticking to that principle. After a time, of course, I stopped having to worry about dangerous reprisals. And today, as I walk the streets of Newark or attend Newark-based events, I am proud of the reception I receive from all elements of the Newark community.

What I can say about my relationship with Ken Gibson is that we were friends before he became mayor and while he was mayor and that we continue to be friends today. There were times while we were both in office when I would press Ken to explain his position on an issue to me, but he never pushed or even asked me to vote in any particular way. He didn't have to. We shared a vision about how to move the city forward.

Emmy Award–winning broadcaster Steve Adubato Jr., PhD,
finds interesting parallels between Mayor Ken Gibson and his
father, North Ward political leader Steve Adubato.

STEVE ADUBATO JR.

It is providential that I have been asked to reflect on memories associated with the election of Ken Gibson in 1970 as the first African American mayor of Newark. Many of my memories already have been recorded in my recent book *Lessons in Leadership*.

In its preface, I describe lessons in tenacity and courage taught to me by my father, characteristics that I did not appreciate early on. I learned some of these lessons from my father's words and others from his actions.

I grew up in the heavily Italian American North Ward of Newark. I was educated in Newark public schools including Broadway Junior High School and then Essex Catholic High School. By the time I entered Broadway Junior High, the school had become predominantly black and Hispanic. Essex Catholic too was very integrated, reflecting the makeup of our city.

As an adolescent in 1970, I found the accepted description of my part of town as an "Italian neighborhood" both problematic and confusing. By then, the demographics of the North Ward had begun changing dramatically, for it was now home to large numbers of minorities. Tensions arose, and the ensuing "white flight" only seemed to exacerbate them. A significant number of the remaining white residents wanted a continuation of a white presence in the mayor's office.

Against this backdrop, my father chose to challenge the political status quo in Newark by taking over the Democratic Party in our section of the city from a party boss controlled by the Mob. My father was told, in no uncertain terms that his efforts would not be a good career move. Undaunted, in 1969, he organized a group of supporters, and in a series of elections that required police protection, they succeeded in winning control of the party.

Thereafter, my father refused to support then-indicted Mayor Hugh Addonizio for reelection. He instead welcomed the candidacy of Ken Gibson. The immediate result was the formation of a strong antiblack vigilante movement in our neighborhood led by a group of Italian Americans who accused my father of betrayal.

I remember death threats against my father that would come in the form of phone calls, pamphlets, and late-night visits from thugs. And it only grew worse over time. My father would rarely travel alone, as it was made clear to him that, as the local Democratic leader in our section of Newark, he was expected to support the Italian American incumbent mayor—even if this mayor was likely to go to jail.

I remember going to school during the 1970 mayoral campaign and hearing white kids say, "What's the matter with your father? What is he, some sort of n—lover?" And then adding, "You must be one too."

I wanted to defend my father, which resulted in arguments and some fights. Yet there was the other side of me that kept thinking, What *is* wrong with my father? Why can't he just go along like all the other Italian American fathers in the neighborhood and support the white mayor, corrupt or not? I remember going to my father one day and asking why he was supporting Gibson. I also remember him being put off by my question—almost shocked by the fact that I didn't know or appreciate the risk he was taking by doing the right thing.

It finally dawned on me. One day, when I was coming home from school and had forgotten my key, I decided to climb into the window of our house. As I approached, I saw a series of holes in the glass. At first, it wasn't clear what I was looking at, but I soon realized they were bullet holes—and they were facing the spot where my father's chair was located when he sat to watch television. I ran to a neighbor's house for help in tracking down my mother. Of course, this alarmed both her and my father, so for the remainder of the 1970 campaign, my two sisters and I were shipped out of our home to live with relatives in a town nearby.

Our family's support for and collaboration with Ken Gibson did not end with his election. Many of my father's most important philanthropic achievements could not have been achieved without Gibson's support. And my entire family continued to support Gibson throughout his sixteen years as mayor. In 1974, for example, while in high school, I was pushed by my father to organize a "Youth for Gibson" campaign to support the mayor's bid for reelection against a local Italian American community icon, Anthony Imperiale.

With little choice, I took up my father's challenge. Our group, with additional recruits from the neighborhood, produced and distributed pamphlets, lawn signs, and other campaign materials. There was still name-calling and threats, but by then I had taken to heart my father's sound advice: "It's OK to be afraid, but never show it."

NOTE

Source: Taken in part from the preface to my book *Lessons in Leadership* (New Brunswick, N.J.: Rutgers University Press, 2016).

> Harold Hodes had served as an Addonizio appointee on the Newark
> Human Rights Commission. Perhaps surprisingly, he details how his
> own political future took shape and grew during the Gibson era.

Harold Hodes

I met Kenneth Gibson when I served on the Newark Human Rights Commission in the 1960s. I was an appointee of Mayor Hugh Addonizio, the person Ken defeated in 1970 to become Newark's first African American mayor. After Addonizio left office, I joined state government as a staff member in the New Jersey Department of Community Affairs, the state agency that municipalities relied upon for community development and financial management assistance. My role at the department enabled me to help Newark secure badly needed financial assistance. When the commissioner of the department who hired me was fired and was replaced by Pat Kramer, the former mayor of Paterson, New Jersey, I decided it was time for me to leave. So I called Mayor Gibson, and he offered me a job as deputy director of a federally funded community development initiative of the Nixon administration.

Soon after I started, my role in the administration expanded. In addition to my primary duties, I was assigned the responsibility for managing the relationship between the mayor's office and the city council. I functioned as an aide to the mayor with an office in the executive suite. It was a fascinating experience made all the more so by the racial diversity of the council.

In my view, Ken's biggest contribution to Newark was his ability to bring calm to the city when it was still reeling from the 1967 rebellion. Steady leadership was Ken's trademark. His guidance was just what the city needed.

Upon taking office, Ken was faced with a teachers' strike said to be the longest in the nation's history. His calm demeanor helped keep the dispute from further getting out of hand. When the strike finally ended, Ken followed up by bringing the parties together in a task force to craft an educational agenda to benefit both students and teachers.

Ken brought highly talented people into his administration. Some were local, others came from afar, but all were eager to participate in addressing the challenges of a major Northeastern city being led by an African American mayor. Additionally, in the early days, Ken was able to attract considerable federal assistance, especially for social service and community-development programs. He was a magnet for talent and federal money.

Ken's leadership ability was recognized over time. He gained national attention when he stated, "Wherever American cities are going, Newark will get there first," a phrase he borrowed from Donald Malafonte, chief of staff to former mayor Addonizio. Indeed, the high point of Gibson's sixteen years in office might be his election as chair of the executive committee of the U.S. Conference of Mayors, which led to him becoming the president of the conference in 1976. He was the first African American to hold the position.

At the time, Gibson caught the attention of President Jimmy Carter, who respected him enough to place his name on the short list for the post of secretary of the Department of Housing and Urban Development. Ken was passed over, however, in favor of Patricia Harris, the first black woman to serve in a presidential cabinet. Ken didn't go to Washington, but staying home had just as much impact. His visibility as Newark's mayor provided positive publicity for the city and helped attract human and financial resources.

I become distressed when I read accounts of Ken Gibson's time as mayor. Many who have written on the subject had no firsthand knowledge of how difficult it was to manage a city as racially and ethnically diverse as Newark. I am still impressed when I recall how Ken was able to somehow find common ground to help resolve the often-conflicting needs and interests.

———

I left the Gibson administration when I was recruited to become Gov. Brendan Byrne's chief of staff. I remained close to Ken, however, which Byrne appreciated, and I vividly recall helping Byrne obtain Ken's endorsement for reelection.

Without a doubt, Ken Gibson made my career success possible.

Grizel Ubarry highlights the significance of Gibson's lack of attention
to the needs of the Hispanic community in light of the critical role
the convening of the Black and Puerto Rican Convention played in
his election as the city of Newark's first African American mayor.

GRIZEL UBARRY

In 1974, as a recent graduate of Rutgers University, I was pleased to have quickly found employment in Newark working as a program coordinator at ASPIRA Inc. of New Jersey, a community-based nonprofit organization serving Hispanic youth. The prior year, I had completed a semester internship at the University of Medicine and Dentistry (UMDNJ) at University Hospital in Newark (now Rutgers Medical School) and was excited about working in this urban center with a large Puerto Rican / Latino population. At that time, there were between sixty thousand to eighty thousand Hispanics, the majority Puerto Ricans, residing in Newark. Puerto

Ricans had been migrating to Newark since the early 1960s. They were concentrated mostly in the North Ward and South Broad Street sections of the city, and at the time, they represented approximately 18 percent of the city's population. Growth in the Hispanic community was happening at the time the white population was leaving the city in significantly large numbers.[1]

Throughout the 1960s and 1970s, the Puerto Rican community was primarily poor and working class. The poor suffered from underemployment, working as day laborers or relying on public assistance. The working class mostly served as laborers, maintenance or factory workers, and in clerical and retail jobs. Households were predominantly Spanish speaking, Christian, and consisting of two to five children living with extended family members. As a community, Latinos lacked political sophistication and were struggling to find their way in a predominantly black city.

Puerto Ricans, for the most part, had been isolated, experiencing a great deal of intimidation by both the black and Italian communities, especially in the North Ward, where a growing concentration of Hispanic families began occupying apartments and homes left behind by white flight. Under both the Addonizio and Gibson administrations, the North Ward political base was strictly controlled by the Italians, who did a fair share of intimidation and voter suppression to keep Puerto Rican residents from organizing and voting.

Politically, Puerto Rican leadership was represented by two types of leaders—the traditional old-school leaders who were older, mostly merchants, social workers, some professionals, and some, frankly, political hacks. The second leadership group consisted of younger activists, many of whom were college graduates or college students. However, among them was a more militant group, including members of the Puerto Rican Young Lords led by Ramon Rivera, the founder and executive director of La Casa de Don Pedro for twenty years. This subgroup of leaders was more vocal, angry, and less willing to compromise. This type of activist leadership was evident in other major cities such as New York, Chicago, and Los Angeles.

During the 1970s, peoples' impressions of Newark were mixed. For some, the city was so engulfed in racial tensions among the city's three largest ethnic groups—blacks, whites, and Latinos—that its future seemed hopeless. For others, Newark's assets, in particular its geographical location as a potential transportation hub for the region, offered significant promise. Some thought that since Newark had hit rock bottom, there was no place to go but up. For them, it was just a matter of time.

The Latino community's relationship with Newark's first black mayor was strained at best. The prevailing feeling among Hispanics at the time was anger and disappointment. In a city where the minority populations—Puerto Ricans and blacks—desperately wanted a change, the two communities had for a brief period united and formed the Black and Puerto Rican Convention (coalition) to agree on issues relevant to both groups and to elect the city's first black mayor, Ken Gibson. However, the ticket, which included a Puerto Rican candidate running for an at-large city council seat, was only partially successful. Ken Gibson was elected, but the Puerto Rican candidate, Ramon Aneses, lost. Many in the Latino community thought that blacks had selectively voted for black candidates but not the entire ticket, fueling their lack of trust.

One problem back in the 1960s and 1970s was that only a small number of Puerto Ricans were registered to vote, which made it difficult for any Latino candidate to win an at-large seat without gaining significant support from blacks. This was a time when the African American community was beginning to feel politically empowered, and voting for someone who did not reflect their history and experience was not something they were ready to embrace.

Dissatisfaction only increased when the mayor appointed just one official in his administration from the Puerto Rican community—to the position of deputy mayor, which many in the community viewed as mostly a

weak and ceremonial position. With less than 2 percent of Latinos participating in the city's workforce during the mayor's first term, it was apparent
that Puerto Ricans were shut out of jobs, services, and training opportunities, as well as discriminated against and harassed by an all-white police
force.

For most of Gibson's first term and for the most part thereafter, the
Latino community remained invisible, voiceless, and powerless.

The worst came in the summer of 1974, on a beautiful Labor Day weekend, where five thousand Puerto Rican residents were enjoying a festival
at the city's popular Branch Brook Park, a disturbance that became part of
the city's turbulent history. This eruption, the start of the "Puerto Rican
Riots of 1974," occurred when mounted policemen, using excessive force,
tried to break up a dice game. A confrontation between Puerto Ricans and
the police followed, leading to several days of disorder, demonstrations,
looting, fire bombing, shootings, arrests, and a curfew. In the end, two
Puerto Ricans were killed by policemen, gunshots wounded five, twenty
policemen and firemen were injured, fifty-one citizens were injured in
ways other than gunfire, and at least seventy-six people were arrested.[2]

The mayor, to his credit, tried hard to diffuse the problem by immediately arriving at the festival scene and encouraging folks to join him in a
walk to city hall to discuss what he assumed were the grievances against
police. His efforts quickly disintegrated, however, when Latino leaders
used the police brutality incident as an opportunity to make demands of
the mayor related to unacceptable conditions experienced primarily by
Puerto Ricans in the areas of housing, education, employment, and the
criminal justice system. The mayor initially refused to hear the demands,
a response that led to more disturbances. Gibson finally agreed to meet
with a handpicked group of Hispanic leaders, known as the Hispanic
Emergency Council, organized by the deputy mayor, instead of meeting
with the younger activist leaders in the community. The mayor during this
incident effectively pitted the two Latino leadership groups against each

other, which eventually backfired, causing even greater disenchantment with his ability to fully understand and engage Newark's growing Latino community.

Working with the Hispanic Emergency Council, the mayor did agree to investigate the claims of police brutality and the deaths of the two Puerto Rican demonstrators. He also directed the Newark Human Rights Commission to conduct hearings on conditions experienced by Latinos. These hearings clearly revealed a community that was impoverished and ignored by city government as well as by corporate and educational institutions. Examples of some of the startling statistics presented at the Newark Human Rights Commission hearings include:[3]

- Sixty-two percent of Puerto Rican high school students were performing below their grade level, with a dropout rate of 66 percent by their senior year.
- Of six thousand Newark city employees, only 2 percent were Hispanics.
- The unemployment rate for young Puerto Ricans ranged between 30 percent and 55 percent.
- Of three hundred thousand units of public housing, only 186 were occupied by Hispanics.
- Major corporations in the city employed less than 2 percent from the Hispanic community, and most of those jobs actually held were janitorial and clerical.

By the fall of 1974 and in the years that followed, Gibson did respond to a number of the demands presented to him by the Puerto Rican / Latino community. Responses included the appointment of a Hispanic municipal judge, the appointment of a Hispanic member to the board of education, and the investigation by the police into the killings of the two Puerto Ricans during the riots. Additionally, there were some minor programs and procedural changes but not much more.

From the beginning of his mayoral leadership, Ken Gibson was never able to achieve a strong political or positive relationship with the Latino community. Much of his effort appears to have been designed to avoid another disturbance while doing the bare minimum for Hispanics, choosing instead to appease the Italians under the leadership of Steve Adubato, who also was skilled at suppressing the Puerto Rican vote. The mayor did not regard the Latino community as a reliable voting bloc that could benefit him, and to a certain point, he was correct. There was no effort on the part of the mayor to mentor young Latinos as a way to engage this emerging, growing minority community. At the end of the day, for Ken Gibson, getting reelected was the most critical factor in his decision-making, without any consideration for serving the city's diverse constituents.

Today, more than forty years and three mayors later, the Latino community represents more than 33 percent of the city's population. It has had three Puerto Ricans serving as city council members for the past ten years, of whom two are at-large members.

NOTES

1. Some of the information contained in these remarks comes from the Newark Public Library's Hispanic Information and Research Center collection of oral histories and papers by leaders including Mayor Gibson in response to the 1974 Newark Puerto Rican Riots.

2. "How Well Newspaper Worked under Stress—Analysis of the Newark Puerto Rican Riots," *Journal of the Center for Analysis of Public Issues* 4, no. 9 (1975): 4.

3. "Newark Human Rights Commission Public Hearing Report on the Conditions of the Hispanic Community," City of Newark, New Jersey, June 1976.

Junius Williams, a Gibson election campaign leader, high-ranking
official in the Gibson administration, and later, an opposing mayoral
candidate, underscores Gibson's missed opportunities—in particular

his failure to take advantage of his position as mayor of the state's
largest city to expand his political influence and power.

JUNIUS WILLIAMS, ESQ.

In the 1970s, the black people we elected and the people who supported
them for jobs, favors, and opportunities were happier to be inside city hall
than they were to continue the struggle. They thought city hall was the end
of the journey and couldn't see beyond its limitations.

On the other hand, some of us vested with momentum and energy saw
the struggle as a continuum. We wanted more power to gain more access
to more distant levels of power, such as state and federal government and
the big businesses downtown. All this required more study, different skills,
and constant leadership development. Our friends in the new black political class wanted to be consummate insiders, integrated into a system that
worked for other ethnic groups such as the Italians and the Irish. They
ignored or didn't understand the limits of power established by whites,
who from their base in the suburbs controlled state government and private
capital. So this new black leadership in the city failed to exert the power it
had, which came from the people in the neighborhoods. Black power,
fueled by black anger, even rage, still existed as a force, yet it was not effectively harnessed. Assimilation was the overriding goal.

Assimilation and accommodation are two words I often think about
even now and shake my head in regret for the pain and sense of futility they produced. These people, many of them my friends, wanted to be
inside so bad that they were willing to give up all knowledge of recent history, just to achieve a seat at the table of mainstream politics in America.

Assimilating into the system of city government brought mostly sym-
bolic victories: "the first black mayor" and a few jobs mostly in city hall
and in the surrounding governmental bureaucracies. But we inherited a
tax structure that was inadequate, and our people were kept out of the
world of private finance. Federal and state programs diminished in size
as the memory of the Newark Rebellion receded. Assimilation alone was

not going to make the governmental and private sectors invest more in Newark.

This desire to be on the inside didn't go unnoticed by the folks who ran the country—the business and political elite of the United States, who controlled things at the time through the Democratic Party. Hence these new elected leaders at the local level in New Jersey were quickly and firmly embraced by the national party and received all the attention any newcomer could possibly desire. Ken Gibson became a member of the National Democratic Council and eventually the president of the U.S. Conference of Mayors. But what good did this do the city in the face of the changing nature of the Democratic Party, guided by President Jimmy Carter and others to his right to become more "centrist" to pick up the white sectors of the population lost to the Republican Party when it appeared black people were getting too much of the American pie?

Ken Gibson was uniquely positioned to make a place for himself in the Democratic Party and change its rightward drift, at least on the state level. At one of our Community Development Administration (CDA) / Model Cities dinner meetings (while I was the director of Model Cities), Larry Coggins, a local organizer, came in looking much defeated. He said, "I told Ken he should let me organize the district leaders in Newark and throughout Essex County, to make Ken county Democratic Party chairman." Boom! There it was. Ken, as the "first mayor," was the highest black elected official in New Jersey's history and one of only a handful of black mayors in the country. He automatically had a following beyond Newark with no competition for loyalty.

Had he authorized Coggins to run district leaders throughout the city and county, including some liberal reform-minded whites and some from among the new Latino population, Ken could have unseated Dennis Cary, the Essex County Democratic Party chairman, and become the party powerhouse in the county. He would decide who "got the line" for countywide and statewide elections (i.e., "Line A," to make it easy for lazy voters to pick candidates on the ballot without moving too far down the ballot), he would have controlled the party's purse strings, and he would have had district leaders to get out the vote in every election in New Jersey for candidates of his choice. Anybody seeking election to the statehouse and ultimately the White House would have to come by him. But Ken told Larry "no," and thus a once-in-an-era opportunity went by.

Later, Ken would run for governor in 1981 and for county executive in 1998 but lose both races. Why? Because he had no organization sufficient to raise money and get out the vote. Had he commissioned Larry and turned us in the CDA loose to get the job done, what would the history books have said?

By the middle to end of the 1970s, black power as we envisioned was a dream deferred.

NOTE

Source: Taken from the contributor's book *Unfinished Agenda: Urban Politics in the Era of Black Power* (Berkeley, Calif.: North Atlantic, 2014).

Charles I. Auffant, Esq., was an impressionable teenager during the Newark Rebellion, and the vivid and violent images he saw on television from his home in a Bronx public-housing project were seared into his mind. This early experience led to a deep and ongoing interest in ethnic power divisions and the city where he is now a clinical professor at Rutgers Law School.

CHARLES I. AUFFANT, ESQ.

The first time I saw pictures of Newark was in 1967. I was a teenager sitting in front of a black-and-white television in my parents' home in the projects in the Bronx. The New York City Housing Authority did not permit residents to have air conditioners back then, and the apartments were like brick ovens. The scenes on the news made me forget the sweltering heat, at least momentarily. I watched in awe as American soldiers aimed their rifles at project buildings that looked just like the one I lived in. "Is this what is happening in the South?" I asked my mother. "No, mijo, that's Newark, New Jersey." We both watched in stunned silence as soldiers unleashed a fusillade at the apartment windows of the projects. The horror was made personal not only because we lived in a Bronx project building that was only a forty-five-minute drive from Newark but also because my mother had told us stories of Newark, a city where she worked for the U.S. Army during World War II. The shocking images continued on the nightly news for the next five days. I silently feared that the soldiers and their tanks would roll into my project next. On the heels of the Newark Rebellion, the city hosted a Black Power Conference, which was attended by the major progressive black civil rights activists. Newark had emerged as a center of the struggle for black power and civil rights in the Northeast. The long hot summer of 1967 saw rebellions in approximately 159 cities, but the images of the state's violent military response in 1967 Newark were seared into my memory forever.

Two years after the Black Power Conference, Newarkers organized the Black and Puerto Rican Convention, which nominated a slate of candidates of color, headed by Kenneth Gibson, the convention's choice for mayor. The Black and Puerto Rican Convention sought to wrest some measure of political power, together with all the benefits that accompanied it, from the white men who wielded it to the exclusion of citizens of color. The Black and Puerto Rican Convention focused on achieving power through electoral politics. Unlike the Black Power Conference, the Black and Puerto Rican Convention was controlled by moderate leaders of the black community and included the city's growing Puerto Rican community. The convention was a positive, progressive coalition of Newark's most oppressed and politically repressed populations. The 1969 convention culminated in the nomination of Ken Gibson for mayor and a slate of seven candidates for city council, one of whom was Puerto Rican.

The coalition supporting Gibson for mayor was broader than the coalition that supported the Black and Puerto Rican Convention. Gibson's support also included a faction of the city's North Ward Italian community led by Stephen N. Adubato. Adubato, who many considered a moderate voice of the Italian North Ward, understood the changes taking place in Newark and realized that the changing demographics of the city would result in a significant change in the city's political leadership. In the 1970 mayoral race, Adubato made a bold move supporting Ken Gibson over the incumbent Italian American, Mayor Hugh J. Addonizio. Adubato was the only white political leader of significance to actively support Gibson's bid for the mayoralty. Adubato's endorsement of Gibson caused many white voters, especially in the racially charged, predominantly Italian North Ward, to brand him a traitor to his race. Adubato, though no supporter of the black power activists, clearly believed that he and Gibson could work together.

Gibson, the insurgent candidate, waged a successful people's campaign that galvanized the city's black and Latino population. Black Newarkers, for the first time in the city's history, defeated the white political machine and won the city's highest political office. Newark was the first major city in the Northeast to elect a black mayor. Gibson's victory was national news, and black folks in Newark literally danced in the streets. Black Newarkers believed that Gibson's victory meant they had finally achieved real power. Newark was an old Northeastern city controlled by various ethnic political machines. Until Gibson's victory, independent black political power had been frustrated. Political power in Newark provided access to resources, to the city's educational system, and to patronage and jobs—from high school football coach jobs to coveted police and fire jobs. Black Newarkers had long been denied these opportunities. Gibson's election broke the chains that limited the city's black community. There was reason for black Newarkers to be dancing in the streets. The Puerto Rican community, at least its progressive sector, was also excited by Gibson's electoral victory even though the Puerto Rican candidate for council at-large was not elected. Puerto Ricans believed that since Gibson was also their candidate, they too had attained a measure of independent political power. Puerto

Ricans, however, would have to wait almost a quarter of a century before they had a reason to dance in the streets.

As with all successful insurgents, Gibson's election forced him to refocus. Gibson had to retool himself from the leader of the insurgency attacking the Newark political structure to the leader of it. He had to build a new political machine, a new political powerbase, to consolidate his power. The city's progressives assumed that this new machine would be built on the foundation of the Black and Puerto Rican Convention. At the time, Newark's fastest-growing Puerto Rican population was concentrated in the North Ward. As was true with the Puerto Rican community throughout the mainland in 1970, Newark's Puerto Rican population was young. They arrived in Newark often lacking English language skills and with poor job prospects. Compounding these limitations, they were also unfamiliar with the culture and politics of New Jersey. Bilingual education was a new concept only recently codified in the Bilingual Education Act of 1968 and still struggling to gain acceptance in Newark. Like other immigrant populations, Puerto Ricans required assistance to adapt to their new home. Unfortunately, there was little help available. Puerto Rican needs were often perceived as personal weaknesses and a drain on already-strained resources. As was true in the context of the black struggle for civil rights, Puerto Ricans expected to benefit from Newark's black-led struggle for political power. After all, that was the promise of the Black and Puerto Rican Convention.

Gibson's supporters had to be rewarded for their continued loyalty and ensured support. In the city's predominantly Italian North Ward, that meant empowering his chief supporter, Stephen N. Adubato. Empowering Adubato rewarded him for his support and strengthened him at the expense of Gibson's Italian North Ward foes. Gibson believed that Adubato's continued support was an essential part of his new machine. Steve Adubato was Gibson's inroad into the North Ward's vote. Strengthening Adubato's North Ward machine served the dual purpose of building the mayor's new political power base and eroding the power of the mayor's political enemies in the North Ward.

To many, however, Gibson's political coalition with Adubato was a betrayal of the principles of the Black and Puerto Rican Convention. Empowering Adubato had a stunting effect on the Puerto Rican community's ability to attain political power.

Gibson rewarded Adubato with the largesse only a big-city mayor can dispense. Steve Adubato eschewed personal wealth; he sought the beneficence a ward boss requires to build a machine. Adubato used the resources made available to him to acquire and renovate an abandoned mansion and several abandoned homes in the North Ward. Adubato acquired these properties on behalf of the North Ward Center, the base of his political machine and the service center of the social services he provided the community. The rehabbed homes became available residences for many of his workers. Adubato obtained grants to run service programs to serve the community. The continuing city largesse Gibson provided Adubato was reinvested by Adubato to provide the community with additional social programs while at the same time further empowering his political machine in the North Ward.

Always sensitive to changing demographics, Adubato had little interest in organizing the white/Italian or Black community; instead, he concentrated his work and efforts on the burgeoning Puerto Rican community. Adubato used the largesse provided by Mayor Gibson to build the most powerful political machine in the city of Newark. The Adubato machine's power emanated from its political control of the Puerto Rican community. In a city where access to jobs, housing, educational opportunities, and often even the most basic governmental services was dependent on political power, the Puerto Rican vote, the essence of that community's political power, was controlled by the Italian machine of Steve Adubato. If you wanted the Puerto Rican vote in Newark, you need not see Puerto Rican politicians—there were none. You had to see Steve Adubato. As the Puerto Rican / Latino community in Newark grew, so did Adubato's power and the services he was able to offer the North Ward community. Gibson and every successive mayor who wanted Adubato's support had to feed his machine, a machine that held a tight grip on power.

Adubato gave Puerto Ricans in his organization low- or midlevel jobs but did not advance them for elected office. Puerto Ricans were the foot soldiers of his machine, responsible to turn out the required number of votes from the districts to which they were assigned. Many Newark progressives believed that Gibson's alliance with the Adubato machine failed to build unity between the city's two largest communities of color. Gibson, they theorized, failed to continue the work of the Black and Puerto Rican Convention to build a new alliance of the black and Puerto Rican communities independent and free from dependence on the Italian machine. Some suggest that the continued repression of the Puerto Rican community under the leadership of Mayor Gibson was a factor in the Puerto Rican uprising of 1974. Despite several attempts, Newark's Puerto Rican community was unable to elect a representative to Newark city government until the election of Luis Quintana in 1994. Clearly, neither the North Ward machine nor Mayor Gibson's empowerment of that machine is the sole reason for the Puerto Rican community's stagnated political growth in Newark. However, the Gibson/Adubato alliance remains one factor in the continued failure of Newark's Latino community to build a base of independent political power.

CHAPTER 3

FRIENDS AND FAMILY

As several of the reflections have pointed out, Kenneth Gibson was a quiet leader who could at times be quite difficult to read. On the lighter side, here are some thoughts from those who knew him best. They provide biographical details that hint at the connection between his private and public aspects.

Elton E. Hill, who worked as a business administrator in the Gibson administration, knew Kenneth Gibson from the time they were children.

ELTON E. HILL

Ken Gibson arrived in Newark from Alabama when he was eight years old. His parents, in 1940, enrolled him in the Monmouth Street School, where I first met him. We became friends, and I am pleased to say we have been friends ever since. We have another personal bond: Ken married my cousin Ann Mason.

There have been, of course, times when I was not in close contact with Ken. We were in different high schools: I attended vocational school; Ken attended Central High School. We both served in the military during the Korean War, but I joined the air force, and after getting married, Ken entered the army.

Upon return from military duty, Ken enrolled in the evening program at the Newark College of Engineering, now the New Jersey Institute of Technology. Upon my return from the military, I got married and pursued a career as an engineering draftsman and carpenter.

People ask me what Ken was like as a youth and whether there were signs indicating his future. No one among our childhood friends would have doubted that Ken could become the first African American mayor of Newark. The calm, strong demeanor he exhibited as mayor was prominent in him as a child. No one back then confused his reserve for weakness. Ken had the determined nature often exemplified in people with great potential. He was also academically gifted. His major passion outside of school was the saxophone, which I believe he began playing at age fourteen.

I also am often asked who Ken considered as role models. One person who immediately comes to mind was George Richardson, who I think ultimately persuaded Ken to run for mayor. George and Ken were both involved in the 1960s struggle for civil rights, though George was the more prominent figure at the time, having been elected to the state assembly. George was not particularly inclined to run for mayor himself, however, so a group of us got the green light to form the "Kenneth A. Gibson Civic Association" and set up a campaign headquarters on the corner of Springfield Avenue and High Street above a sweater shop. I was the president of the association and got some of my friends in the construction trades to volunteer time to produce signs for Ken's historic mayoral campaign.

Ken had other help. Poet LeRoi Jones (Imamu Baraka) returned to his hometown to support Ken. He, with others, such as Robert Curvin, Oliver Lofton, Harry Wheeler, Bill Mercer, John Caufield, Miguel Rodriguez, and Gus Heningburg, organized the Black and Puerto Rican Convention that endorsed Ken as their candidate.

At the time of Ken's election, I was working at the Newark Housing Authority. While I was doing OK in terms of supporting my family, I knew that I could be doing even better. So Ken and I discussed a possible position in his administration. Ken said that I could be the city's assistant business administrator but insisted I first go back to school—which I did, earning a BS degree from Rutgers University and a master's in public administration from Fairleigh Dickinson University.

As a result, I was able to serve in the Gibson administration as an assistant business administrator from 1970 to 1979, when I became the business administrator. In addition to the normal duties of a business administrator, I was Ken's primary liaison to the Newark Municipal Council and the "grassroots" community.

These days, I am still often reminded of the opportunity given to me by my friend Ken Gibson. This is so especially when I am approached by people who thank me for the job opportunities offered them.

What I take away from those days, years ago, are memories of a friendship, of course, but also the thought that one should never be afraid to accept a reasonable challenge. Ken certainly wasn't, nor was I, thanks to his example.

Harold Gibson, the mayor's brother, tells a story about the mayor's childhood and of his own achievements both with and apart from his famous brother.

HAROLD GIBSON

Although Ken was destined to make significant news later in life, my brother's first newsworthy action took place when he was a child in Enterprise, Alabama, in July 1937, before my fourth birthday. While playing with a toy balloon that was equipped with a brass horn that blew when the air was let out, my brother sucked on the balloon stem and unintentionally swallowed the tiny horn. When he exhaled deep breaths, a strange noise came from his throat. Young children in our community were usually relegated to medicines like 666 Cold Preparation or castor oil for most illnesses. So our mother decided to give him castor oil to stop the honking sound. Upon being confronted with this prospect, Ken readily owned up to our mother about having swallowed the brass horn.

Our father rushed him to a local physician, who recommended a throat specialist in a nearby town. After several unsuccessful attempts to remove the horn, the physician advised my father to take Ken to another specialist at faraway Jefferson Hospital in Philadelphia, Pennsylvania, where practice on such issues was well noted. An article in the *Enterprise Ledger*, our local newspaper, told how my father "sold his hogs," took his life's savings, and set out for a place he had never visited before. The surgery was successful, and Ken never got close to another brass horn–equipped balloon. Were it not for the action of our father, there might never have been a Mayor Kenneth A. Gibson. It certainly would allow Ken to give a speech without undue distraction.

Ken was elected mayor in June of 1970. The preparation for that successful campaign began with a warm-up—his finishing third in the election of 1966. In 1970, my brother successfully defeated Mayor Hugh J. Addonizio, becoming the first black mayor of a major Northeastern city. My name was no longer Harold or the nickname Hatch, but I was tagged the "mayor's brother." My love, loyalty, and support of my brother were such that I would allow no obstacle to interfere with his tenure, which spanned sixteen years.

During his terms in office, Ken became a national spokesman for big American cities. He also was elected president of the U.S. Conference of Mayors. One day, while I was visiting Ken in his city-hall office, his secretary buzzed him and said, "You have an important call on your private line." He asked, "Who is it?" She replied, "The President." He asked, "President of what?" She answered, "The President of the United Sates." I quickly excused myself so he could talk privately with President Jimmy Carter. Later, I found the subject of the call was an offer of a cabinet-level position in President Carter's administration, an indication of the political height my brother had reached.

During those years, Ken and I maintained a close family tie. As mayor, Ken also recognized that as a police commander, I had a special relationship with the people of our city and, in fact, law enforcement officials throughout the country. And as a result, Ken occasionally sought my opinion on important matters, which I was happy to give when we both thought it helpful.

From 1970 to 1986, I was employed by the Newark Police Department. Among my assignments included: assistant commander of the homicide squad supervising ten detectives, commanding officer of the southern district detective squad, and commanding officer of the housing patrol unit, which provided law enforcement services to all the public-housing buildings in the city.

To improve my standing, I did undergraduate study at Livingston College in the Rutgers University system. I later received a law degree at Seton Hall University Law School.

Camille Savoca Gibson, the mayor's wife, describes how she met the mayor, how their relationship evolved, and what she learned from him.

CAMILLE SAVOCA GIBSON

I first met Ken Gibson on the occasion of my twenty-third birthday. I was working in the public information office in city hall at the time, down the hall from the mayor's office. I recall Harold Hodes and Dennis Sullivan having organized a celebration in the office in honor of my birthday and them inviting Mayor Gibson to attend. I have been in awe of the man ever since.

Because of the significant difference in our age, I viewed Ken in the early days as a father figure. In fact, in many ways, he reminded me of my father, and in some ways, he raised me along with his daughters. Over time, however, our relationship evolved to a point where we were on more equal footing. We became confidants.

Ken has always had a calm and calming personality, was always fair-minded, and was always family oriented. These are some of the major traits that attracted me to him—traits that caught the attention and earned the respect and admiration of my family. He also has always been highly principled. I recall, for example, the time the Ku Klux Klan applied for a parade permit. While the parade would have been legal, Ken refused to issue the permit as a matter of decency.

Although difficult at times, I have tried over the course of my life to practice many of the lessons and values that I learned from my husband.

One thing I learned from Ken was that revenge is often a self-defeating impulse.

I recall having to rely on that lesson many times over the years. It took much effort, for example, to remain civil in the presence of Sharpe James, who had released his nasty campaign literature during Ken's 1986 reelection bid.

Sharpe and I had one amusing encounter a while after Ken left office and after he and I started a consulting business in Renaissance Towers in downtown Newark. We had a Doberman puppy at the time that stayed with us in the office. One day, Sharpe came by to visit, and the puppy tore after him. Sharpe, startled, exclaimed, "Did you sic that dog on me?" I frankly wished at the time that the dog had been older and more capable of inflicting harm. Instead of offering a snarly response, I invoked Ken's principle and politely stressed that the puppy was only being playful. Since then, I have always been able to greet Sharpe warmly with a hug and a kiss. It is what Ken would have wanted me to do. He holds no grudge at all toward Sharpe.

The city council was even tougher to tolerate. During Ken's first four years in office, while the old guard was still in place, it was "us versus them." As I recall, it took a full eight years before Ken enjoyed respect from any part of the white community—including residents of certain neighborhoods and their representative council members. However, after 1978, there was at least some degree of peace. And as I recall, it was Councilwoman Marie Villani whose presence helped make for a more workable relationship.

In dealing with the council, Ken also relied heavily on his chosen liaisons—first Harold Hodes, then Barbara Bressler.

It probably should come as no surprise that I have many happy memories working side by side with Ken. In 1979, I became the personal secretary to the mayor, replacing Helen Demerick. In that capacity, I came in direct contact with numerous political notables of the time. I recall, for example, the extreme contrast between Ken and Mayor John Lindsey of New York

City. Ken was always modestly dressed and rode around in a checkered cab. Lindsay, on the other hand, had the look of a Hollywood actor with a flashy air—and he would arrive here and there in a red Cadillac.

I remember how handsome I thought Jerry Brown was and the joy associated with the visits from Bill Bradley. Gerald Ford stopped in, which was exciting. But the most memorable association at the time was Ken's friendship with Jimmy and Rosalynn Carter.

Given the hostile and racially divisive environment in Newark at the time of Ken's election as mayor, I was constantly concerned about his safety. Members of his security detail were always on call but were with him only one at a time. I lived in the Ironbound section of Newark at that time, which was within walking distance from city hall. I recall members of the security detail occasionally camping out at my home when they thought they might be needed. This practice became so prevalent that I had a Centrex telephone installed in my home for an immediate line of communication to Ken.

In retrospect, the years spent in city hall with Ken, the years in business that followed, and the years we are now spending together have provided memories so pleasing that they have practically blotted out the difficult times. I can now put out of my mind instances of rock throwing, the threats, and the nastiness in campaigns—much of it emanating from the North Ward. We even had a sitting councilman knock down Ken's door to threaten him.

But with the passage of time, I can now say, "It's all good. Ken is my hero, and I just want to be the wind beneath his wings."

CHAPTER 4

TRYING TO MAKE CITY
GOVERNMENT WORK

From 1970 to 1986, Newark suffered from more than its fair share of urban ills. Mayor Gibson focused his efforts on the delivery of services, housing, education, policing, cooperation with the business community, and the restoration of faith in government. The reflections that follow reveal the wide variety of vantage points and approaches that those people involved took in trying to make Newark work better. They also give us a feel for the sense of mission and teamwork that many of the people who worked for the city felt. Of course, progress was slow, obstacles were daunting, and successes were hard-won.

Rev. James A. Scott, a clergyman who served as the chair of the Education
Task Force in the aftermath of the nation's longest teachers' strike,
describes the slow pace of meaningful change on a difficult issue.

Rev. James A. Scott

I remember Mayor Kenneth Gibson from the dual perspectives of a black clergyperson serving a middle-class congregation in the heart of Newark and an educator employed by Rutgers University. After the successful 1970 campaign, the new mayor asked me to chair a "blue ribbon" commission on education. My selection was not happenstance. Gibson wanted to establish that his administration would involve citizens of diverse backgrounds and not use city-hall appointments to court or repay loyalty. Also, he was trying to impress the skeptical that he meant what he said about developing a new sense of community.

The clergy had supported the new mayor but not with unbridled enthusiasm. We liked his insistence that Newark was worth rebuilding, which meant radical changes in the political culture and relations between city hall and people in the streets. We resonated as he identified issues essential to rebuilding the city. Clergy agreed that improvements in employment, housing, education, health services, and police–community relations were key to renewal. We were delighted the new mayor viewed these issues as intertwined. The clergy also were of a mind that no lasting community could be built on foundations of race baiting. But the clergy differed sharply as to how these issues should be met. There were widely divergent views in our churches, ranging from endorsement of black power to toleration of the old political order.

Black clergy, however, perceived that centrist perspectives were probably much deeper and engrained among blacks than the media depicted. And yet we also knew that the survival of our churches was entwined with Newark's progress, so we had a vested interest in social change.

Gibson, as a candidate in 1966 and again in 1970, was measured in his dealings with nonwhites. The absence of stridency reassured us because we feared that more racial conflict would spur some of our church constituency—upwardly mobile working-class and middle-class persons—to flee a city that was barely surviving. We knew many blacks grappled with whether living in the city could be justified, considering the sacrifices demanded in safety, schooling, high taxes, and dysfunctional government—in other words, the general decline in the quality of life.

The mayor had done his homework before asking me to work with him on an education task force: He assured me that the task force would have adequate funding. He was in the process of engaging a top-flight staff. He suggested a timeline that was short and manageable, with the task force having the option to change it. He assured me that the education task force would not be "window dressing," that it would be an essential apparatus in the search for better schooling.

Gibson was confident that a task force, representing many different sectors of the community, would be the best approach to changing schooling. He had talked to professionals, planners, and educators, including noted psychologist and educator Dr. Kenneth Clark, and there was the consensus that a task force would be successful. But the mayor was not overly idealistic—ready to conclude that improvement in schools would solve all the city's problems.

I understood that Mayor Gibson didn't expect the task force to encumber itself with all the city's educational challenges. Among those hurdles were the looming prospect of a state takeover of schools, the teachers' union flexing its muscle about contractual issues, school-board meetings that were often raucous and filled with racial rants and jockeying by neighborhoods for scarce resources, not enough seats provided by the schools if all students attended classes, school buildings that were in some cases substandard, control of jobs (there were more jobs in schools than any other city unit), and finally, the fact that the schools at the time were perceived as underperforming, even though large allocations of monies were available for teacher salaries. But the mayor made it clear that these matters, though pressing, were not areas for the task force to investigate.

In retrospect, I ask myself, What exactly was our mission? As I look back, I realize that the task force could do little to change the infrastructure of schools. Our optimism began to pale as we tackled our job. We examined reading programs and asked ourselves what could be done on a short-term basis to improve student achievement. We were hampered by two decisions: first, we feared being caught up in hostility—and losing focus—if we interacted too closely with school personnel, administrators, and teachers; second, we thought that we understood what community residents, especially parents, wanted schools to do.

The short timeline and incessant demands on schools (teacher strikes, charges against key administrators, threats of state takeover, and ploys to reform that fizzled) shifted the ground of our investigation and left us looking helpless; in the political context, we had limited strategic options, and the public knew little about our task. The political establishment had no stake in our enterprise.

Perhaps our most serious failure was not examining the effective or successful programs that actually existed in Newark's schools. We were aware that some schools, including a few in what were considered ghettoes, performed at or above standards set for Newark schools and, in some cases, surpassed national averages. We didn't examine the role of school leadership, for, if done poorly, we worried that could have been too easily misinterpreted, hardening judgments about why schools fail. I don't mean that the task force overlooked school leadership, but we didn't examine it closely enough to isolate desirable variables that could be considered while evaluating and helping other schools.

I can't identify the moment when the mayor realized the task force would accomplish little. We finished our work with assurances from him that we had done a creditable job. But the basic elements of the educational experience for Newark students were to remain, and when the task force finished its work, little in schools had changed.

Still, there were accomplishments. Though not earthshaking, what we did forecast a new direction for Newark. Gibson had appointed a task force of blacks, whites, and Latinos to work on changing a critical institution affecting the urban scene. So we were pioneers in a sense, for the task force involved business leaders and community organizers, representatives from traditional social welfare agencies, colleges, the clergy, and parents. If nothing else, we proved that disparate groups, with different visions for schools, could work together. Creating conditions for the democratic pursuit of public interest for schools was no small achievement.

Mayor Gibson quietly opened the window to such planning. He was moving in defiance of the political culture that wanted change based on models of the old patronage system. His dependence on planning and inclusion dismayed black power champions because they wanted—more immediate and narrowly—the redistribution of benefits as the first step in social change. Planning would involve seeking professional assistance. Many in Newark looked on with disfavor when consultation with professionals was suggested, precisely because they believed outsiders couldn't understand what was happening in our city. Planning was slow and arduous, involving monitoring and not quick payoffs. Planning also required political acumen, and I now understand the toughness of Gibson and his resolve to lay foundations for a new, planned city.

The most important contribution Gibson bequeathed Newark was melding black rage into the fabric of political enterprise. It is doubtful that he took seriously the exaggerated expectations of the black community and the media, when recognized as a messiah or at least someone who might usher in an era of prophetic change. But I feel that Ken Gibson understood, better than most of us, both the potential benefits and dangers of black rage. He didn't play to the masses and attempt to identify with every expression of blackness. Seldom did he wear a dashiki, and generally, he eschewed the language of extremism. I felt he understood black rage while not seeking to cap or deny its effect in shaping both our views and status.

Gibson wanted to build a healthy black community, and improved education was a bedrock necessity. He knew that black rage must be tempered and fitted to coexist within a political environment. Rather than call on blacks or whites to take the first steps toward the creation of the new political environment, he tried to encourage the task force to seek the creation of a community that would transform goals for schools. He was daring enough to undertake something that had not been attempted in Newark's recent history. That it failed wasn't surprising; that it was launched represented a positive development for blacks in the city's political life.

I don't suggest that Mayor Gibson was effective or prudent in all his moves. While the task force was taking shape, he made appointments—or approved them—that compromised his long-range strategies. But he had the courage and intelligence to return to core values. I feel that he politely dismissed the education task force in order to salvage other important components of educational reform.

Constructing a new environment entails changes in vision and spirit. The first black mayor knew his vision would shape the city's political life for a generation or more. This became a spiritual crusade. Governance—and control of city hall—was not an opportunity to divide the spoils, it was a mandate to find and transmit moral principles, build, and do the greatest good for the largest number of people. And in this regard, the mayor clashed with both blacks and whites who were shortsighted.

However, despite the limited progress in changing the city's social ills, Gibson did manage to hold office for sixteen years. He didn't deliver everything he hoped, but his integrity and spirit were mildly contagious, and for a time, his was the only "show" that promised a brighter future. The appeal he communicated to black clergy suffused the churches and moved into the streets. Slowly and surely, life in this city improved.

Mayor Kenneth Gibson met extremism in the black community and angry resistance in the white community, all the while plodding toward rebuilding a shaken, fractured city. The education task force was an example of his determination to involve the people of Newark in new ventures of reform that were important for the city. He challenged inertia and political paralysis. The education task force may have failed at full reform, but it opened a few windows and doors that helped the populace understand that social change was within reach and the entrenched political culture could be altered within a new model of governance.

Diane Johnson, who was the regional director for the federal Department of Housing and Urban Development, expresses her frustration in what she sees as Newark's failure to take advantage of federal funds.

DIANE JOHNSON

It is with a sense of frustration that I recall Newark and the Gibson Years. As an advocate for the needs of Newark, especially following the 1967 rebellion, I am of the mind that the city did not take anything close to full advantage of the financial and other opportunities available to it at the time.

In some ways, it is also a challenge for me to identify any particular person, including Mayor Gibson; department of city government; or ancillary city agency to blame for this underutilization of programs. Overall, I would attribute the city's failure to fully utilize available funding to three primary factors: (1) the proverbial "too many cooks in the kitchen," (2) a general lack of sound planning, and (3) a general lack of understanding of the value of certain programs and how they worked. My assessment of the period derives from my perspective back then as the field director in the Newark Office of the U.S. Department of Housing and Urban Development (HUD).

In the years following the 1967 rebellion, Newark enjoyed an unprecedented flow of state and federal dollars into its various coffers. To his credit, Ken Gibson proved to be an emissary that was credible and attractive to both state and federal officials. On the other hand, once the money reached the city, it was unclear who was responsible for carrying out the mandates and objectives of the individual programs. It was also unclear whether those in charge fully understood how to take full advantage of the programs once available.

On behalf of HUD, I did, of course, look to the city's business administrator. There was also a Community Development Administration (CDA), a Model Cities Program, a Mayor's Planning and Development Office (MPDO), a Planned Variation Demonstration Program, a Mayor's Policy and Review Office, a nonprofit corporation called the Newark Housing Development and Rehabilitation Corporation (HDRC), and so on. In addition to this litany of city-related departments and agencies, I had to factor in the operations and responsibilities of the Newark Housing Authority. While I suppose I could have held Mayor Gibson accountable for the chaos associated with city-related operations, he had very little influence over the operations of the troubled Newark Housing Authority.

We at HUD had assigned it that official status, labeling it a "troubled housing authority" based on poor performances in a number of critical areas. As mayor, Gibson had the authority to appoint just one of the seven housing authority commissioners—while five were appointed by the city council, and one was appointed by the governor.

Gibson had little control over the Newark Housing Authority; he also had little control over renters, and from the get-go, he faced housing challenges. From his first year in office, 1970, until 1974, he had to deal with what turned out to be the nation's longest public-housing rent strike ever.

The housing authority and its clients, the renters, posed one challenge: federal officials were flummoxed by all the "cooks." There were too many. It became extremely difficult to monitor the city's use of the extensive flow of money and thereby equally difficult to offer assistance.

With respect to the matter of sound planning, I believed, as did other federal officials at the time, that an engineer, such as Ken Gibson, would be naturally inclined toward establishing sound planning principles and capabilities. But that was not the case. What I found confusing in this regard was the fact that there appeared to be a planning department of unprecedented size but apparently one of little clout or vision. With better planning at the city level, federally and state-funded programs would have been better utilized and residents better served.

Newark, for example, had a near-total lack of understanding of the value of HUD's Section 108 Loan Guarantee Program. Under the terms of that program, cities were empowered to transform a small portion of their CDBG (Community Development Block Grant) funds into federally guaranteed loans large enough to pursue important economic revitalization projects.

Cities such as Newark could receive loan guarantees equal to five times their CDBG entitlement amount. There were plenty of competent developers operating in Newark at the time—among them Cecil Sanders, Oliver Lofton, Walter Barry, and Sandy Gallanter—but the city failed to take advantage of the Section 108 Loan Program.

To be fair, I can see how certain programs deemed successful actually looked like they could be detrimental to the city. The Section 8 Rent Subsidy Program was a case in point. Because Section 8 vouchers could be transported out of the city of Newark, the program had the potential for contributing to the city's population drain.

But while the city, unfortunately, underutilized the level of federal funding, the audits at the time suggested that the federal money, if not used wisely, was at least used legally.

And if Ken Gibson deserves credit for that, he also should be honored for something else: his low-key style and friendly personality. You would bump into him on the street and find him eminently approachable. His manner, as much as anything, made him the right person for the troubled times.

James "Jack" Krauskopf, from the Office of Newark Studies, describes an innovative program that took on difficult challenges and had many significant successes, including the creation of the Newark Watershed Conservation and Development Corporation.

JAMES "JACK" KRAUSKOPF

I came to Newark in 1971, about one year after Ken Gibson was first elected mayor of Newark, to direct a new Office of Newark Studies that would provide the mayor with staff support beyond what he had at city hall. The idea was to work on projects that were longer-term and less immediately political than his operations there. Over time, we worked on Newark watershed planning, cable-television franchising, renegotiating leases with the Port Authority of New York and New Jersey, education reform, public radio (WBGO), the recruitment of senior department heads in city government, and more. Many talented young students and professionals managed, developed, and staffed those projects, among them Terrence Moore, Mildred Barry Garvin, Donald Harris, Richard Roper, Bob Ottenhoff, and Marty Klepper.

Bob Curvin, one of the strategists for Gibson's election, conceived of the Office of Newark Studies. Bob was for all his life a political and moral beacon for Newark in the many roles he played; he is now much missed and is remembered in part through his insightful book on Newark politics and mayors—*Inside Newark: Decline, Rebellion, and the Search for Transformation*—including a vital chapter on Gibson. Working with Gordon MacInnes, director of the Wallace El Jabar Foundation (later the Fund for New Jersey), and other New Jersey foundation officials, Bob saw the need for an office to provide programmatic and analytic advice that the mayor would need beyond what he would get from his city-hall staff. Howard Quirk of the Victoria Foundation and Carl McCall of the Florence and John Schumann Foundation were among the important supporters.

The office was a vehicle for foundations to collaborate in assisting the new city administration, and during my five years of experience, Mayor Gibson showed that he appreciated and respected it as a nonpolitical vehicle. I had access to the mayor's office and always felt that my rapport with Ken was strong.

Administratively, the office was a unit of Rutgers University through its New Brunswick–based community-affairs division. George Tapper was the key university link to the office, and we also had good support from Rutgers–Newark officials, including Vice President Malcolm Talbott, law-school dean Willard Heckel, business-school dean Horace DePodwin, George Sternlieb and his colleagues at the Center for Urban Policy Research, and President Edward Bloustein.

Paul Ylvisaker, senior urban grant-making official at the Ford Foundation and former commissioner of the New Jersey Department of Community Affairs during the 1967 Newark riots, initiated one of the major projects for the Office of Newark Studies—an analysis of the Newark watershed property in the northwest corner of New Jersey, which supplied water for Newark and suburban customers in the state. Encompassing thirty-five thousand nearly pristine acres, the watershed had been saved as an asset for Newark by candidate Gibson, who went to court to prevent his predecessor as mayor, Hugh Addonizio, from selling off the land.

Ken was a strong advocate and client for the watershed conservation and development plan produced in the office by Terry Moore as a means for Newark to preserve the land and water resources, ensure only limited development that would not jeopardize its primary purposes, develop recreation and environmental-education uses for residents of Newark, and make it affordable for Newark to maintain the land. As mayor, he personally chaired the nonprofit corporation that was established to manage the land. Although there have been abuses by watershed management subsequent to his administration, the corporation was successfully launched under Gibson and effectively developed by Moore and colleagues such as counsel Phillip Elberg, who was able to challenge the high property-tax assessments by the rural municipalities where the watershed was located.

The Office of Newark Studies played a facilitating role in renegotiating the city's lease with the Port Authority of New York and New Jersey. During the Gibson administration, the port authority was led by its long-term formidable executive director Austin Tobin. The lease on land for Port Newark and Newark Airport had years to run, and the port authority had no legal obligation to renegotiate it. However, it became clear in discussions that Gibson, as a new and popular black mayor of New Jersey's largest city, had some leverage because the port authority did not want to be publicly criticized as an unfair operator on about 20 percent of Newark's land.

Ken was able to get increased rental payments amounting to several million dollars over the life of a renegotiated lease. The victory, modest as it was, showed Ken's clout as the leader of an aggrieved city.

Another Gibson administration accomplishment was its identifying of an underutilized board of education radio frequency that was ultimately converted into WBGO, a public radio station that is popular with all who love jazz. Robert Ottenhoff made the analysis while a Rutgers urban-planning master's-degree student in the office, then conceived of the idea for a Newark national public radio station, and then went on to operate the station. He eventually became the chief operating officer at the Public Broadcasting Corporation, was made the president of Guidestar (the source for information about nonprofit organizations), and is now the CEO of the Center for Disaster Philanthropy.

The office established a mayor's task force on education reform through the work of Donald Harris, a corporate executive, and Richard Roper, then a recent Princeton University Woodrow Wilson School MPA graduate with a subsequent long public-service career, including serving as planning chief at the port authority. (Richard, of course, also became the director of the Office of Newark Studies along the way.) This broad-based education task force was an expression of Gibson's interest in improving the public schools, a continuing challenge to the current day.

The Office of Newark Studies developed model cable-television franchises for what was then a new area for local governments. In this regard, the technical analysis and review of agreements established in other cities was essential to Newark receiving good service for its residents and some revenue. A law student, Martin Klepper, became our expert and was instrumental in the creation of franchise documents.

We also recruited staff for city government at the mayor's request, an example being the position of director of the department of health and welfare. These and other office projects emerged from a combination of city needs, opportunities for progress, and Ken's determination to make the city better.

What connects all of the people mentioned, especially those of us working for the Office of Newark Studies, was a desire to work on issues important to Gibson. It was the right mission, and I think my colleagues would affirm our commitment to it and to him.

Dennis Cherot began working for Newark city government during the Addonizio administration. He became an integral member of the team

that brought about significant achievements in health care—an area
in which the mayor is particularly proud of his accomplishments.

DENNIS CHEROT

I am not a Newark native, but because of my experiences working there, it
is the city with which I most identify.

I came to Newark in 1964, having been recruited out of college to work
at the Prudential Insurance Co. Six years and several jobs later, I was
offered a position in Newark's Model Cities Program in the Addonizio
administration. I started my employment a few months prior to Ken Gibson's election as mayor. I remember being elated that a black man had
been elected to run a major U.S. city, but I also was concerned that I might
be perceived as an expendable holdover from the previous administration,
which might make my career in the city short lived. I was not politically
involved, nor did I know Mayor Gibson or any member of his team. Fortunately, someone—I credit Donald Tucker—saw something in me worth
retaining, and thus began my tenure with the Gibson administration,
which was to last until he left office. I remember feelings of enthusiasm in
being a part of Gibson's team.

He surrounded himself with bright, dedicated individuals who believed
in their ability to make Newark a better place. He also provided ample
opportunities to grow and gave us responsibilities that in other circumstances would not have been possible. I personally served in grant-funded
positions but also as an assistant business administrator and ultimately
served in the mayor's cabinet.

The highlight of my professional life was Mayor Gibson's appointment
of me as director of the city's department of health and welfare. It was
an awesome responsibility; I was responsible for overseeing all municipal health issues and providing health services to thousands of needy
residents. My portfolio included monitoring food safety, addressing
communicable-disease issues, operating several health centers, and managing the municipal welfare department. However, as any schoolteacher

will tell you, one remembers the students who caused the most problems. For me, most problems were related to housing violations that seriously impacted health conditions.

Newark is a city of older buildings that were constructed before any real concerns about lead-based paint. Lead poisoning was a serious problem in Newark, adversely affecting child development and even causing death. Detecting and remediating was a major concern. The problem was that lead-based paint cannot simply be painted over but must be stripped from surfaces before repairing and repainting, a very expensive undertaking. Thus we began a never-ending push-and-pull process with landlords and homeowners to bring buildings into compliance. Landlords who wanted to avoid the cost of remediation were adept at seeking delays in court, paying fines as an alternative to remediation, or simply abandoning properties and thereby forcing the city to address the problem.

Another housing issue grabbed our attention every winter. That was the problem of insufficient heat for apartment dwellers. The department was literally inundated with complaints of little or no heat. Again, the cost made unscrupulous landlords creative in their attempts to avoid their responsibilities, but the code enforcement staff deserved credit for vigorously addressing this problem.

Housing issues could also be used to score political points. I remember one very cold Super Bowl Sunday when I received a call at home from Councilman Earl Harris concerned about a no-heat matter that required my immediate attention. I visited the building and found that the situation was indeed intolerable. I decided that the building should be vacated, and I placed the tenants in a hotel for the night. This, however, did not stop the councilman from publicly criticizing me about the handling of the situation. As I've indicated, the role was challenging but one that gave me the opportunity to work with a great team of professionals and staff.

After leaving the city, I worked as a senior vice president at two hospitals—Interfaith Medical Center in Brooklyn and Liberty Medical Center in Baltimore. My final position before retiring was as the president/

CEO of Total Health Care, a federally qualified health center, in Baltimore, which is one of the largest medical facilities in the state. During my tenure, I increased the number of patients we serviced from thirteen thousand to more than thirty thousand. I also expanded our services to include not only primary care but also mental health and dentistry services as well as pharmacy and substance-abuse care. I attribute these accomplishments to what I learned from my experiences working in Newark. Working there taught me to be an effective manager.

I can recall hearing Mayor Gibson say in an interview with the *New York Times* that his most gratifying major accomplishment had been improving Newark's health services. I hope, in some small way, that I was a part of helping him achieve that.

Philip Elberg, Esq., an assistant corporation counsel for Newark,
became deeply involved in hotly contested battles involving the use
of Newark's Pequannock watershed lands and also did the legal work
associated with several projects initiated in the Office of Newark
Studies including the creation of Newark Public Radio—WBGO.

PHILIP ELBERG, ESQ.

After graduating from Rutgers–Newark Law School, I was hired by Newark's corporation counsel William Walls as an assistant corporation counsel in the law department. I replaced a friend, Roger Lowenstein.

Newark City Hall was filled with smart people committed both to making a difference and to trying to help the city's first African American mayor succeed. City hall also included too many people who were invested primarily in retaining their jobs and had little stake or interest in the ambitious changes that the newly elected mayor promised and the city needed. Among that dedicated group I recall well were Jack Krauskopf and Richard Roper of the Office of Newark Studies, along with Terry Moore and Sue Sullivan, who were heading up the watershed project, and Bob Ottenhoff, the founder of WBGO. Later, I worked with Bob Holmes when he assumed responsibility for the thirty-five-thousand-acre Pequannock Watershed.

Much of my work was the product of initiatives originating in the Office of Newark Studies. That office developed programs and effective ways for Gibson to transition from the administration of outgoing-mayor Hugh Addonizio—and where possible to do so—without having to funnel money through the municipal council. Among the initiatives was the study that led to the incorporation of the Newark Watershed Conservation and Development Corporation.

Early in the twentieth century, Newark purchased thirty-five-thousand-acres of rural land located in three New Jersey counties and five municipalities to the north of the city. Near the end of his term as mayor and knowing that political change was coming to the city, Mayor Addonizio attempted to convert the city's water department to a municipal utilities authority (MUA). That move would have led to transferring the title to a new institution, controlled by individuals personally associated with the outgoing rather than the newly elected mayor. Gibson, then a city engineer, campaigned in opposition to Addonizio's MUA plan and pledged to stop it. He filed a lawsuit with the assistance of civil rights attorney Leonard Weinglass seeking to block Addonizio's efforts and preserve the watershed lands for future generations of Newark residents. As Gibson told the story, he used his last dollar to fund the lawsuit. In Weinglass's version of the same story, he never received the dollar. Addonizio's plan to deliver control over the watershed to his friends was created as the land was increasing in value—an increase fueled by suburban migration and a proposed highway interchange linking Route 287 with Route 23. It also occurred against a backdrop of the *Mount Laurel* court decisions that were focused on eliminating exclusionary zoning in municipalities such as the watershed towns and against a backdrop of the open-space movement, then in its nascent stage.

Studies, funded primarily by the Ford Foundation, were conducted, and plans were devised focused on appropriate ways for Newark to manage this vast area. The study conclusions led to a land-use plan that called for mostly open space with limited housing development. The plan also called for the creation of an entity to advise on the management of the tract. I created that advisory entity—the Newark Watershed Conservation and Development Corporation (NWCDC), a name that symbolized the two different aspects of the plan.

From the start, the watershed communities presented strong and at times hostile resistance to the implementation of the development element of the watershed plan. I recall that our initial attempts to advance housing came at the time of the Kawaida Towers controversy in Newark. Residents in the watershed communities loudly expressed their concerns and unambiguous objections to what they perceived to be what the plan was clearly not—a relocation plan for Newark residents. The hostility and resistance to any form of development by Newark incredibly included fires in the watershed that seemed to follow any signs of progress that Newark made toward the implementation of the plans, which was most often through litigation and court decisions.

The newly elected mayor supported the NWCDC but seemed to be careful about picking his fights and chose not to challenge the "old guard" at city hall that controlled the operation of the water utility. In the end, the watershed towns stopped the development plans but found that they could not have it "both ways" because their adamant opposition to development led directly to our recapturing millions of dollars for the city of Newark in the form of tax refunds for lands that were overassessed based on the suburban communities' claims that they were undevelopable.

After I left the corporation counsel office, I was retained to advance another plan devised in the Office of Newark Studies—this one to transfer a radio-station license owned by the Newark Board of Education to a new and independent nonprofit entity, Newark Public Radio. The station, WBGO, had been languishing, with limited resources, for years in a small space in Central High School. It was an underutilized asset, even though its valuable FCC (Federal Communications Commission) license reached the entire metropolitan area. The Office of Newark Studies, with funding provided by the Corporation for Public Broadcasting, hired Robert Ottenhoff, a broadcaster and graduate of the Rutgers City and Regional Planning Department, to conduct a study to determine how the asset's value might be maximized to better serve residents of Newark and the region. I did the legal work associated with the transfer and the creation of a new entity. I worked with Bob to structure and select the board of trustees, drafted bylaws for the new organization and participated in the negotiations that culminated with the transfer of the station's license from the Newark Board of Education to the newly created Newark Public Radio. The station, still WBGO, was created with the mayor's consistent support. WBGO has become a premier jazz and public-affairs station and an important Newark and New York metropolitan-area cultural institution.

> Editor Robert C. Holmes, Esq., just out of Harvard Law School, worked
> through the struggles and successes of his early career in both municipal
> and state government. At one point, he found himself in the middle of
> the volatile issues surrounding the Newark-Pequannock Watershed.
> Through that and other experiences with the mayor, he describes
> the "learning under fire" that he shared with other young people in
> the administration as well as coins the term *Gibson University*.

ROBERT C. HOLMES, ESQ.

Like others asked to contribute their reflections about Newark and the "Gibson years," the passage of time has taken a toll on me. Perhaps the passage of time will also serve as a filter that leaves behind only the most salient and indelible memories. Among such memories is my time spent at, what I like to call, Gibson University.

By May 1970, when Ken Gibson was elected as the first African American mayor of Newark, I was in Cambridge, Massachusetts, working on my law degree at Harvard University. I had entered law school in September 1967 and was a semester behind my entering class because I needed to complete my military training at Fort Dix related to my enlistment in the New Jersey National Guard. Having received a draft notice in 1968, my mentor, Raymond Brown, Esq., helped me fulfill my military duty with the guard rather than the regular army.

In December 1970, Newark—and its new mayor—would enter my consciousness in a new and dramatic way. Just before completing my law degree, I met Junius Williams, who was on campus at Harvard seeking law students who might be interested in working in New Jersey's largest city. Newark was still reeling from the effects of the deadly riots that seriously damaged the city's national image. The new mayor had appointed Junius as the head of a major federal initiative known as the Model Cities Program. The program included a wide range of operations intended to improve living conditions in America's declining cities.

Due in some part to my childhood memories, family ties, and other associations with Newark, I was captured by Junius's recruiting efforts, and I accepted a job in the Gibson administration. Throughout my college and law-school years, I had been involved with causes designed to increase advancement opportunities for African Americans, and this seemed ideal to continue on that course. I found myself beginning my post-law-school career as the executive director of a nonprofit corporation called the Newark Housing Development and Rehabilitation Corporation (HDRC). The HDRC was created by the city upon the recommendation of the Office of Newark Studies and was charged with developing and administering housing policies and plans for the city.

I remember my initial impressions. I was surprised that a position such as the head of housing policy would be entrusted to a recent law-school graduate with little relevant experience. I was further surprised to find that I was given tremendous latitude to hire staff and structure corporate policies. Though this was not at all what I expected to encounter in what I perceived to be a political appointment, here I was, and to be clear, I was not on my own. To assist with the initial structuring of the HDRC, the mayor had retained the services of the Washington, DC–based consulting firm Skidmore, Owings, and Merrill. A principal of the firm, Richard "Dick" Tager, took the role of advisor to me and to the board of directors. Board members, including Mayor Gibson—who served as the chairman—regularly attended meetings and were involved in decision-making. For additional support, the city had an excellent planning department, headed by Al Shapiro and staffed with competent planners such as Jeanette Brummell and Susan Stevens, to provide me with much-needed and appreciated backup.

No matter the quality of the team, I painfully recall how difficult it was to attract developers to the city. Ultimately, only low-cost—or even free—land became the primary inducement for developers. Unfortunately, this policy quickly proved to be counterproductive when speculators adopted a practice of "land banking" (aggregating and holding parcels of land in anticipation of future increases in land values) rather than developing the land as they had promised.

There were positives too. Because of respect for Mayor Gibson, the U.S. Department of Housing and Urban Development (HUD) provided us with easy access to their officials. As part of a national program called "Project Rehab," during my tenure as director of the HDRC, we were able to rehabilitate hundreds of housing units in the city and were publicly described by HUD as the best Project Rehab in the country. We were also able to construct a 420-unit housing complex on an abandoned inner-city reservoir, which is still aptly referred to as the "Reservoir Site." As part of Mayor Gibson's vision for improving health care as a way to revitalize Newark, we launched a series of neighborhood-based health centers, the first of which was called the Gladys Dickinson Health Center, named for a person who was well-known for her community service.

During the spring and summer of 1973, I got a firsthand experience of the way that politics and governing work hand in hand. It was campaign season for the office of the governor, and Mayor Gibson supported the candidacy of an Essex County prosecutor, Brendan Byrne. When Byrne was successful, as a reward for his support, he gave Gibson the opportunity to recommend individuals for high-level positions in the new administration. Gibson recommended me. Following a role on the transition team for the Department of Community Affairs (DCA), I was appointed by the governor to the position of assistant commissioner for that department. At the time, I was the highest-ranking African American in state government. Because the DCA provided a voice for municipalities at the state government level, I was able to maintain a meaningful connection to Newark.

Early in Byrne's second term, I returned to Newark to head the Newark Watershed Conservation and Development Corporation (NWCDC), another innovative idea from the Office of Newark Studies. The NWCDC was charged with providing stewardship for the thirty-five-thousand-acre Newark-Pequannock Watershed lands while allowing limited access for recreational purposes. The watershed covers parts of five municipalities and three counties north of the city of Newark. The lands had been acquired by the city at the turn of the nineteenth century to provide quality drinking water to Newark residents as well as to satisfy a formidable demand for water from burgeoning Newark industries, including leather-tanning operations and breweries.

The NWCDC was also responsible for advancing a land-use plan funded by the Ford Foundation. The plan called for limited development, with the vast majority of the land remaining open space. It is important to note here that notwithstanding the fact that the lands were acquired primarily for the purpose of providing the city with a predictable source of clean water, it was not the case that all of the thirty-five-thousand acres of land were environmentally sensitive for this purpose.

A notable exception to the general principle that municipally owned lands are tax-exempt is the fact that in New Jersey, municipally owned watershed lands are taxable at a common level with privately owned land. Municipalities in which Newark's watershed lands are situated attempted to have it both ways: they were taxing Newark watershed land at a high rate, as if developable, while at the same time zoning the land as if the land were only good for conservation purposes, which would have allowed Newark to pay a much lower rate.

Under the guidance of the board of directors, with Gibson as chair, the NWCDC developed a legal strategy for the watershed that called for pursuing two courses of action at once. On the one hand, the corporation initiated lawsuits brought pursuant to the New Jersey Supreme Court's landmark *Mount Laurel* rulings, which declared exclusionary zoning unconstitutional. Simultaneously, the corporation initiated lawsuits in the form of tax appeals that sought to reduce assessments and provide tax rebates on lands that watershed communities claimed were undevelopable yet taxed at rates generally associated with development potential. While the watershed communities held fast to their opposition to Newark-initiated development within their borders, Newark recovered millions of dollars in the tax appeals.

As the NWCDC tried to implement the part of its legal strategy that called for limited development, the watershed communities resisted with a hostility that threatened to spill over into violence. Threats against me as executive director reached a level that prompted me to seek state-police protection. Signs I had posted inviting hunting, for example, were replaced with signs calling for an "open season on coons." Similar signs were left on the windshield of my car. Numerous improved parcels within the watershed, including a recently constructed campsite for Newark youth, were destroyed by arson. A councilman from West Milford Township, the watershed community with the largest share of watershed land, dared to show a minimal level of support for Newark's positions and was recalled from office. Ironically but not necessarily surprisingly, local activists who opposed Newark-initiated development on watershed lands were not opposed to fellow residents negotiating with Newark for locally initiated development.

In this highly charged atmosphere, local community activists demanded that Gibson appear before them to assure that Newark would not be expanding into their communities. I recall being amazed at one of the questions that was suggested to be posed to Mayor Gibson. The question was whether Gibson would be the mayor over any sections of the watershed lands developed by Newark.

At my request, Gibson faced just such a hostile crowd while demonstrating the positive characteristics that served him so well and that, I think, contribute to his lasting legacy. Arriving on a red-eye from Asia, the mayor met one day with local activists in a hall in Hardyston Township. Reminiscent of a major element of his timely value to the city, Gibson was able to calm an otherwise angry and suspicious group with his unshakable and self-assured demeanor. Through this seemingly simple appearance, Gibson showed me that he was loyal to his managers, that he paid attention to detail, that he was committed to the needs of his city and his constituents over his own personal comfort or gain, and that his calm and reasonable approach could win the day.

It was, however, only the day that was won. In the end, residents of the watershed communities rallied around stern opposition to any development by Newark on lands owned by Newark within its vast watershed holdings, preferring instead to struggle to make payments against judicially mandated tax refunds.

After twelve years at the watershed corporation, I left to become the first African American partner at the New Jersey law firm Wilentz, Goldman and Spitzer and, later, a law professor at Rutgers Law School in Newark.

I conclude these reflections with this: I am a proud graduate of Edison Township High School, Cornell University, Harvard Law School, and Gibson University. Each of these institutions contributed significantly to the quality of my life and my career.

Editor Richard W. Roper began a varied and vital career as a public-policy leader when he became the head of the Black Organization of Students at Rutgers–Newark. Through various high-level appointments in government and academia, he has maintained an impactful connection to Newark. As does his colleague Robert Holmes, he credits Mayor Gibson with providing an incubator that nurtured his career in urban policy and social justice.

RICHARD W. ROPER

I arrived in Newark on my twentieth birthday in 1965. I came looking for work so that I could finish my schooling at West Virginia State College and later at Rutgers University–Newark, where I earned a degree in economics. At Rutgers, I helped establish and lead the Black Organization of Students (BOS), an organization that sprang from the campus chapter of the NAACP. The members of the chapter and I shared the view that the NAACP was too timid in its approach to the civil rights struggle, so we decided to establish a more assertive entity and return the NAACP's student charter to the parent organization in New York City. Immediately after my graduation, Ralph Dungan, New Jersey's first chancellor of higher education, invited me to join his staff to help launch the state's newly formed Educational Opportunity Fund (EOF), a program designed to assist underrepresented minority students—primarily African Americans—gain access to and complete college. The program was a direct response by the Richard J. Hughes administration to the 1967 Newark Rebellion.

A year later, in 1969, I was married and on my way to Princeton University to pursue a master's degree in public policy. And after completing the program, I returned to Newark and put my newly acquired skills in advanced economics, statistics, research, and policy analysis to use in urban revitalization.

Robert Curvin, someone I knew from my undergraduate days at Rutgers who was then pursuing a PhD at Princeton, told me to consider joining a newly created office assisting the recently elected black mayor of Newark, Kenneth Gibson. I said that I was interested, and he put me in touch with the director of the Office of Newark Studies (ONS), an office situated in the mayor's cabinet but administered for the City of Newark by Rutgers University.

The director of the office was Jack Krauskopf, a guy who had graduated from the Woodrow Wilson School of Public Policy at Princeton a few
years before me and had spent several years in the administration of Carl
Stokes, Cleveland's first black mayor. Jack hired me to set up an education task force to be composed of key Newark public-school stakeholders committed to addressing the complex issues that had beset the city's
school system for years and had led to the longest teachers' strike in the
nation's history. I guess Jack thought I'd be up to the challenge of putting the task force in place, since I had addressed education policy and
politics as the key issue in my master's thesis. I did, indeed, set up the task
force and recruited Donald Harris, someone with experience dealing with
education politics. Harris at the time was serving as an education-policy
staff assistant to U.S. senator Walter Mondale. He also happened to be
the son-in-law of Dr. Kenneth Clark, the man who framed the argument
that helped Thurgood Marshall achieve success in the 1954 Supreme Court
school-desegregation case *Brown v. Topeka Board of Education*.

Once the education task force was up and running, I felt that I should
move on to another challenge—serving as assistant to the director of the
New Jersey Division of Youth and Family Services (DYFS), a newly created state agency focused on child welfare. The director of the division,
Fred Schenck, a black guy with considerable talent who would later play
an instrumental role in my joining the Carter administration, assigned me
the task of crafting a plan to establish a statewide, state-funded system of
childcare programs. The system would augment what then existed in the
state's bureau of childcare service. I spent a year working on the plan but
eventually concluded that I was not cut out for the isolation required to
complete the plan. Out of the blue, I received a call from someone inquir-
ing about my interest in leading a statewide education-finance-reform
research project that was being created at the Newark Urban Coalition in
Newark.

I returned to Newark as the director of the New Jersey Education
Reform Project and spent the next two years attempting to give visibility

to and provide a voice for New Jersey's urban school districts desperately in need of enhanced public-school funding. My interaction with the state legislature and the executive branch of state government prompted Mayor Gibson to offer me a job as his legislative aide, a position I accepted in 1974. One year later, when Jack Krauskopf resigned his post at the ONS to accept an appointment in the cabinet of the governor of Wisconsin, Gibson appointed me Jack's successor.

Over the three years that I led the Office of Newark Studies, I had the opportunity to put my interests in public-policy formation, community development, and social-policy activism into play. The first initiative undertaken by the office during my tenure was setting up and staffing a task force to examine ways that Newark's tax-exempt properties might contribute to the city's revenue base. The task force was chaired by Horace DePodwin, dean of the Rutgers Business School, and had representatives from the business, civic, religious, and municipal government sectors. The group struggled with a troubling reality: tax-exempt properties made up almost 60 percent of the city's landmass. These properties, including churches; schools; municipal, county, state, and federal buildings; and property leased to the Port Authority of New York and New Jersey, received substantial city services but did not contribute a penny to cover the cost of those services.

The task force concluded that selected tax-exempt properties should make payments to the city in lieu of taxes and drafted legislation to that effect. The legislation focused on state-owned properties and mandated that state government should provide some fiscal relief to the communities in which they were located. The New Jersey payment in lieu of taxes (PILOT) legislation was introduced in the assembly by members of the Essex County delegation, passed by both the assembly and the senate, and was signed into law in 1977. I vividly recall Newark North Ward councilman Anthony Carrino calling me after receiving the task-force report to express his pleasant surprise at its quality and its likely positive impact not only for Newark but for all cities hosting state-owned property.

I also assumed responsibility for completing a couple of projects that began during Jack's tenure. One was an insurance-redlining study that was being conducted by George Hampton, a Newark native and Rutgers University–Newark graduate who was beginning his career in urban planning. The study examined the extent to which banks in the city were denying loans to residents of the city's neighborhoods, especially those with heavy black populations. The findings were unambiguous, and the negative impact on neighborhood revitalization was staggering. The report called for immediate action by the federal government to force changes in the banks' behavior. Mayor Gibson found the study convincing but was unwilling to push for action for fear of alienating his business community. The study languished.

The other inherited project was led by Robert Ottenhoff, who had been hired by Krauskopf to explore what might be done with the languishing radio station that was licensed to the Newark Board of Education. Bob had almost completed the research and analysis associated with the project when I assumed leadership of the ONS. Shortly thereafter, he submitted his findings and a recommendation that the station's license be transferred to a new nonprofit entity in order for the station's potential as a community resource to be realized. Newark Public Radio Inc. was created to serve as the licensee. I was named to its board of trustees.

While the logic of creating an independent, freestanding entity to own and operate WBGO was sound, the politics of separating the station from the board of education was daunting. Key members of the board were reluctant to give away what they regarded as a valuable asset, even though the asset was not being used. The matter was resolved at a meeting in the mayor's office involving Carl Sharif, the board president; Mayor Gibson; and me. Carl, who also served as an aide to the mayor, was loathe to give up the station and argued that the children of Newark would lose if the board did not retain it. I argued that the board lacked the resources and the interest necessary to maximize the asset the station represented. I maintained that Newark and the region would benefit from allowing the station to be managed by a nonprofit that would focus solely on its utility as a public radio station providing news, public affairs, and other information services.

The mayor, who at that time appointed all board of education members and kept undated, signed letters of resignation from each, agreed with my argument. The license transfer was approved by the board at its next meeting, and Newark Public Radio Inc. acquired the license in 1977.

One other major initiative of the ONS during my stewardship was the creation in 1976 of Newark Emergency Services for Families (NESF). The nonprofit twenty-four-hour crisis-intervention program has operated, with foundation support, ever since.

I left the ONS and Newark in 1978 to join the Carter administration. I had been offered a position as special assistant to the secretary of commerce Juanita Kreps, and I accepted.

Looking back on this exciting period in my life, it is fair to say that Ken Gibson provided the incubator in which my engagement with urban policy and social justice was nurtured. He made possible the launch of a journey that has been the source of both professional satisfaction and personal fulfillment. I will ever be grateful to him for the opportunity he presented when I was but a young man.

Jerome Harris echoes a reference to "Gibson University" as a platform to describe lessons learned through his association with the Gibson administration.

Jerome Harris

I, along with a considerable number of others, have described my education and training as including some time at Gibson University. This is a reference to the fact that many of the lessons I came to rely on over the course of my career were learned during the time I was associated with the administration of Newark's first African American mayor, Kenneth A. Gibson. As I reflect on that period in my life, I can vividly recall the lessons I learned as well as the individuals associated with imparting those lessons to me. Like any of life's lessons, some of those I learned during the Gibson era were painful, amusing, or both. Looking back, I can recall the good, the bad, and the ugly. Overall, I have a positive view of that period in my life.

Prior to my arrival in New Jersey from New York in 1965 to attend Rutgers College in New Brunswick as an undergraduate student, I had very little exposure to or interest in the affairs of the city of Newark. To me, Newark was just a stop along the Northeast Corridor rail line. I did, on the other hand, have a growing interest in the condition of black people wherever they were located, especially within Rutgers University. It is interesting to note that there were no students from Newark among the twelve black males in my freshman class at Rutgers University. I became active in the black student movement and eventually became the president of the Student Afro-American Society (SAS) for the Rutgers–New Brunswick campus. In the spring of 1968, I met student leaders from the Black Student Unity Movement at Rutgers–Camden and the Black Organization of Students at Rutgers–Newark as each organization presented demands at the Rutgers Board of Governors meeting following the assassination of the Rev. Dr. Martin Luther King Jr. The BOS leadership included Richard Roper, Joe Brown, Vicki Donaldson, Vivian Sanks King, Harrison Snell, Arthur Bowers, and Rod Bohannon. From this emerged a coordinated effort involving the BOS, BSUM, and SAS to demand that Rutgers become more accessible and relevant to the communities in which the university had a significant presence. The 1969 BOS takeover actions of Conklin Hall in Newark are legendary. The protest actions by black students in Camden, Newark, and New Brunswick brought about changes that forced Rutgers to function as the "State University of New Jersey," perhaps for the first time.

In the spring of 1970, Ken Gibson was making his second attempt to become Newark's first African American mayor and the first African American mayor of any major Northeastern city. Rutgers University–New Brunswick students were aware of the historic significance of the election, including the efforts of Amiri Baraka, through his Committee for a Unified Newark (CFUN), to mobilize volunteers for the campaign. Many students such as Deforest "Buster" Soaries and Kaleem Shabazz responded and worked in the May election and the June runoff. In my capacity as assistant to the dean at the newly opened Livingston College campus, I helped provide transportation and other logistical support to the Rutgers University–New Brunswick students seeking to volunteer. Memories of the June election night celebration still excite me.

In 1973, thanks to Rod Bohannon, I was introduced to Sam Shepherd, an aide to Mayor Gibson, who recruited me for the position of director of the Newark Urban Institute, a HUD-funded work-study program. After interviews with David Dennison, the director of the mayor's policy and planning office, and Mayor Gibson himself, I was offered and accepted the job. The Newark Urban Institute was an internship program that sought to attract bright college students to be planted in all areas of municipal government. It is relevant to say in the context of my marching orders as director of the institute that Mayor Gibson proudly expressed as a principle of his governance style attracting to Newark the best and brightest young talent available. In keeping with this mandate, we were able to attract students from the nation's leading universities, including Harvard, Yale, the University of Pennsylvania, and Rutgers. Further in keeping with the theme of attracting the best and brightest available young talent, we included among our interns Paulette Brown and Zulima Farber. Paulette Brown went on to become a prominent attorney and the president of both the National Bar Association and the American Bar Association. Zulima Farber went on to become a partner in a prominent New Jersey law firm as well as the first Afro-Cuban attorney general for the state of New Jersey. In what might be characterized as a "shadow government," our interns were placed throughout municipal government. And so my lessons as a student at Gibson University had begun. Lesson number one: municipal government is far more complex than it appears from the outside. Learning about the complexities would serve me well throughout my career.

The advent of Gibson's first bid for reelection in 1974 was the basis for lesson number two: governing a city has two distinct components. There is an operational side (which I had learned through lesson one), and there is a political side (which I had a lot to learn about). The new set of lessons included learning how grassroots ward-based politics works and how to marshal and deploy resources and voter support in hotly contested elections. My principal instructors for lesson two were Harry Wheeler and Elton Hill. I also began to understand, through my observation of Dan O'Flaherty's work, the importance of data-driven campaign strategies.

The third major lesson related to my association with the Gibson administration came because of my being assigned on election day in 1974 to be Gibson's representative in the election district where his opponent, Anthony Imperiale, happened to live. I was treated exceptionally well by Imperiale supporters, leading me to lesson number three: when you find yourself in a position of power and control, there is no need or reason to be abusive to your opponents.

When federal funding for the Newark Urban Institute ended, my job was transferred to the Mayor's Policy and Development Office (MPDO). At the MPDO, my duties expanded to include a leading role in the creation of the city's first Community Development Block Grant (CDBG) application. Neighborhood hearings associated with that process gave rise to my next lessons, for which I can either credit or blame the administration's chief community organizer, Clarence (Larry) Coggins. Larry Coggins had primed resident expectations related to the upcoming CDBG funding toward a belief that CDBG funding would result in new housing for those who had been displaced by "urban removal" or were living in substandard conditions. This was not at all the primary focus of the CDBG application. At a public hearing held at the Springfield Avenue Branch of the Newark Library, community residents expressed in no uncertain terms their dissatisfaction with the "bureaucratic bullshit" we presented. Lesson number four: in order to avoid a disastrous disconnect between the plans and policies of elected officials and their constituencies, one must learn how to manage expectations and be ready to feel the heat.

As I continued to grow my role in the Gibson administration, the lessons continued to unfold. I recall, for example, how I learned the lesson of "don't burn bridges." When a key administration official, Donald Tucker, was elected to the city council, I was assigned to oversee the program he had administered. I proceeded to attempt to assume leadership of the program and staff without first understanding the shoes I was stepping into. In this transition, Donald and I got off to a very bad start. I survived, and no bridges were burned, and Donald and I went on to become very close allies in an effort to bring about improvement in the living conditions of New Jersey's African American population, primarily through the creation and management of the New Jersey Black Issues Convention (NJBIC). The NJBIC continues to this day.

I left the Gibson administration in 1977 but not before developing close relationships with other young professionals who had been part of "Gibson University." In part inspired by his election and in part disillusioned by the fact that our ideas about the future of Newark and its residents were not being realized, a number of us from the "young crowd" began a series of conversations about what to do next. We called ourselves the "Friday Group." By the time I reached state government, the Friday Group was evolving into what later became the New Jersey Public Policy Research Institute (NJPPRI) drawing from both the Friday Group and from the Gibson University graduates then serving in state government. This would have been around 1979.

In 1981, while I was the city administrator in Plainfield, I was approached to play a leadership role in the "Gibson for Governor" campaign. I suspect that I was asked in large part because of my involvement with Gibson's 1974 reelection and the work of the NJPPRI. I quickly recognized from this assignment that Gibson was a more astute politician than many, if

not most, observers gave him credit for. He recognized that the seat was
open and that African Americans needed to be exposed to the possibility
of having someone represent them at the highest level of government in
the state. In the Democratic primary, Gibson came in third, out of a field
of thirteen, garnering in the neighborhood of ninety-five thousand votes
(about 15 percent of the total votes cast). He enjoyed solid support from
black elected officials from across the state. This campaign experience
yielded some of my most important lessons. I learned, for example, the
importance of having county party organization support when involved
in a statewide primary election; I learned to use the term *connective tissue*,
by which I meant to describe how relative success in a statewide election
could have a ripple effect on outcomes for African American candidates
in local elections; and I learned that the "connective tissue" (money and
volunteers) could contribute to political momentum above the state
level—for example, Jesse Jackson's run for president of the United Sates
in 1984.

I was also asked to play an active role in the "Gibson for Governor"
campaign in 1985, with a new set of lessons to follow. Gibson again ran
third, this time garnering eighty-four thousand votes—or 26 percent of
the total votes cast. In my opinion, we underperformed in 1985. The campaign failed to build on the momentum of the 1984 Jesse Jackson presidential campaign. My lesson learned was that "connective tissue" for African
American candidates for elected office is real and valuable. On the other
hand, it is unstable and hard to sustain for races for statewide office. In
New Jersey, for example, we did not see another serious run for statewide
elected office by an African American candidate until 2013, when Cory
Booker ran unopposed in a special election for a seat in the U.S. Senate.

I put my campaign experience to work in the role as senior advisor
to the 2017 Democratic Primary campaign of Jim Johnson. Johnson ran
second in a field of eight to now-governor Phil Murphy, garnering 110,000
votes, which represented 21.6 percent of all votes cast. The "connective

tissue" did not work in Johnson's favor because the Murphy campaign secured the early endorsement of most black elected officials in the Democratic Party and all the county party organizations. As I put these reflections together, I find it significant that Johnson is the only black candidate to mount a primary challenge for the most powerful governorship in the United States since Mayor Gibson's 1985 campaign.

There are too many examples of my application of the lessons learned and applied over the course of my career to include in this summary of my reflections about that period in Newark's history. I must say that the experiences and relationships forged in this period were and are invaluable. I, like many others, owe much to Kenneth A. Gibson, including these lessons for which I am grateful:

- Be systematic in developing solutions to problems.
- Surround yourself with the brightest and the best.
- Always show grace when under pressure.

Larry Hamm, who describes the ups and downs of his relationship with Mayor Gibson, describes the mayor as a calming and believable individual.

Lawrence "Larry" Hamm

I am a product of Newark. I arrived in the city just before my first birthday, and I have had some involvement with the city ever since. My fundamental character and who I am derives from my relationship to Newark.

By 1970, when Ken Gibson was elected as the first African American mayor of Newark and of any major Northeastern city, I was enrolled as a student at Arts High School. These were the days of two teachers' strikes in the city—the first in 1970 and the second in 1971. The 1971 strike was said to be the longest in U.S. history.

I had a role in the ferment: I headed a student walkout. While in high school, I organized a group called the Newark Federation of High School Student Councils, an organization generally supported by school-system higher-ups. Among my initiatives was to invite social activist Imamu Baraka to address the group. Truth be told, I had never been exposed to a person like him before, and he had a profound impact on me.

Inspired by the words and experiences of Baraka, I organized a student walkout intended to influence the ongoing teachers' strike. My plan was to have hundreds of students from various Newark schools descend upon the Gateway Hilton Hotel—where negotiations were taking place—with student demands. We students were facing the real possibility of not graduating if we missed thirty-five consecutive days of school.

Initially, I thought I had made a terrible mistake when it appeared no one would join me in the walkout. Then, to my delight and relief, hundreds of students did join me in a march to the Hilton, where we proceeded to take over two floors associated with the ongoing negotiations. It seems now like a radical approach we took as we expressed our demands, but the reality is that political consciousness often begins with radical behavior.

It is at that time and that event that I first met Ken Gibson. I found the mayor to be a calming and believable individual. I and, I am sure, other young fatherless men in our group saw him in some ways as a protective father figure. We trusted him and took him at his word when he said that he would take a serious look at our demands.

Mayor Gibson kept his word. He had the president of the board of education appear at Arts High School to speak with students. That meeting in turn led to a meeting with Don Saunders, the chief negotiator for the teachers. I organized student leaders from eight high schools for that meeting. As a result of the meeting with Mr. Saunders, some of our demands were met.

Mayor Gibson went even further. Soon after the meeting with Mr. Saunders, a man named Pete Curtin, an aide to the mayor, arrived at my home on Twelfth Street. He had been sent by Gibson, and his purpose was to inform me that the mayor wanted to offer me a position on the Newark School Board. After much soul-searching—I was also planning to start college at Princeton University that fall—I agreed and became the nation's youngest school-board member. During that summer of 1971, I also served as an aide to the mayor.

My commitment to the work of the school board caused me to withdraw from Princeton in the middle of my first semester. The board became a full-time job for me for one year. During that time, I continued to move closer to Imamu Baraka. In fact, I even changed my name to Adimu Chunga. With Baraka's referral, I became an aide to Central Ward councilman Dennis Westbrook. Also during this time, I was a delegate to several conventions focused on various social-justice issues, and my work on the board had taken the form of organizing students around a host of demands. We were eventually identified as a group by our 101 demands.

By the end of my first term on the school board, I had fallen out of favor with Mayor Gibson. This resulted in me not being reappointed. While I am uncertain about the specific basis for the mayor's loss of confidence in me, I am certain about his negative feelings in this regard. In an article in the *Star Ledger*, Gibson described my appointment to the board as the worst decision of his administration. I guess that in his view, I did not toe the line, and my close relationship with Amiri Baraka probably didn't help matters.

Not being reappointed actually turned out for the best. It allowed me to return to Princeton University, where I graduated in 1978 cum laude. I was also accepted into a Princeton doctoral program where I completed two additional years of study.

I did have one additional political encounter with Mayor Gibson. In 1974, I joined a political ticket for a seat on the Newark Municipal Council. We called ourselves the Second Community Choice Team. Against Gibson's Community Choice Team, everyone on our ticket lost.

Vicki Donaldson was another of Mayor Gibson's appointees to the Newark
School Board. She reflects fondly on her personal relationship with him.

VICKI DONALDSON

I was early in his camp, before the 1970 campaign, when coffee klatches
were the way to get the message out and the money in. My stepfather was a
block president, and our basement saw lots of politicos. I was there in the
trenches with his early supporters, the "Gibson Girls."

The first thing you noticed back then were his eyes—always focused,
looking at you straight on, never evasive, never uncertain. You never really
had to guess with him. He was refreshingly transparent.

He could be enthusiastic enough, but he was never much at jumping
for joy or fist pumping. A cheerful greeting, "Hello, Mr. Mayor," could
often be met with a bland "How you doin', Vickie?" A major accomplishment might get a dry "good job." Conversely, a chastisement would rarely
stir more than an "OK, it has to be my way. . . . I'm the mayor here."

There was not much difference in happy or sad—just different kinds
of smiles.

These, admittedly, are somewhat superficial personal observations, but
I write this knowing that more-critical eyes will be focusing on his policies,
his legacy, and the political history he made. This is a reflection about how
he impacted my life and how I will always remember and respect him. He
was my mentor.

I have always been an activist, first in the Deep South, where marching
and almost dying became the tools to fight oppression, and then, more
boldly, when we dared to speak loudly at Rutgers, challenging institutional
racism. We had discovered a love for our community and brought it with us
to the university. We fought the medical-school fight, the labor-union fight,
the welfare-rights fight, the Model Cities fight, the school board fight, and
so many others. We did not go unnoticed.

Our efforts were not unrewarded. When Ken (as we affectionately called him privately, with Mr. Mayor being our official designation), took the oath, some of us were called to do the work. We were not insiders, the real politicos, but we were the troops who constituted the workforce—writing the policies, defining the procedures, revamping a system that had excluded us into one that embraced us. Sometimes we worked for the mayor and the people; sometimes we had to choose to work for the mayor or the people. This was, after all, a political system, and there were rules. Learning the rules and how to use them would be the one great gift that I picked up from the mayor. He taught me how to "count to five."

Democratic systems work by majority rule. In Newark, the magic number was often five, for the most influential of these bodies in Newark were the nine-member city council and the board of education. Meetings of these boards in the Gibson era were often attended by hundreds of people. School-board meetings often involved controversy with impassioned, forceful cries for economic parity and empowerment.

The school board was the largest employer in the city, with more than one hundred school buildings and several thousand employees, serving a population that was increasingly African American. A school system once known as one of the best in the nation became the focus of attention as the transition from white control to black control began.

Ken Gibson made momentous strides in some of his political appointments. He did the required things, and then he did things that his "bright young people" had pushed for. One was to appoint a student to the board of education—a vibrant young man named Lawrence Hamm, who was just experiencing a political awakening. He was the youngest person appointed to a school board in the state, and he went on to become a firebrand and, as such, often was at odds with the office of the mayor.

The deliberate, willful, and focused Kenneth A. Gibson, counseled by those young and daring people, somehow also got him to appoint me to the board of education. I'd like to think that the choice was because I was overwhelmingly qualified, but more likely, I was a balance to the fiery Adimu Chunga, as Larry Hamm had evolved to be called. So at age twenty-three, I became a member of the Newark Board of Education.

I remember getting an urgent call that I was to meet with the mayor. I arrived nervous and frightened. I had absolutely no clue of what was to happen. When told by the mayor's aides that I would be appointed to the board, I was overwhelmed: "Why me? I'm not ready. . . . Oh shit!" And then: "My mother and my grandma are going to love this!" I had about five minutes to absorb, recompose, and march into the mayor's office. His eyes—his eyes—told me that it was real.

The mayor explained why he chose to appoint me. He thought that I was bright, a team player, and I would provide balance to the board. He asked me to be involved in three issues that were paramount at that time: the teachers' strike, getting a new superintendent of schools, and working with the board president, Charlie Bell, to give some stability to the board. I think that I did all three.

The mayor reappointed me to another three-year term. Afterward, however, I declined to be considered for another reappointment because I wanted to go to law school. He wished me well, and we have remained friendly at all times.

During my six-year tenure on the board, the mayor had many issues that I could not support—mostly personnel issues. I didn't do patronage, so I excised any opportunity to become a real player. Above the fray, I focused on policy and rewrote the policy manual. And as for voting, I was usually a part of the four-person minority on critical issues.

Kenneth A. Gibson called me only a few times during those six years. Once, he phoned to ask me to support a teacher's contract—and I did. Once, he checked in to share his concern about possible graft and to warn me to stay clear. I thanked him, and I did. Once, he asked me to support someone as a principal who was not only unqualified, in my view, but also tied to a political opponent, and I couldn't.

What Ken taught me was how to count—on the school board and in life. When school-board members Helen Fullilove, Fred Means, George Branch, and I would approach the mayor on an issue with an intense longing and desire to defeat the majority of five, the mayor would listen, consider, and then decide whether we would win the day. He never blinked. He could announce that we would likely lose—or win—by calmly saying yea or nay.

Once, when we got up and were leaving after one of his "nays," I glanced back to see him walk a slow, deliberate but seemingly tortured walk toward his office window. Ever polite, I yelled, "Thank you, Mr. Mayor," and he said, "Remember, Vickie, you always have to count to five."

I think that it is fairly safe to say that I love Ken Gibson for the boost he gave me. I honor him because he took a chance on a young woman, empowered her, and gave her the opportunity to grow.

Hubert Williams, Esq., an African American, was named police director during a period—not unlike current times—when relations between police and the African American majority were frayed past the breaking point. He describes, in detail, a multiple-point program on which he and Mayor Gibson worked closely to try to improve policing in Newark.

HUBERT WILLIAMS, ESQ.

My recollections of Ken Gibson as mayor are most vividly recalled in the context of my tenure as director of the Newark Police Department from 1974 to 1979. It is also significant to note, I think, that I spent twelve years in the ranks of the department as a uniformed officer, including a stint as a lieutenant. From these positions and with these perspectives, I have a firm understanding of the law enforcement–related challenges Mayor Gibson faced during his four terms in office, how he prioritized these challenges among the many he faced, and outcomes associated with his efforts to meet these challenges.

At the time of Gibson's election in 1970, the perception that police routinely abused their authority and used excessive force was rampant in the African American community. The arrest, in July 1967, of a black taxi driver by a white police officer outside the Fourth Precinct and rumors that the taxi driver had been brutally beaten inside the precinct set off a chain of events that resulted in the deaths of twenty-six civilians and millions of dollars in property damage. These events caused numerous businesses to leave Newark and much of the white middle class to move to the suburbs. Mayor Gibson recognized that the use of excessive force and abuse of authority by the police could be the fuse that would set off another rebellion. To minimize that possibility, he ordered the police department to curtail the use of excessive force and to take other measures to gain the trust of the black community.

The 1967 rebellion had a devastating psychological effect on the people living in the city. While some residents left Newark, others remained but lived in fear. These psychological effects divided the city along racial lines, including among the members of the municipal council; negatively impacted the municipal budget; and generally set the city back in the decades that followed. It is worth noting that almost every rebellion that occurred across the nation in the 1960s was precipitated by an event between the police and a member of a minority community. Mayor Gibson's concern about the potential for another rebellion occurring in his city—and the need to bring about reforms to prevent it—was well-founded. As a result, the mayor endeavored to strengthen the bond between the police and the public by improving the nature of interactions between them and by reducing the abuse of authority and the use of excessive force by officers.

One reason reforming the police department proved challenging was that there existed a unique relationship between the department and elected representatives on the municipal council, several members of whom were police officers on leave from the department. These council members would regularly attempt to use their power and influence to obtain special treatment for their friends and associates remaining in the department. At one point, four of the nine council members were former police officers. In addition, one council member's brother-in-law served as the president of the Fraternal Order of Newark Police. I can offer an anecdote to exemplify the challenge this situation presented. As police director, I was often faced with strong requests for particular moves within the department. One such request involved the appointment of a captain to command the city's North Ward precinct. My refusal to comply with a particular request resulted in my home being picketed by a group led by North Ward councilman Anthony Carrino and a North Ward activist named Anthony Imperiale. When the mayor backed my decision, this same group, armed with weapons, stormed his office after kicking down his door.

When seeking to understand the challenges facing the mayor in his attempts to reform the police department, one must factor in the department's complex political environment, its quasi-military structure, the fact that the municipal council was responsible for approving the police department's budget, and the fact that the municipal council had the power of confirmation of the appointment of a police director.

Mayor Gibson supported a public-safety and law enforcement strategy that can be grouped into five basic categories:

1. Elimination of the stigma of corruption that characterized the department.
2. Reduction in the use of deadly force and abuse of authority by the police.
3. Advancement of accountability and productivity.
4. Creation of a better relationship between police officers and the residents they served.
5. Development of law enforcement leaders of the future.

Elimination of the Stigma of Corruption

The most pressing item on Mayor Gibson's agenda with respect to reforming the police department was the elimination of the stench of corruption. This issue had been elevated to prominence as a result of a grand-jury presentment during the administration of Gibson's predecessor, Hugh Addonizio. The department was cited for its failure to enforce gambling laws. This matter surfaced at a time when a significant increase in the use of narcotics was occurring throughout the country. The huge amounts of money associated with trafficking narcotics and gambling were at the same time emerging as major law enforcement problems.

Mayor Gibson's initial appointment of a police director was John Redden. Redden had earlier served as the deputy chief of police and as the commander of a special gambling enforcement unit under Mayor Addonizio's police director, Dominick Spina. Mayor Gibson's appointment of Redden sent a powerful but mixed message. On the one hand, Redden's appointment signaled a focus on the elimination of corruption within the department as a high priority. On the other hand, the appointment represented a break with the tradition of having the ethnicity of the police director correlate with that of the mayor and the political base that elected the mayor. Not long after his appointment, Redden resigned, as he was unable able to gain the trust and confidence of the black community in the department promised by Gibson. Mayor Gibson replaced Redden with Edward Kerr, who was at the time serving as a lieutenant on the force. Kerr was the first African American in the city's history to serve as director of the department.

Kerr's undoing came as a result of the awkwardness associated with seeking accountability from officers who previously had authority over him and who would again have authority over him when he returned to his civil-service position as a lieutenant on the force. Recognizing my independence as a lawyer (I received a Juris Doctor degree from Rutgers–Newark Law School in June 1974), Gibson approached me to be Kerr's successor. Not only was I a lawyer, but I had no intention of ever returning to my civil-service position as a lieutenant on the force. While I had some regrets about leaving my position as the executive director of Newark's High Impact Anti-Crime Program, I did accept the mayor's offer to become the police director.

Coming into the job, it was my belief that I would be unable to resolve the police-corruption problem by way of an exclusive reliance on the resources available within the police department. I believed that a fundamentally different approach would be required. What I envisioned was the establishment of a joint task force with the county prosecutor's office that would merge the resources from the two agencies to create a gambling enforcement and corruption unit. My concept called for combining the legal talent and skills of the prosecutor's office with the experience and skills of savvy investigators in the police department. If political considerations could be worked out and mutually acceptable policies agreed upon, it had the potential of creating a powerful new weapon for law enforcement to deal with the problem at hand: police corruption.

Essex County Prosecutor Joseph Lordi and I discussed the matter at length and ultimately agreed to establish a joint investigative team. We then held a joint press conference in my office to announce the new unit. At the same time, I dismantled the old gambling enforcement structure within the department and transferred personnel associated with that unit to the patrol division, a move that bolstered the department's field operations. The joint corruption and gambling enforcement squad expanded the scope of the police department's gambling enforcement capacity by enabling the department to target high-level offenders who had previously been beyond the reach of the department.

Moreover, the establishment of the new unit dealt a major blow to anyone seeking to protect a gambling operation by paying off corrupt police officers, while the transfer of personnel previously assigned to the bureau of investigation to the patrol division helped offset the losses in our field operations resulting from layoffs. All these changes also served to address issues raised by the grand jury in its presentment issued years earlier.

Reduction in the Use of Deadly Force and the Abuse of Authority

This matter was deeply troubling to me because it undermined public trust, which results in the loss of public support for the police, which in turn affects the department's ability to control crime and provide for public safety. To gain an insight into the magnitude of the problem, I examined the penalties meted out for violations of department rules and regulations over a period of years. From this exercise, I concluded that while the rules and regulations were basically sound, penalties were ineffectively low even for serious violations, amounting in most cases to mere "slaps on the wrist."

Moreover, the problem was systemic. Command-level personnel were reluctant to charge officers with excessive use of force and abuse of authority, and even when they did, the officers would likely be charged with a lesser offense. In addition, even though internal affairs had the principal responsibility for the enforcement of department rules, its personnel were insufficiently rigorous in the pursuit of investigative leads into the more complicated and serious charges. As a result of these findings, leadership in internal affairs was changed and most of its personnel assigned to other areas of the department.

Advancement of Accountability and Productivity and Efficient and Effective Use of Police Resources

Throughout a prolonged period of social unrest, the police department found it necessary to develop various innovative programs to compensate for decreases in personnel and finances. I believe that the department emerged from the turmoil as a leaner, more productive, and more sensitive organization and that it was more responsive than ever to the needs of the citizens of Newark.

One important new initiative was the Accountability and Productivity Program. This program was based on a major effort to introduce standard management practices into the department; it operated under the slogan "As the department decreases in size, it becomes more and more important to ensure that maximum efficiency is realized from existing resources." Under this program, a formalized policy of strict accountability for all ranks and personnel was introduced. The policy carefully outlined the specific responsibilities of all personnel, according to their rank and functions within the department. This program, coupled with a newly created productivity-monitoring process and an official warning system to rectify inefficient or incompetent behavior, succeeded in markedly improving both individual and unit productivity throughout the department.

Creation of Better Community Relations

To accomplish this objective, top leadership in the department held community forums and met with people who lived and worked in every section of the city. The forums were designed for department personnel to listen to concerns and to develop effective responses to the issues raised. We learned much from this process. It also brought the department closer to the community and enabled us to respond to new concerns more effectively.

Community relations were also enhanced by way of these specific new programs:

- Sexual Assault and Rape Analysis Unit
- Team Policing Project
- Decoy Unit
- Victim Service Center
- Modernization of Communications Center
- Employment of Civilians as Communication Clerks
- Office of Management Improvement and Professional Development
- Investigative Case Screening Initiative
- Target Area Red Team
- Crime Analysis Unit
- Newark Comprehensive Crime Prevention Program
- Rapid Response to Robbery Program
- Hazardous Waste Task Force

Development of Future Law Enforcement Leaders

No less significant than the other elements of Mayor Gibson's five-point strategy for improving police services was his effort to provide an opportunity for leadership positions for individuals in groups who had previously been systemically excluded from such opportunities. Blacks and other minorities have historically been denied such opportunities on the grounds that they lacked the experience to qualify for higher-ranking positions. Mayor Gibson took significant political risks in this regard, but the result was an impressive list of future leaders.

By reaching down to lieutenants to fill the position of police director, Gibson skipped over four higher-level positions. In doing this, he contributed to overcoming the handicap that blacks had historically experienced through discriminatory practices. I am personally appreciative of the mayor's courage in this regard, having been one such lieutenant who was elevated to the position of police director. In return, I have made it a feature of my administrative practices over the years to take similar risks with respect to hiring and promotion policies. These practices have worked wonderfully well for me. I found my efforts in this regard were rewarded with a cadre of young and energetic officers who were loyal, hardworking, and deeply committed to our mission.

Alan Zalkind, similar to Hubert Williams, served Newark in the area of crime prevention. He takes great pride in what he sees as the police department's significant innovations during his time.

ALAN ZALKIND

I was hired by Mayor Ken Gibson in 1973 to be the deputy director of the Newark High Impact Anti-Crime Program, a federally funded program to reduce stranger-to-stranger crime. I worked for Hubert Williams, the executive director, who subsequently became the director for the Newark Police Department. I succeeded Hubert as executive director of the anticrime program in 1974, remaining in that role until 1977. From 1977 through 1980, I worked in the mayor's office as the director of constituent relations.

It was an especially exciting time to work in Newark. The federal government had created many innovative opportunities for urban areas through its Great Society programs. In addition to such noteworthy programs as

Medicare, Medicaid, and Head Start, Washington had begun offering a host of block-grant and economic funding programs to aid troubled communities. Based on Newark's demographic, educational, and economic conditions, the city was an ideal place to test many of these efforts.

But change, if it were to come, would require more than money; it would require effective local leadership. And fortunately for Newark, that came in the person of Ken Gibson, who was elected as the first African American mayor in a major city populated with predominately minority residents at a time of great urban unrest.

The mayor would need special skills to navigate competing interests, institutional and organizational biases, a suspicious business community, and an inherited workforce that had been loyal to his predecessor. He had them. Most important, he had to create and maintain the trust of residents who were historically distant and suspicious of local elected officials. In my view, Ken Gibson was successful in that regard as well.

He was humble and self-effacing. He employed individuals who were extraordinarily talented—many who went on to great success in the public and private sectors after their service in Newark. Gibson's own extraordinary talent was to engage competent professionals and profit from their expertise without ever feeling threatened by their abilities.

Gibson's ability to satisfy differing and divergent interests and reach a consensus was special. While he could forcefully advocate for the city's interests, the discussions in which he participated were seldom if ever contentious. When there was honest disagreement, the mayor would find compromise.

I have worked directly for numerous elected officials in my career as a manager in the public sector, including two mayors and four county executives. Without question, Ken Gibson ranked among the best.

The Newark High Impact Anti-Crime Program

To place my comments about the mayor in perspective, it may be helpful to understand my role as the executive director for the Newark High Impact Anti-Crime Program, the program that brought me to Newark during the Gibson administration. This special initiative was created by the Law Enforcement Assistance Administration (LEAA) to address the public-safety issues affecting the nation, specifically urban street crime, of which Newark had plenty.

Crime had escalated nationally to record levels at the time, and states and local jurisdictions were demanding remedies even though public safety was not considered a federal responsibility. Public safety became the number-one domestic issue as public unrest escalated during the period of civil rights and Vietnam War protests. This volatile situation was compounded by a basic distrust within urban communities of police, the courts, and the whole corrections system.

In response to the concerns regarding crime in America, the U.S. Justice Department identified eight cities and dedicated $20 million for each to reduce stranger-to-stranger crime. The focus would be on five of the seven major serious offenses: murder and nonnegligent manslaughter, forcible rape, aggravated assault, robbery, and burglary. Offenses related to auto theft and larceny were not targeted.

The cities selected to participate were Atlanta, Baltimore, Cleveland, Dallas, Denver, Portland, St. Louis, and Newark. One of the federal government's criteria for inclusion was the size of the resident population, which had to be within the three hundred thousand to one million range. The cities selected were geographically mixed with differing criminal justice systems.

Newark and the other cities were required to conduct a comprehensive analysis of their criminal justice systems and to develop innovative strategies to reduce crime. Among the challenges faced by the selected local jurisdictions was the reality that many of the rules, procedures, and services provided by the criminal justice system were established not by the cities but by their counties (courts and jails) or by their states (courts and prisons). The ability to communicate and coordinate with these broader jurisdictions would be critical to the success of our endeavors in Newark.

Besides these larger governmental entities, Newark and the other cities would have to communicate effectively with their local residents to effectively develop the expected remediation plans.

To place the situation in perspective, Newark's 1970 population was 382,000, and that year, there were 48,656 serious offenses, including 374 murders. By 1972, that number rose to 48,915, with 383 murders. Based on criteria selected to assess each city, Newark ranked the worst of the eight cities.

In response to the initiative, Newark was able to create twenty-seven separate programs affecting every aspect of the criminal justice system. The initiatives included a program to improve street lighting, a new communication system for police, a drug treatment and diversion program, and a rape analysis and investigation unit in the police department.

After the initiative ended in 1978, Newark cited progress in these areas:

- Burglaries were reduced by 7 percent, murders and rapes were reduced by 9 percent, robberies were reduced by 10 percent, and aggravated assaults were reduced by 16 percent.
- Several of the programs became institutionalized with state and local resources.
- Communication and coordination within the criminal justice system among the jurisdictions became routine.
- Trust within the community for the police increased.

Ken Gibson's Leadership

Why do I think so highly of Ken Gibson and his leadership? Why do I regard my time with him as so important to my own professional development? A listing of his special abilities answers all.

- Ken had an astute understanding of politics and power (on all levels).
- He had a deep respect for the city's residents and an appreciation for the importance of providing effective services.
- He was loyal to his staff and demonstrated a willingness to engage

Gibson enjoys Governor Brendan Byrne's support. Gibson reciprocated with support for Byrne's campaigns for governor of New Jersey.

Kenneth Gibson with Anthony (Tony) Imperiale, a staunch opponent of Gibson during the mayor's first two mayoral campaigns.

Kenneth Gibson with Harry Wheeler. Wheeler ran against Gibson in the 1970 mayoral campaign and later became a key member of Gibson's administration.

Gibson attends a meeting of the U.S. Conference of Mayors hosted by President Ronald Reagan. Gibson was elected the president of the U.S. Conference of Mayors in 1976.

Gibson chats with President Jimmy Carter in the mayor's office. The two executives were mutually supportive.

Gibson displays one of his many talents and interests.

Kenneth Gibson with Junius Williams. Williams served as Gibson's campaign manager for the 1970 mayoral campaign and later joined Gibson's cabinet as the head of the Model Cities Program.

Kenneth Gibson with Amiri Baraka. Baraka chaired the Black and Puerto Rican Convention that ultimately resulted in Gibson's election in 1970 as the first African American mayor of Newark and of any major Northeastern city.

Moderator and panel from the October 7, 2018, symposium titled "Reflections on Newark, N.J. 1970–1986, 'The Gibson Years.'" From left to right: George Hampton, moderator; Hubert Williams; Grizel Ubarry; Robert Holmes; Lieutenant Governor Sheila Oliver; New Jersey state senator Ron Rice.

Lawrence (Larry) Hamm speaking from the audience at the October 7, 2016, symposium. Also pictured are Susan Stevens, a member of the City of Newark Planning Department during the Gibson years and an unidentified participant.

Barbara Kukla speaking at the October 7, 2016, symposium.

Kenneth Gibson surrounded by family and friends at the October 7, 2016, symposium. Pictured from left to right: Rev. Deborah Stapleton (Gibson's sister-in-law), Camille Savoca Gibson (Gibson's wife), Kenneth Gibson, Harold Gibson (Gibson's brother), Sheila Oliver (lieutenant governor of New Jersey.), and Cheryl Fuller (Gibson's daughter).

Newark Public Radio (WBGO)—founded in 1977.

New Jersey Performing Arts Center (NJPAC)—proposed for construction by
Governor Tom Kean in the mid-1980s.

Victoria Human Services Plaza—home of Emergency Services for Families, founded in 1978.

them in the decision-making process.
- He had superb mentoring skills.
- He had a special knack for communication with other elected
  officials—especially when it was needed to gain consensus on issues
  that appeared to be irresolvable.

> Soon after the election of Gibson in 1970, Roger Lowenstein was hired
> into Newark's Law Department just two years out of law school. He
> recalls both positive and negative aspects of that two-year experience.

ROGER LOWENSTEIN, ESQ.

Central to my recollection of the Gibson administration are vivid experiences and events that occurred during the mayor's first term in office. The matters addressed in the paragraphs that follow speak to my sense of what working for Mayor Gibson and the City of Newark was like for a Jewish Newark native.

To me, the election was a true revolution. On election night, I was dancing in the street in front of the mosque, and some of us, more sure-footed than this skinny white boy, climbed up on top of a bus to keep dancing. I was part of the "Newark Law Commune," which included lawyers for Tom Hayden and the Students for a Democratic Society (SDS) folks who, prior to the riots, were active in the Central, South, and East Wards. To us, the coming of the Gibson administration represented a defeat of the corrupt white oppressors, a defeat of organized crime by the good guys.

Ken Gibson realized, if not immediately before the 1970 election, at least immediately after, that he didn't need one white vote to get elected mayor. Of course, he got a bunch of white votes; he just didn't need them. So when going about the business of making appointments, he was keenly aware of the need to see black faces in important jobs. So for example, when Dick Debevoise, a prominent Newark lawyer, offered to take a leave from his law practice and be the city attorney (head of the law department), he was refused, even though he offered to do it without pay. Bill

Walls and Al Lester, both African Americans, were appointed, and I was
hired as an attorney under them.

Life in the law department was an important learning experience for
me. I was only two years out of law school. And I was treating it as a full-
time job, whereas everyone else was busy building their private practices
on the side. So I got a lot of responsibility and no supervision, not that
I wanted any either. My first big case was the Newark riot-damages case
A & B Auto Stores v. Newark, a compendium of all the millions of dollars
in claims for riot damage made by insurance companies that had paid off
their insureds and were now coming after the City of Newark for reim-
bursement pursuant to a Civil War–era statute that made the city strictly
liable for all damages. Losing the case might have bankrupted the city. The
case was pending before the New Jersey Supreme Court, and the city's
brief had been written by Charlie Handler, an Addonizio lawyer who, in
my esteemed view, had phoned it in. My first legal action was to ask the
court for permission to file a supplemental brief. It was granted. I then
proceeded to research the statute (which was passed in the wake of bloody
Civil War draft riots in New York and elsewhere) and to make the argument that what happened in Newark in 1967 was a rebellion, not a riot.
In my lefty radical–community, we always referred to it in those terms, so
why not get the supreme court to agree?

At the very end of the brief, I threw in a technical argument based on
the concept of subrogation, the legal doctrine that allowed the insurance
companies to stand in the shoes of their insureds. I argued that subrogation was an equitable principle that was discretionary, not mandatory, and
here the court should exercise discretion and not apply it. Oral argument
was amazing—I was all by myself, age twenty-seven, arguing in front of
a court I had just clerked on (I was the official driver of Justice Proctor's
station wagon, taking the chief justice and two others to the train station
after argument), and at the other table were ten of the highest-paid lawyers in the state. I needn't have worried. The chief justice wasn't about to

let Newark go bankrupt. He skipped the rebellion argument and held that subrogation was discretionary and it wouldn't be applied here.

I loved working in city hall, and I loved having the city and all its employees as my clients. I became friendly with the longtime city clerk Harry Reichenstein (easily 120 years old) and with the city councilmen, especially South Ward councilman Sharpe James. The only other lawyer who showed up every day was Bill Hodes, a friend who I recommended hiring, and often at lunch, we would walk up Broad Street to Market, make a right, and disappear downstairs into Steel's Billiard Parlor to shoot pool. We were the only white faces. Ever. We went there so often that I earned my own cue that sat behind the counter and had my nickname tacked onto it. Everyone had a nickname at Steel's. My nickname was "Lawyer." When Bill also earned a cue and a nickname, he was "Other Lawyer."

When we took over the law department, I found a box of Hugh Addonizio's official mayoral stationery. It was beautiful—and expensive! It was gold leaf with the official Newark seal and everything. By this time, he was in federal prison. I couldn't just let the box sit there. So I sent a bunch of fake (Free Hughie!) Addonizio letters to my father and various friends and acquaintances in the radical left, assuming they would know that the letters were fake. The letters said something like "Dear _____, Now that I am settled here in federal prison, I've had an opportunity to reflect upon my tenure as mayor and my criminal behavior. I realize that I have terribly misjudged who my friends were and who are my enemies. I particularly want to apologize to you for not realizing we were really on the same team. My brothers in struggle here in custody join with you in fighting government oppression! Right on!" I sent the letter to a bunch of folks, but only Tom Hayden took it seriously. Tom was working out in Los Angeles with Lenny Weinglass on the Ellsberg case, and according to Len, who called me very upset, Tom had tearfully put the letter up on the (Free Hughie!) office bulletin board. Len begged me to call Tom and tell him it was a joke. I never did.

The law department was not immune to the expectation that its members would contribute to the mayor's fund-raising efforts. About two weeks after I began working in the department, I arrived one morning to find two $100 tickets to the mayor's picnic on my desk. I hadn't ordered any tickets. I was puzzled, so I went to see my boss, Bill Walls, but of course, he was not in. His extremely savvy secretary, Mary Kornegay, asked me what the problem was. I told her there must be some mistake because I had no intention of going to the mayor's picnic. She laughed and told me, "Nobody said you have to go to the picnic. You can just buy the tickets and stay home!" I noticed that she had some tickets of her own on her desk. Now I began to understand.

Continuing my saga of Newark Law Department experiences, one day, there was a disaster on Broad Street. An old water main (we still had hundred-year-old wooden mains in some places) burst and created a giant sinkhole that jammed up traffic and water service for a long time. It was a mess. A huge amount of city services were required to get things back to normal—easily six figures of expense, maybe seven. Luckily, this was the kind of thing we were insured for, and I was assigned the task of managing our claim. We had an entire city department to manage our municipal insurance. The department head was Pearl Beatty. I knew her from the campaign. She was a nice person, a real politician. She was rumored also to have a special relationship with the mayor. I went to Pearl and asked her to please pull the policy covering this disaster. She assured me that she would get right on it. Actually, all Pearl had to do was simply call the city's broker and get the policy from him. But despite many calls, the broker was not responding. Then it turned out, to use a Newark expression, the broker was "in the wind." And he was in the wind because there were no insurance policies. He was simply pocketing the premiums and paying the occasional claims himself. He was way ahead of the game until the Broad Street sinkhole. He couldn't cover that, so he simply disappeared. Some have speculated that someone as savvy as Pearl must have been in on it, and if she was, her boyfriend was too. But I didn't then—and I do not now—make such speculation, other than to say that the various departments did in fact run like fiefdoms with little or no oversight, reminiscent of the old commission form of government.

My final recollection involves a personal disappointment. Someone offered Newark a grant to create a municipal "ombudsman" department that would have some umbrella-oversight responsibility to resolve administrative issues across the various departments. It was designed to help with citizen complaints. I went to Ken and asked to be appointed the ombudsman. After all, we didn't have to pay for it. I never was appointed, and I don't remember if anyone was. I think it just went away. As did I after two years.

CHAPTER 5

AN IN-DEPTH LOOK INSIDE CITY GOVERNMENT

MAYOR GIBSON'S RIGHT-HAND MAN

David Dennison left New Jersey government to work for Mayor Gibson at the beginning of the mayor's first term. Until 1978, Dennison was the mayor's trusted confidant and aide in a series of positions that culminated in his being named as the executive director of the mayor's policy and development office. He provides us with an up-close view of the nearly overwhelming challenges involved in making a troubled city, with unique bureaucratic complexities, work as well as it could. Dennison guides us through the often dizzying "alphabet soup" of city agencies and their dynamic relationships to one another to describe some solid achievements.

DAVID DENNISON

In August 1970, I was working as the director of the Model Cities Program and Community Development Administration at the New Jersey Department of Community Affairs. One morning, I got a call from Junius Williams, the director of Newark's Community Development Administration (CDA), offering me the deputy director position. Junius wanted me to start work within a week. The CDA was also responsible for administering Newark's Model Cities Program. I thought the request was crazy but, after thinking about it, concluded it would be an extraordinary opportunity to get in on the ground floor of the administration of Newark's first black mayor. After a discussion with my wife, I resigned from my state job, and within a week, I was working in Newark. I didn't even ask about pay. My primary interest was to do what I could to help Newark's first black mayor.

On my first day, I walked into the director's office, located in a retail space of a Branford Place office building, just a few blocks from city hall, and observed Junius sitting behind a big desk with papers and folders stacked about a foot high. "Welcome to Newark and CDA," he said. "This desk and everything on and in it is yours." He gave me an orientation, introduced me to Mamie Hale, the office manager, and Carol Jones, my secretary; said his office was on the second floor; and then told me that if I needed anything to talk to Ms. Hale and left. I glanced through the stuff on my desk and realized that I had inherited a mess.

Somehow the folders got sorted with help from Ms. Jones and others who probably felt sorry for me. I quickly got up to speed on the CDA's authority and responsibilities. After the initial folder review, I studied the city ordinance that created the CDA to understand the legal basis from which to manage. The most important aspect of the CDA ordinance was that the agency was part of the mayor's office and by law answered directly to the mayor and not to or through anyone else, such as the city business administrator, which created the potential for competition, even conflict.

The potential for tension was heightened by the fact that the CDA's role included that of primary procurer of flexible federal and state funds coming into the city. The scale and flexibility in applying these funds in a real sense established our operation as a "shadow government" within city hall. In view of this, I expected disagreement and pushback from other city officials, the city council, certain community organizations, and many community activists.

Not surprisingly, the unit of city government most uncomfortable with the CDA and Model Cities' direct line to the mayor was the office of the business administrator, which oversaw the city's departments and agencies. Both the business administrator and the CDA director were overseers of funds managed by city departments and agencies. The business administrator was responsible for monitoring departmental and agency programs that relied upon city-appropriated tax-based funds. The CDA director by ordinance was empowered to monitor city departments and agencies using grant funds received from federal and state government. The tension created by this arrangement can be summarized by the cliché "Whoever has the gold makes the rules."

Despite this arrangement, the offices and programs that were the recipients of one or both sources of funds easily understood the different reporting requirements and were grateful for the expanded access to resources.

The triangle structure linking the mayor, the business administrator, and the CDA director was most problematic when the two disagreed about a policy for which both had a role. Good communication should have resolved any problem but too often did not. Adding to the tension was the fact that in addition to managing the influx of significant state and federal dollars, the CDA was assigned the special task of managing the city planning office and providing staff support to the city's planning board. That gave the CDA additional clout but also responsibility.

Of course, it was politically advantageous for the mayor to have sources of flexible grant funds under his direct control and separate from municipal tax-based funds. I knew that for this arrangement to work, the mayor, the business administrator, and the CDA director would have to respect each other and work together. The structure was intended to generate healthy but synergistic tension but had to be mastered by all to be effective. I was ready to ride this train despite the potential for interoffice conflict. I saw the potential for extraordinary opportunities to benefit the city in general and Newark's black and Puerto Rican folk in particular.

Money Is Found

After becoming established in my new position, I at one point began a review of the financial status of the Model Cities Program, and I discovered a windfall of sorts. I discovered that the program had been approved in March 1970 under the Addonizio administration and that none of the approved $5.6 million had been spent or obligated. Projects were planned, but none had started. Our task, then, was to quickly review the projects in order to determine what revisions might be needed to meet Gibson's goals to improve conditions for all who lived or worked in Newark.

We had flexibility in terms of how to spend large sums of state and federal funds but soon found that represented both a blessing and a curse. On the one hand, the administration could hire with considerable freedom, which meant we could find work for many more people. On the other hand, that meant more people looking for a reward for their political support of the mayor than could possibly be accommodated. Eventually, most stakeholders accepted the reality that not everyone could be included in the spoils of success. We simply moved ahead with the hiring.

Early on, I ran into another challenge. I discovered that most of the CDA staff did not know how they fit into the organization. I believe that most, including longtime employees, had never seen an organization chart. We set up interim organizational structures to implement Gibson's goals and objectives. But before we settled upon a formal structure, we tested numerous structural reorganizations, and we revised as we learned more about our needs.

I learned that major functions in the CDA operation had not been initiated—from contract monitoring to program and project evaluation. So we took steps to address these important issues.

There was a citizens' advisory board that provided valuable input from residents of Model Cities' neighborhoods. The board kept us on track with regards to the needs of the community and helped ensure that our work led to desired outcomes. Patronage matters relating to the city generally were handled by Elton Hill, the city's assistant business administrator, but we received our share of inquiries, and it proved unsettling to staff and affected productivity. We did, however, find it helpful to retain, at least on a temporary basis, some program coordinators from the previous administration in part because of their institutional memories.

In time, I realized that I needed a chief planner to assist in managing things. I picked Zinnerford Smith for the role. I also added Dennis Cherot to my support team. These two men greatly lightened my workload. Zinn and Dennis ensured that despite the myriad challenges, we could still finish critical assignments on time. They helped determine ways to establish priorities and to deal with backlogs due to system overload.

We were a capable group, I believe, from the top down. Our combined CDA / Model Cities Program leadership group consisted of Junius Williams, me, Donald Tucker, and Larry Coggins. We each brought different but complementary skills to the table. I was the only outsider and the new kid on the block. While the other three knew each other well and had worked together, I had to learn about how this leadership group could function in pursuit of common objectives. Fortunately, we found respect for one another and continued as a strong and productive team.

How did I wind up on this team? My invitation to come to Newark was based solely on my having worked for Paul Ylvisaker, the commissioner of the New Jersey Department of Community Affairs. Ylvisaker, a former program director at the Ford Foundation, had applauded my skills as an administrator and my knowledge of federal and state community development and Model Cities regulations. In addition, my academic background in education, community organization, and public administration was an asset. I had also spent three years working in the U.S. Department of Housing and Urban Development, Philadelphia, Pennsylvania, regional office as an urban-renewal representative—in which capacity I managed millions of dollars of grant funds that had flowed to New Jersey.

Developing a Plan

Once we began to settle down, the leadership team had to assess how best to take advantage of our assets and the doors that Gibson's prominence opened for us. I recall, for example, the fact that Directors of the New York / New Jersey Federal Regional Council met quarterly in Newark to assist us with the preparation of applications for various federal grants. We had similar access to and assistance from departments of state government. Because of Ken Gibson, we were included in the key committees established by the U.S. Conference of Mayors. From these positions, we were able to work on federal legislation that would benefit Newark. We understood that access to key places and people was not enough. We also needed "staying power"—the capacity of a carefully selected staff to continuously mine the opportunities presented. And this, of course, included developing a plan for interfacing with other city departments and agencies as well as with the business community.

Early on, we concluded that jobs, the education and training of employees, and service delivery would be necessary for the sustainability of the Gibson administration. Providing services to all the people was Gibson's stated goal. We knew, however, that he wanted us to place a special emphasis on enhancing the living conditions for black and Puerto Rican residents of the city.

The team knew that to gain long-term growth and development for Newark's various constituencies, we first had to identify the resources at our disposal and then prioritize among interventions. We knew, for example, we were in a prime position legally as a result of our authority to manage the most-flexible financial resources coming into the city. We also knew that Newark's location geographically was a major competitive advantage and supported a major airport, a major seaport, important transportation systems, easy access to New York City, higher-education institutions, and major financial and insurance institutions. To take full advantage of these assets for the benefit of residents, we had to attract people who were capable of effectively interacting with public and private decision makers.

In addition to funding our own initiatives, we were often called upon to assist with fund-raising for mainstream city-hall programs and projects. Our planners, for example, went to work writing grant proposals for the police and health departments. Such efforts afforded our operation an opportunity to learn about the inner workings and priorities of many city departments and agencies.

Basketball at Night

Newark's reputation as a city that prudent people avoided after dark came to my attention one day in August 1971 when a group of us at the CDA were talking about basketball and I asked if there were any good holiday tournaments in the area. Everybody laughed. When I asked why, the response was that most tournaments occurred in the late evening, when it was dark, and that couldn't happen in Newark. From this conversation, I decided that Newark should host a statewide Mayor's High School Invitational Holiday Classic basketball tournament sponsored by the Model Cities Program and that it be coordinated with the board of education. The event would be held in the Model Cities Area in the Central Ward at Central High School and would be scheduled in the evenings with community-event monitors but no police.

I thought that I had found a way to test whether, contrary to popular belief, blacks in Newark, especially youth, could recreate after dark safely and sensibly.

A committee was formed to make this tournament happen. The board of education handled statewide high school invitations; posters and advertisements were developed, and tickets were sold. Numerous community organizations became involved, and word quickly spread citywide. Schools from across the state as well as local ones were invited and competed. Jackets were ordered, and photos were taken. Courtsides were jammed with spectators, but there were no untoward incidents. When the balls finally stopped bouncing, a team from Camden was crowned the winner, while a team from Newark's Westside High School took second.

We were all proud of our city afterward. The absence of police did not go unnoticed, nor did the fact that folk could gather in Newark after dark and have fun.

New Federal Initiatives

Things changed quite dramatically in July 1971 when President Richard Nixon instituted a new urban initiative called the Planned Variations Demonstration Program. The new two-year federal program, which covered twenty cities, was designed to demonstrate the feasibility of community-development special-revenue sharing within existing Model Cities Programs. The program was designed to help cities better coordinate the use of federal funds in solving critical urban problems, help cities set local priorities, and reduce the red tape that comes with seeking and accepting federal grants.

On the morning of April 11, 1972, in a meeting with Mayor Gibson, I was advised that I would be directing the new Planned Variations Demonstration Program. While unexpected, the new assignment did not catch me entirely off guard. My staff and I were much aware of the importance of this program to the mayor, given the significant increase in federal funding we were receiving.

An important element of the new Planned Variations Demonstration Program was the Chief Executive Review and Comment Component (CERC), under which the participating city's chief executive would have the opportunity to comment on the effectiveness of this and other federal funding initiatives. I was the mayor's choice to manage the bureaucratic CERC review, in part because of my knowledge of federal programs and regulation and experience in strategic thinking.

Among its many successful attributes, the Planned Variations Demonstration Program helped put Newark in a qualifying position when President Gerald Ford in 1974 initiated the Housing and Community Development Act, which led to city grants through a program that operates in Newark to this day.

By now I was wearing several leadership hats, for I also was named director of the Mayor's Policy and Review Office (MPRO), which had been newly established to handle the CERC process. I had this new responsibility while remaining the deputy director of the combined CDA and Model Cities Program.

And wearing several hats, I had to deal with the business administrator, the finance director, some members of city council, federal housing and urban development regulators, and interested neighborhood community organizations and community activists. With demands coming from every direction, I opened four offices in four locations. In order to lead MPRO and continue to perform my other duties, I designed a schedule that allowed me to spend time at all locations. This was taxing but good exercise, as I had to walk up and down Broad Street from office to office.

More changes were in store. Near the end of December 1972, the mayor made a big leadership decision regarding the CDA and Model Cities Program. Our leader, Junius Williams, was fired. The mayor asked if I would serve as acting director, and he also noted that he might merge the two offices, the MPRO and CDA. My plate was already full, but I accepted the challenge. In the following days, I continued to visit all four offices during the week but not necessarily all on the same day.

I believe that it was sometime in June 1973 that a decision was made to merge the CDA, Model Cities, and the MPRO and to create the Mayor's Policy and Development Office (MPDO). And I was named its executive director. Subsequently, my office was moved to city hall just a few doors from the mayor's office.

As time went by, Gibson was reelected mayor, and Donald Tucker was elected to the city council. We replaced Tucker with Barry Washington, a mature longtime Newark resident who was a highly qualified professional from the Prudential Insurance Co. and who was an expert on budgets, finance, and contracts.

Another important change soon occurred, this time in the leadership of our city planning division. The New Jersey Civil Service Division had conducted examinations for the position of city planning officer. Wilbert Allen, a planner in our city planning division and a longtime resident of Newark, came out number one on the statewide list. I promoted Wil to the position of city planning officer; the first black person to hold that position.

In his new position, Wil and his planning staff soon determined that the city's comprehensive plan was wanting, and they went to work updating it to reflect the values and vision of the Gibson administration. After that task, the MPDO City Planning Division set out to produce an urban development policy for the city, one designed to arrest the physical, social, and economic deterioration of the city's various neighborhoods and to promote balanced growth over the next four years. The document was to address the needs of residents in the various neighborhoods—including providing improvements in housing conditions, in education opportunities, in health services, in community facilities and recreation, and in commercial and industrial facilities.

In my estimation, the citizens of Newark eventually became the beneficiaries of increased programs and services that resulted from policies informed by citizen participation, sound planning and careful monitoring, and importantly, the involvement of my staff in numerous community meetings. Comments from residents at these meetings in most cases had a positive impact on our program development decisions.

An example was housing. During this time, certain priority projects not overseen by city departments or agencies continued to be funded by the MPDO. Among them were housing development and rehabilitation programs implemented by the Newark Housing Development and Rehabilitation Corporation (HDRC), one of several nonprofit entities created by CDA Director Junius Williams at the behest of the mayor, on the recommendation of the Office of Newark Studies, to expand his capacity to deliver on campaign promises.

To advance a focus on physical development activities, Gibson engaged assistance from a Harvard intern, Tom Massaro, who stayed on after graduation as a mayoral aide. Tom was assigned the task of coordinating an ad-hoc group the mayor called the Mayor's Development Team. The team consisted of business administrator William Walls, me; Wil Allen;

the executive director of the housing authority, Robert Notte; the deputy director of the housing authority, Robert Aprea; the executive director of the Newark Economic Development Corporation, Al Faiella; the city engineer, Al Zack; and the director of the Newark Transportation Council, Robert Bakke. The Greater Newark Chamber of Commerce president, David Rinsky, also participated in meetings of the team.

We created a living, dynamic organization to create policy, planning, and implementation programs, being adaptable as the environment we lived in changed. The results or outcomes over the years were highlighted by our ability to attract millions of dollars to the city that greatly assisted city departments and agencies in spite of the turbulence those flexible funds seemed to create.

We acquired a baby's hospital, created a drug rehabilitation center, set up an urban institute, improved street lighting, and made other infrastructure improvements. The evolution of the MPDO, I believe, demonstrated a high level of professionalism on the part of devoted and competent employees who were receptive to community concerns.

Pumping Station

One of my last challenges before resigning was to test what was known as the "municipal corporate collaborative management approach" to grantsmanship. This was an attempt to get a grant approved for a much-needed pumping station in the industrial section of the city close to Newark International Airport. The effort was occasioned by the fact that the city experienced severe flooding in this area during heavy rain. The excess water would overwhelm sewers, forcing area businesses into financial hardship, as they had to close temporarily and send their employees home.

For over twelve years, Al Zach, the chief engineer, tried unsuccessfully to get a federal grant to abate the problem. I, accordingly, asked the mayor to let me develop a proposal to submit to the U.S. Department of Commerce. I told him that it would require the highest level of cooperation from the business community and the full participation of any related city departments and agencies. Gibson approved my request, and I enlisted the assistance of the Newark Economic Development Authority (NEDC), one of the mayor's public/private nonprofit quasi-governmental agencies, which received most of its funding from the MPDO.

We met with representatives from the business community and reached an agreement that the NEDC would work with the MPDO to collect data from the businesses affected by the flooding. MPDO planners took the research data and material gathered at various meetings and worked with Zach and his staff, the NEDC, the NRHA, and the consulting firm Barton Aschman Associates, who had produced additional technical data that were needed. Finally, a proposal was prepared and submitted to the department of commerce.

In April 1978, the federal economic development administration announced a $4.9-million grant to spur business development and eliminate serious flooding in the industrial area. The announcement included mention of the fact that approval of the grant was prompted by a special industrial survey conducted by the city to determine the causes of the exodus of local businesses. A major portion of the grant was used to construct a pumping station to accelerate the draining of stormwater into the Newark Bay.

Congressman Peter Rodino, applauding the effort, estimated that the flood-control measure would "halt the exodus of business from Newark and stabilize the jobs of nine thousand workers."

It was an accomplishment that made us all proud.

CHAPTER 6

WORKING WITH THE ANCHOR INSTITUTIONS

City governments can only do so much. Every great city also must depend on a host of anchor institutions that have, at least, as much to do with the welfare of the citizenry as the municipal government itself. Of course, it is critical that these institutions work symbiotically with the host city and not drain resources that are crucial to both.

As several reflections have pointed out, Newark has had a complex and varied relationship with its anchor institutions—the corporations, commercial enterprises, state and federal organizations, nonprofits, colleges and universities, and religious and cultural centers—that, along with all the layers of government and the citizens, make up the fabric of a city.

Mayor Gibson, to his credit, understood that all these enterprises contribute to a city's strength and character. Relations with them were to be nurtured.

Al Koeppe experienced Newark as a student, as a lawyer, and as a
high-ranking business executive. He describes Gibson's businesslike
problem-solving style and his relationship with the business
community, which he saw as key to boosting his city.

AL KOEPPE

My recollections of Ken Gibson and of Newark can be arranged into three time periods:

1. 1964–1978: In this span of years, I was a student at Rutgers University, a lineman for N.J. Bell, a law student, a judicial clerk, and a trial attorney for the New Jersey Department of the Public Defender. During

this time, I vividly recall events surrounding the 1967 Newark civil unrest and was struck by the formidable challenges facing the city and its leadership.

2. Post-1982: After a stint in Washington, DC, I returned to Newark and eventually became the chief executive officer of New Jersey Bell-Atlantic, PSE&G, and, after retirement, the nonprofit Newark Alliance. My perspective on Newark, the city and its government, was colored by my experiences as a lawyer and senior executive during this time.

3. After 2014: This period was occasioned by the election of Ras Baraka as mayor and my selection by the mayor to serve with Ken Gibson as cochairmen of the new mayor's transition team. This third encounter with Ken taught me much about the mayor and his approach to problem-solving.

As we might expect, Ken, an engineer, approached Newark's formidable challenges analytically and methodically. Even out of office and in his role as cochair of the transition team, Ken would demonstrate an ability to dissect a problem and deal smartly with its individual parts. As a member of the team, Ken would allow everyone to have his or her say and then, with deft skill, would summarize the issues and move the team along to the next steps in the process of preparing the new mayor for challenges he would likely face.

Ken's effectiveness as a team member confirmed my belief that he always understood and embraced the role of a leader. In this regard, I can recall one of his earliest decisions as mayor. Soon after being elected, Ken called a meeting of the chief executive officers of the major companies then operating in the city. To my knowledge, no mayor had done that before. They came to discuss their companies' futures and the future of the city.

I see two significant features about the man emanating from this act. First, it demonstrated Ken's understanding that he was, himself, a CEO who could and should discuss Newark's challenges with persons of similar status. Second, it provided a glimpse at Ken's priorities. His meeting with CEOs reflected his view of the unique importance of securing and advancing the quality of life in the community for all its members.

Later, as I watched the reactions of a diverse cross section of people living and working in Newark to encounters with Ken, it became apparent that the man had—and continues to have—the presence and charisma of a bona fide leader.

With hindsight, I can also see how Ken's steady, unemotional style could be viewed eventually as a weakness as well as a strength. A careful approach to problem solving is always a good strategy. But it can also be confused with a lack of enthusiasm. And in 1986, the mayor was easily defeated by an energetic and emotional Sharpe James.

The truth is, by 1986, Ken may have been a little worn-out. That year, the unemployment rate had begun rising again, and there were renewed concerns about public safety.

But the challenges Ken faced over sixteen years should never be overlooked. He inherited a broken city. Few at the start had confidence that anyone, especially a politically inexperienced engineer, could improve matters. But Ken did, and he continues to be highly regarded within all sectors of Newark.

Vincente Perez worked at a nonprofit called the United Community Corporation. Newark, perhaps more than other cities that have greater financial resources, has always depended on a vital network of nonprofit organizations to address its social and economic issues. As with virtually every observation of life in Newark, there is a racial/political overlay to his reflection.

Vincente Perez

My family roots are in San Juan, Puerto Rico. I did not relocate to Newark until 1982. Before that time, however, I was exposed to Newark by way of summer visits to the home of my sister, who had moved to Newark in 1968.

Most of my recollections about the years between 1968 and 1982 are related to the activities of my sister and her husband, Raoul, who was particularly active in city affairs. Raoul's contributions were such that after he died, the city dedicated a street in the North Ward in his name and honor.

Raoul, an actor, was regularly featured on channel 47 television. He was also a founding member of the "Golden Age of Spanish Broadcasting" and the creator of a bilingual newspaper dedicated to reporting news about Newark's Hispanic population. The paper emanated out of city hall, and I believe that Raoul worked under the guidance of Bernie Moore, who served at the time as Ken Gibson's director of information.

About a year after I relocated to Newark, I was invited to join the board of trustees of the United Community Corporation, commonly known in Newark as the UCC. This organization was among the early Community Action Programs (CAP agencies) established in Newark and funded initially under the Economic Opportunity Act and later under the Community Development Block Grant Program. The UCC was well funded and was at the time the largest CAP agency in the state.

Although the UCC had been created during the Addonizio administration, Gibson supported the organization throughout his sixteen years in office. Beginning with the UCC, in my view, Ken Gibson built a network of social service organizations that continues to have a positive impact on the residents of Newark. For example, the UCC created so-called delegate organizations that in time became independent and established an important presence in the city. These organizations include the FOCUS Hispanic Center for Community Development, the International Youth Organization (IYO), the Elizabeth Avenue Community Center, and the Newark Pre-School Council, just to mention a few. Gibson also supported La Casa de Don Pedro, the New Community Corporation, and Episcopal Community Development Inc.

While the UCC and other similar organizations functioning during the Gibson years were an important adjunct to city government for the delivery of service to the city's residents, they were not without problems of their own. As I think back, I believe that many of the problems faced by these organizations were emblematic of the racial and economic tensions existing at the city government level. The tensions sometimes were exacerbated by crass political maneuvers and allegations of conflicts of interest.

An example comes to mind. Let me preface the example with a description of the UCC Board of Trustees. There were eight political representatives, including a representative from each of the five wards plus three at-large representatives. There were seven additional representatives from the private sector and seven more representatives from the constituent population. On one occasion, political members of the board tried to sell fund-raising tickets for their campaigns—putting their political interests ahead of community needs as perceived by the board's community representatives.

Despite such political intrusions, the UCC was able to deliver a wide range of needed services. These included an emergency food program, an after-school program, alcoholic rehabilitation initiatives, job training, and a homeless-shelter program.

While I do appreciate Gibson's support of the various social service and community development organizations during his tenure—including several organizations largely dedicated to serving the Hispanic community— I can also say confidently that things are very different today for Newark's Hispanic community than they were during the Gibson years. By different, I mean that life in Newark for Hispanics has improved significantly. I note, for example, the significant increase in Hispanic representation on the municipal council, on the board of education, and on other boards and in other strategic positions affecting the quality of life for Hispanic residents of the city.

The voices of Hispanics in Newark are being heard like never before—a hopeful sign for the future.

Richard Cammarieri, of the New Community Corporation
(NCC), describes the intersection of the church and a nonprofit
agency in neighborhood-based community development.

RICHARD CAMMARIERI

Following the civil disturbances of July 1967, what came to be called the
Newark Rebellion by many of its residents, activism in Newark took two
separate but related directions. One focus was political, the goal being
to elect a mayor and city council that would reflect what had become a
majority-black electorate. The other focus was on changing the material
conditions within which people lived—improving housing, child care,
health care, and employment. It would mean creating a new environment that would foster a sense of community and provide opportunity
for advancement.

In many ways, Ken Gibson was at the intersection of these interre-
lated and complementary impulses: electoral political organizing and
neighborhood-based community development.

In terms of politics, Gibson ran for mayor in 1966, more or less testing the waters for a black candidacy. While he did not win, his voting
totals were encouraging, and he became a favorite to run for mayor in
1970 when many black residents felt the demographics were in their favor
and serious political organizing could spell the difference. At the center
of black political organizing in Newark was Amiri Baraka—then called
Imamu Amiri Baraka. Spurred on by the ethos of black power and cultural
nationalism, Baraka and his followers were in the vanguard of galvanizing
the local black and allied electorate and raising national awareness of the
Gibson campaign because of the recent memory and impact of the Newark Rebellion.

In terms of community development, Gibson worked as the chief engineer for the Newark Housing Authority (NHA). In some ways, one can
think of a public-housing authority such as the NHA as a kind of proto-
community development corporation. It planned and built affordable

housing, managed it, and provided some level of social services for residents. With this background, Gibson had a context for understanding and supporting the work of the core founders and planners of the New Community Corporation (NCC), a community development organization, which was spearheaded by a young priest named William J. Linder.

The people who participated in founding the NCC were longtime workers for racial and social justice in Newark. In addition to Linder, they included Joseph Chaneyfield, Timothy Still, Willie Wright, Alma Bateman, and Robert Curvin, the leader of the Newark CORE organization. The genesis of the NCC was rooted in the social and pastoral work of Queen of Angels Catholic Church, a church of black parishioners, where Linder was assigned; the church had a legacy of social activism that went back to the 1930s led by black lay women.

The NCC standard-bearers were known and had credibility as workers for equity and justice in Newark. And Gibson joined them to become part of the founding board. Interestingly, both Gibson and Linder had engineering backgrounds—Linder having studied engineering before entering the priesthood. As such one can imagine both having an appreciation for designing, operating, and maintaining smoothly operating systems, something Gibson hoped to do with city government and what NCC hoped to achieve with resident-driven community development.

As Linder states in his memoir—*Out of the Ashes Came Hope*—the election of Gibson in 1970 was "the dawning of a new day." He wrote that Gibson, unlike the prior Mayor Addonizio, "understood the urgency of repositioning political goals in tandem with a progressive social agenda."[1] In many ways, one can see connective social tissue between the kind of urban populism that resulted in Gibson's victory in 1970 and the focus of the NCC on community uplift rooted in "community governance on a scale that was considered humane and authentic," as described by one historian of the NCC's creation and growth.[2]

Overall, the NCC maintained positive relations with the Gibson administration throughout the mayor's sixteen-year run. The organization fully hit its stride in the latter years of Gibson's tenure, between 1975 and 1986, constructing or rehabilitating over 2,200 units of rental housing made affordable for low- and moderate-income seniors and families. Like many community development corporations around the nation, the NCC established a parallel and complementary civic structure within the city, providing employment, housing, and social services.

Another point Linder makes in his memoir is that "New Community was a perfect fit for Gibson's agenda and simultaneously served to legitimize the mayor's efforts in housing development, while restoring hope and trust between Newark residents and the city."

Ultimately, he continued, under Gibson's leadership of the city, the "NCC had prospered and gained prominent recognition. Gibson and New Community were a winning combination."

Monsignor William Linder, the longtime leader of the Queen of Angels Catholic Church and one of the founders of the New Community Corporation (NCC), was at the forefront of the program that Mr. Cammarieri describes. He gives us a largely personal reflection on the mayor.

Monsignor William Linder

Politics had been a part of my life from almost the time I was in the crib. It was the dinner-table conversation that I heard growing up. My father was an active, politically connected Republican, although Hudson County where we lived was primarily Democratic. He was also an admirer of Wendell Wilkie, who supported some progressive ideas. And my father exposed me at a young age to a wide variety of political activities and the democratic process.

When I arrived in Newark as a young priest assigned to Queen of Angels Church in the Central Ward, Hugh Addonizio recently had been elected mayor. Over the next several years, I discovered the reality of just how corrupt, racist, and unjust politics could be under the Addonizio administration.

To be precise, what I saw of daily government and political affairs was downright sacrilegious. I knew from my upbringing that political representatives were supposed to look out for their citizens' best interest. In Newark, every man fended for himself. Truthfully speaking, when it came to Newark, at New Community we never fully trusted the local government because we didn't want to be beholden to a system that we knew was crooked.

That was until the dawning of a new day, when Kenneth Gibson was elected as Newark's first black mayor. Gibson, unlike his predecessor, understood the urgency of repositioning political goals in tandem with a progressive social agenda. After all, before serving as mayor, he'd been the chief engineer for the Newark Housing Authority. He knew the housing situation all too well, and as an NCC board member, he knew what we were all about.

Ken surrounded himself with the smartest people. He wasn't intimidated by their intellect. He was respected in the community, and that's why I asked him to be on the NCC board.

Later, I got to know Ken as the mayor through Tom Massaro, the city's development officer. Tom, who was like a trusted son to Ken, worked with New Community to coordinate our efforts with the city. The NCC also did well with U.S. Department of Housing and Urban Development. The department visited the NCC because we threw big events for groundbreakings. We often got the secretary of housing and urban development to come, and of course, that made Ken Gibson look good. So Ken and I got along well.

During Mayor Gibson's tenure, New Community invested heavily in Newark's revitalization. In 1977, construction began on New Community Associates, a 225-unit building for the elderly. That was followed by the acquisition of Roseville, which also was for seniors. These were the first two of six senior-citizen residences that New Community acquired and built.

The idea of equal opportunities for housing was important to Ken, which was why we built so much housing while he was mayor. He helped guide all kinds of mortgage money into Newark. Ken was also good on affirmative action, and that's why we had so much activity getting African Americans into the construction unions.

New Community was a perfect fit for Gibson's agenda. It served to legitimize the mayor's efforts in housing and restored hope and trust between Newark residents and the city. In keeping with his housing goals, Gibson established the nonprofit Housing Redevelopment Program and appointed Massaro, then only twenty-seven, as its director. And Massaro then appointed me to the executive committee of the nonprofit housing program.

Perhaps understandably, Gibson's nonprofit housing agency posed a threat to the more established Newark Housing Authority—in part because of the government perks the NCC was receiving to increase low-income housing. The Newark Housing Authority was still under the control of the old Addonizio regime, which caused the mayor tremendous anxiety. The roots of corruption ran deep in Newark, and when Gibson took office, doing business, public or private, often entailed physical risk.

But Gibson, in the face of such challenges, was buoyed by the fact that he was elected the first black mayor of a major Northeastern city. He attracted a strong allegiance of black support, and I strongly believe that the spirit of black nationalism, so right and ripe at the time, acted as a bulwark for him. Amiri Baraka was certainly a force in the city, and I think the Mob, also a significant influence in the city, thought twice about the repercussions if they tried to go after Gibson.

This "mandate" from the people afforded Gibson the freedom he needed to move forward in housing. Massaro noted that Newark's Neighborhood Improvement Program offered homeowners an Urban Development Action Grant to spruce up the outside of their homes, making them more weather-efficient and aesthetically pleasing, which was the basis of the program.

This initiative allowed Gibson to bring the U.S. Secretary of Housing and Urban Development, Patricia Harris, the first black woman to serve in that post, to Newark on more than one occasion. When Secretary Harris was in town, the NCC was naturally included in Newark's showcase of housing development. We held elaborate groundbreaking ceremonies and dedications whenever we got the word that she was coming to town. The NCC had a way of making the mayor shine.

Other officials in Jimmy Carter's administration followed, such as Marcy Kaptur, the domestic policy advisor. Now a congresswoman from Ohio, Kaptur would forgo the fancy hotels during her visits and lodge at St. Rose of Lima Rectory, where I served as pastor. I had a great deal of respect for her as a public servant, and we became good friends.

The mayor was successful in getting Washington, DC, to focus on the plight of Newark. What the NCC was accomplishing made Mayor Gibson proud, considering he was an original board member. More important, under his leadership, the NCC prospered and gained prominent recognition. Gibson and New Community were a winning combination.

Saul Fenster, the former president of the New Jersey College of Engineering (now the New Jersey Institute of Technology) offers a brief description of the hopes for a better Newark after 1967.

SAUL FENSTER

Mayor Ken Gibson was an enthusiast of his alma mater, the Newark College of Engineering, now the New Jersey Institute of Technology. Ken was the first African American mayor of a major Northeastern American city and proud of it. The burden of leading Newark was immense, as his tenure followed a period of deindustrialization and a population decline of over one hundred thousand. But hope began to rise after the civil unrest of the summer of 1967. And Mayor Gibson, elected in 1970, helped put Newark on the path to rebirth. I recall a conversation with Ken in which the mayor said optimistically that he envisioned a future of growth and development for the city. But things were never easy. Gibson faced many challenges, somehow met many of them, and he remains a credit to the college that helped launch his professional and political career.

> Zach Yamba was the longtime president of Essex County College.
> He describes how he worked with Gibson to make sure that
> this academic anchor institution remained in Newark.

ZACHARY "ZACH" YAMBA

It was never inevitable that Essex County College would establish its roots and grow to its current impressive scale in the city of Newark. On the contrary, in the late 1960s, it appeared that the college was destined to become a suburban institution like most of its counterparts around the state.

A group calling itself the People's Council emerged in 1970 and issued a manifesto demanding that the main campus of Essex County College remain in Newark. The council consisted of faculty, administrators, and students. And there were others behind the scenes, including Dr. Mary Burch of the Leaguers, Msgr. William Linder of the New Community Corporation, and many others. Leading that campaign was Kenneth Gibson, who went on to become the first African American mayor of Newark. In the end, it was Gibson's stature and commitment to the outcome that ensured that Essex County College would indeed become a Newark-based institution.

When I became the fifth president of the Essex County College in May 1980, I felt proud and privileged to have had the opportunity to build upon the foundation established for the college by the People's Council in 1970. Having retired in March 2010, after twenty-nine years, but then having been asked to return on an interim basis, I have had additional opportunities to contribute to Essex County College expanding even further while meeting the formidable challenges of the early twenty-first century.

For all the opportunities and joy my time at Essex County College has given to me, I will be forever grateful to those who had the interest, foresight, and stamina to set Essex County College on a steady and productive course. I count particularly among such people Ken Gibson, who following his election and reelections as mayor helped establish countless institutional changes that continue to serve the residents of Newark as well as those who choose to work, learn, and be entertained in this important city.

> Gene Vincenti, who spent more than three decades working
> at the Rutgers–Newark campus, describes how an institution
> needs to grow with a city in a way that benefits both.

GENE VINCENTI

I do not mean to sound boastful, but I was recently told by someone, "You know so much about this city I just assumed you were born and raised here." I was neither born nor raised in Newark. My introduction to the city occurred in September 1967, when I was an incoming freshman at Rutgers University–Newark. This was, of course, just after the 1967 rebellion and three years prior to the election of Kenneth Gibson as the city's first African American mayor.

Once I got to Newark, I never left. I have been described as an "adopted son" of the city. Following my undergraduate study at Rutgers, I enrolled in a two-year MBA program at the business school. My first job following my Rutgers degree work was with the Rutgers University Budget Office in New Brunswick. I spent four years in that position. Then, for thirty-four years, I worked on the Rutgers–Newark campus, beginning in the budget office, moving to assistant provost, and ending my career there as executive vice chancellor.

I can recall my first meaningful orientation to the city was provided by Junius Williams and political activist Tom Hayden. I believe that we met in a church on James Street. What impressed (or perhaps, stated more accurately, *depressed*) me most about that orientation and other discussions about Newark was the extraordinary level of negativity people felt toward the city. I remember asking myself, Why does no one seem to care about Newark? At that time, I challenged myself to a three-part mission: first, understand and answer the question; second, learn what I might do about the negative image; and third, figure out ways institutions like Rutgers University could help.

Little of my early work on the Rutgers–Newark campus involved community affairs. Provost James Young handled such matters himself. I do vividly recall one of my earliest assignments, a recollection that helps me understand the challenges Gibson must have faced when he became mayor. I was assigned the task of allocating office space among four university departments. As I tackled the assignment, it quickly became apparent that it would be impossible for me to make everybody happy. No doubt Mayor Gibson had a similar realization when he took office. He was to govern a racially divided city while somehow attracting desperately needed outside investments. Newark's recent past was not exactly a selling point for Kenneth Gibson.

Although still not directly involved with the mayor's office, I did connect with the city through my work related to university facilities planning and development. Then-provost Norman Samuels and I realized that Newark was an anchor city for Rutgers University and that the university needed city support for its Newark-based development. Upon reflection, I can say that during Gibson's tenure, feedback from the city ranged from full support to cautious neutrality. Our projects did not always move ahead smoothly. We at times banged heads with Liz Del Tufo and other historic preservationists, and from the university itself, there was always the question, Why are you spending so much money in a city like Newark?

But during Gibson's time, we were able to complete many significant projects. We built the Golden Dome Athletic Center; completed a much-needed parking garage; developed an admissions office for the business school; acquired 15 Washington Street; developed the first student housing for the campus, advancing an interest of the mayor to make Newark a true college town; and laid the planning groundwork for two particularly significant buildings: the Talbott Apartments, opened in 1988, and the Stonesby Apartments, opened in 1990.

There's no doubt that these projects helped both the university and the city. There's also no doubt that these and other projects would not have been possible without the support of the Gibson administration.

> Frank Askin, Esq., a longtime professor at Rutgers School of Law
> in Newark and a famed civil rights attorney, details how the school
> responded to the civil rebellion in 1967 with direct legal assistance, clinical
> programs, and a nationally recognized minority students' program.

FRANK ASKIN, ESQ.

There was much disagreement over the cause of the so-called Newark riot in the summer of 1967. The police and city administration placed blame on civil rights agitators such as playwright LeRoi Jones (later to become Imamu Amiri Baraka) and Tom Hayden. Hayden and some of his colleagues from the Students for a Democratic Society (SDS) had set up shop in Newark's Central Ward under the name of the Newark Community Union Project (NCUP) shortly after the issuance of the famous SDS Port Huron statement.

There was no doubt that the black population was seething with grievances against the predominantly Italian American city government. The immediate spark was a demonstration in front of the police station protesting the arrest and beating of a cab driver named John Smith. When some members of the crowd began throwing bottles and rocks, the police attacked, launching four days of police vengeance against the essentially defenseless black community, resulting in twenty-six deaths.

A report commissioned by Governor Richard Hughes and issued the following February called for an investigation of the Newark Police Department, which it accused of allowing the use of excessive and unjustified force and (permitting) other abuses of Negro citizens. It further accused the state troopers assigned to riot duty of engaging in a pattern of police action for which there is no possible justification.

The postriot legal response was organized by the local ACLU and the young Newark Legal Services Corporation, which was spawned by Lyndon Johnson's War on Poverty and whose local branch was chaired by the dean of Rutgers Law School, Willard Heckel. Dean Heckel was a devoted humanist who opened the doors of the law school as the headquarters for volunteer lawyers, including members of the law-school faculty who were recruited to provide representation to the hundreds of people arrested during the disturbances. These lawyers also organized a federal civil rights suit against the police force for the needless death and destruction unleashed against the black community.

Having been appointed to the law-school faculty immediately upon my graduation in 1966, I eagerly answered Heckel's call to join the defense team and suddenly became a practicing lawyer. This was also my introduction to Morton Stavis, the dean of New Jersey's civil rights bar, who was directing the suit to put the Newark Police Department in federal receivership.

Like many such lawsuits, this one did not result in a legal remedy, but it became an effective political tool in the interest of the client—Newark's black community. It was one of several public actions that helped mobilize the majority population of Newark to elect the city's first black mayor, Kenneth Gibson, in 1970.

My own introduction to law practice was an eye-opener. I was assigned to represent a middle-aged man who had been rounded up by police and charged with rioting. When I interviewed my client, he told me that he was peacefully standing at a bus stop waiting for his wife to come home from work to escort her home. He also told me there was a teenager already under arrest in the police car who could verify his account. I was able to track down the teenager through police records, and he confirmed my client's story. I assumed my witness's testimony would result in a quick acquittal. The prosecutor didn't even bother to cross-examine my witness, but the judge inexplicably found him guilty. I thus discovered there was not much justice to be expected for poor black defendants charged by white police officers. Fortunately, the judge just sentenced the defendant to time served, and that was the end of it.

My second "riot" case had a better but equally unexpected result. My client was Tom Hayden and his NCUP buddies. They had been charged with trespass for picketing a supermarket accused of overcharging its black clientele. It so happened that as a law student, I had been in a course with the legendary civil rights attorney Arthur Kinoy, who had been recruited to join the faculty by Dean Heckel in 1964, after leading the Southern civil rights bar in the early 1960s. Professor Kinoy taught us about federal civil rights statutes that he had utilized successfully in the South. Among them was the federal civil rights removal statute, available to criminal defendants who were unable to find justice in state courts. I decided to try it out and filed a removal petition to the U.S. District Court in Newark. Under the statute, jurisdiction was immediately divested from the state court pending the filing of a remand petition by the state authority. Apparently, the attorneys for the City of Newark knew nothing about the procedure and never filed a petition. So the case languished in the federal court, and that was the last I heard of it.

One other consequence of the "riot" was the adoption of Rutgers Law School's pioneering Minority Student Program (MSP). Dean Heckel was appalled by the paucity of indigenous lawyers to represent the minority community in Newark and New Jersey. My own graduating class had only three African American members, and this was reflected generally in the bar. The courthouse was populated by white lawyers and justice personnel and predominantly minority persons as criminal defendants. Black lawyers were about 1 percent of the New Jersey bar, and Hispanic lawyers could be counted on the fingers of one hand. Heckel was determined to change that demographic. He appointed me to chair a committee to determine how to diversify the student body.

My committee worked through the 1967–1968 academic year to adopt a plan. Opponents feared that we would dilute the intellectual capacity of the school by bringing in unqualified students. We finally established a goal (not a quota) of admitting twenty minority students the first year and forty in subsequent years and established a standard that applicants had to have graduated in the top half of an accredited college or university. That partially mollified some critics, who believed that we would not find that many qualified applicants. We also proposed to expand the student body so that rejected white applicants could not complain about reverse discrimination.

Fortunately, the law-school faculty (which numbered only nineteen at the time) included other strong civil rights advocates in addition to Heckel and Kinoy. One was Alfred Blumrosen, who had a long history as a federal administrator in efforts to combat racial discrimination in housing and employment, including a stint as a special counsel to the Equal Employment Opportunity Commission (EEOC). Another strong supporter was Professor Ruth Bader Ginsburg, who had not yet become an advocate in her own right but whose sympathies clearly resided with those who had faced historic discrimination.

The faculty finally approved the plan; the rest is history. The Rutgers Minority Student Program has been recognized throughout the legal academic community as the most successful diversification program in legal education. It has transformed the bar and bench in New Jersey while also having an impact on many other states. Rutgers remains today—as the MSP prepares to celebrate its fiftieth anniversary—probably the most diversified law school in the country, not counting historically black schools. Racial diversification also quickly expanded to include gender diversity, as second-career women began descending upon the law school.

The changing demographic also had a profound effect on the curriculum. Minority students and their female allies together with former Southern civil rights workers who had followed Arthur Kinoy to the law school began demanding a curriculum more suited to producing practicing lawyers who could quickly represent their various communities. The result was the establishment in 1970 of the most extensive clinical program of any law school in the country, starting with the Constitutional Litigation Clinic and the Urban Legal Clinic in 1970, soon to be followed by a Women's Rights Clinic, an Environmental Law Clinic, and a Labor Law Clinic.

The Minority Student Program and the clinical program remain today as the flagships of Rutgers Law School in Newark.

George Hampton, who along with editors Holmes and Roper is a prime mover of this project, describes his coming of age in Newark. His personal and professional development coincides with many of the most dramatic and important events of the Gibson era. Through his professional experience in higher education, he describes the cooperation between a city's power centers that is required if a city's anchor institutions are to work well within the total framework of a city.

George Hampton

I have come to understand over the years that contrary to common belief, the rise and fall of American cities is not dependent solely on the policies and programs of an incumbent administration. A city's fate can also be significantly affected by the people who come to the city to reside, work, worship, or learn. When I was a young man working in the Ken Gibson administration, I used to ask city employees, "Where do you live?" I always found it amusing that people would answer by telling me about the town where they reside, yet they would spend close to half their daily living (breathing, eating, driving, walking, and working) in Newark. They were "living" in Newark, and their routine actions and thoughts dramatically affected Newark's successes and failures. Newark's people (residents, students, employees, and others) were advocates, idealists, politicians, and practitioners who implemented policies and initiatives through anchor institutions operating within the city's borders. Such institutions can include, among others, state and county government agencies, community organizations, businesses, and institutions that compose the area's academic community.

I have had an opportunity to be involved with the affairs of Newark from various perspectives, including several associated with major anchor institutions. My reflections can be organized into six categories, each representing a different perspective: a high school senior, a college student, a Newark employee, a state government employee, a community-organization employee, and an executive with a major institution of higher education. Each of these perspectives is informed and enhanced by the fact that, throughout the time involved, I was also a Newark resident.

High School Senior

In 1966, when Ken Gibson first ran for mayor, I was a senior at the mostly black South Side High School. I was an honor-roll student and president of the student council, but I was not happy about past race relations in my city or prospects in that regard for the future. The nation's black power and awareness movement had just begun to affect me. I was disillusioned and tired of reading books or watching movies in which blacks were nonexistent or were depicted as second class or as buffoons, criminals, or derelicts. The media—newspapers, television, and especially history books—routinely projected subliminal messages suggesting the inferiority of black Americans. I recall with disdain my white American-history teacher saying, "The native North American Indians proved to be too proud and too fierce to make good slaves, and so early American settlers chose the Negro instead." I thought, How dare white professionals write about, infer, conclude, and ultimately define the character of my ancestors and my race? I became angry. As a black high school student, I felt disrespected and powerless because I was unable to channel my frustrations in a meaningful way.

I also found the negative imagery about Newark and its residents depicted by the media and by urbanologists—who should have known better—to be offensive. In later years, I saw "urban planners" as "urban haters"—professionals who were always ready to tell you what was wrong with a city, in this instance, Newark, while using statistics related to crime, unemployment, welfare, and poor schools to make their case. These professionals were big on numbers but rarely offered solutions to Newark's problems. If Newark residents wanted a better life for their families, they seemed to have only one choice, and that was to move—if they could afford to. I noticed my city becoming more and more racially divided, with ever-expanding ghettos of the poor. But I also took notice of the role and power of protest, advocacy, politics, and public policy in serving the needs of those remaining behind in the city.

During the mid-1960s, some racial tensions were elevated in Newark due to a proposed new medical school / hospital complex that initially called for the displacement of thousands of Newark residents, most of whom were black. Contributing to the tense environment was the existence of government "urban renewal" programs and policies that were really "urban removal" programs. These programs, plus a host of other factors, contributed to the general erosion of the quality of life for Newark's black residents, helping trigger the city's 1967 rebellion that claimed the lives of twenty-six residents and caused millions of dollars of damage.

In 1968, state, city, and community representatives collaborated on the creation of an agreement intended to quell the underlying causes of the rebellion. The document, which was labelled the "Newark Agreements," has historic significance embedded in a number of key provisions: (1) reduce the proposed medical complex's displacement and land acquisition by two-thirds, (2) provide for employment and training opportunities for area residents related to the medical-complex construction, (3) provide for permanent employment opportunities associated with the medical complex, (4) provide for minority student enrollment, and (5) provide for access to health services for area residents.

In the years following the adoption of the Newark Agreements, local dissension and distrust persisted. The community called for an entity that could help resolve disputes arising from the implementation of the Newark Agreements. Because of these demands, the Board of Concerned Citizens (BCC) was created, which was to serve as a communications vehicle that would cooperatively work both within and outside of the medical complex to share information and to provide a forum for conflict resolution. Two outstanding presidents of the new organization were Dr. Carroll Levy, the first president, and Mary Mathis Ford, the longest-serving and last president. The BCC lasted for more than forty-two years—from 1971 to 2013—and served as a community-board model that has been duplicated on all five of Newark's university campuses and in other universities.

College Student

Today, there is a building on the Rutgers University–Newark campus named after Bessie Hill, called Hill Hall. In 1967, my high school senior year, Bessie Hill, a black woman and member of the Rutgers University Board of Governors, spoke with me and encouraged me to enroll as a student at the predominantly white Rutgers–Newark campus. In addition to a paucity of black students, Rutgers–Newark at that time had virtually no black employees, faculty, administrators, or suppliers. These facts seemed even more unusual to me given the predominantly black makeup of Newark.

Going to Rutgers–Newark and majoring in urban studies/planning was a defining moment in my life. I discovered that the few black students on campus were keenly aware of local, state, and national politics. At Rutgers–Newark, black power and Pan-African ideology were omnipresent. There was, for example, a constant struggle to establish the correct cultural identity and proper nomenclature for black Americans: Should we be called coloreds, Negroes, Afro-Americans, blacks, or African Americans? I met many bright, articulate black students who were passionate about advocating for social change. While a freshman, I bonded with fellow freshmen Tom Roberts, Claude Singleton, and Doug Morgan, and we learned from audacious student leaders such as Richard Roper, Joe

Brown, Marvin McGraw, and Vickie Donaldson as we formed the Black Organization of Students (BOS). With Bessie Hill, Bob Curvin, and Gus Heningburg as our mentors, we challenged the university's discriminatory admissions policies through protests, including sit-ins in the provost's office and in Conklin Hall.

Our Rutgers–Newark protests merged ultimately with off-campus community advocacy. Older adults—such as State Senator Wynona Lipman, Donald Tucker, and Junius Williams—helped mentor us in our effort to become effective advocates for the underprivileged and voiceless. We joined welfare-rights organizations, protested housing-discrimination policies, and picketed the relocation of the hospital / medical complex. Ironically, two of the original BOS student protestors, Vivian Sanks-King and I, went on to become vice presidents at the very same medical school I described earlier. A third BOS protester, Douglas Morgan, became a director at the medical-school complex. Today, the University of Medicine and Dentistry of New Jersey (UMDNJ) is part of Rutgers University. Richard Roper, the first president of BOS in 1967–1968, now serves as a member of the Rutgers University Board of Governors.

Many of the original Rutgers BOS students (e.g., Tom Roberts, Claude Singleton, Doug Morgan, Richard Roper, and Joe Brown) got their first professional jobs in the Gibson administration after serving as volunteers in his second campaign in 1969–1970. We all loved Newark—the city, its people, and its potential to grow and prosper. As young idealistic, energetic professionals, we couldn't wait to use our education and skills to make a difference in the city and improve the quality of life of its residents.

Donald Tucker, a community advocate who became a Newark city councilman and state assemblyman, used to call us "BOS AGAIN," meaning that the former Rutgers–Newark college students were morphing into seasoned political activists and public-policy advocates. In the sixties, we were students at Rutgers who created BOS; in the early seventies, we worked as key administrators during Gibson's first term. As we became skilled in civic engagement, my high school student's feelings of anger and powerlessness had found solace in my ability to articulate and influence progressive change for the disenfranchised and marginalized residents of Newark and other urban communities. Because Gibson was elected, the door was opened for a cadre of young people.

City Government Director

At the beginning of Gibson's first term, at age twenty-seven, I was hired by Junius Williams to be the deputy director of the Interim Assistance Program (IAP), a program designed to duplicate several of the goals of the larger Model Cities Program (MCP). The South Ward was the target area for the IAP, and the Central Ward was the target area for the MCP. These federal programs were funded to create jobs and stimulate economic recovery in the inner cities that had been devastated by civil unrest in the sixties.

In 1974, I was hired by Jack Krauskopf, the director of the Office of Newark Studies, to be the project director of a so-called Redlining Project. The Office of Newark Studies was an agency administered by Rutgers University, received funding through grants through the city, and served as a public-policy / research arm of Mayor Gibson's office. With Jack, I coauthored the report "Residential Mortgage Lending in the City of Newark 1975" a study of the mortgage-lending practices of twenty-six banks doing business in the city. The report demonstrated that residential neighborhoods primarily inhabited by blacks and other minorities were denied access to mortgage-based loans. Basically, these neighborhoods had been "redlined." Upon completion of the report, Ken Gibson sent the study and its recommendations to the twenty-six bank presidents and chief executive officers who were encouraged to meet with the mayor and select staff. Once their exclusionary practices were exposed, the banks agreed to create a multimillion-dollar mortgage pool program for specifically targeted neighborhoods in Newark. Mortgage pool program funds protect banks against potential losses by sharing the risks associated with loans made in low- and moderate-income neighborhoods. In later years, the federal government created the Community Reinvestment Act, which duplicated several of the policies of the former mortgage pool programs, such as those created in Newark.

The Redlining Project caused an epiphany: I realized that "the pen really is mightier than the sword." If I could conceive, I could achieve; I realized that my newfound education and skills could make a difference for those in Newark who mattered to me.

State Government Employee

In 1976, I was hired as an executive assistant to the commissioner of the New Jersey Department of Environmental Protection (NJDEP). Ken Gibson had much to do with me getting the job. Working in state government was a real eye-opener for me. I was surprised to find that not everyone carried the same affinity or love for Newark as we young professionals who were from the city. I was amazed and disheartened to see how state bureaucrats seemed to view Newark and other cities. They were contemptuous of the reasons Newark was on the decline. Far too often, bureaucrats blamed urban communities for the challenges they faced. They "blamed the victims," Newark's residents, for poverty and social problems.

The attitude of state elected and appointed officials had a significant impact on the allocation of state resources. The attitude of residents living in suburban and rural communities in the state had a significant impact on who got elected or appointed, which in turn had significant impact on the allocation of state resources.

Community Agency Consultant

In 1978, I left the NJDEP and was hired by Gus Heningburg of the Greater Newark Urban Coalition (GNUC). Gus asked me to direct a research study on the federal government's Local Public Works Program II (LPWII). In 1977, Congress took the unprecedented step of requiring that 10 percent of every LPWII grant awarded from a $4 billion local public-works construction program be awarded to minority business firms. The program was intended to be an immediate stimulus for minority businesses and minority employment. The program, administered by the Economic Development Administration (EDA) of the U.S. Department of Commerce, resulted in 486 separate grants in New Jersey with a total dollar value of approximately $221 million being awarded to public agencies in the state of New Jersey. While the EDA reported that the program in New Jersey was exceeding the 10-percent goal, many minority contractors insisted that the program was a failure.

The GNUC's study concluded that although about 77 percent of the New Jersey grantees did achieve minimal levels of minority participation, time constraints and the economic-stimulus goals of LPWII caused the program to be a subordinate objective from the perspective of program implementers. The study also found numerous discrepancies in the program including (1) the EDA was reporting MBE (Minority Business Enterprise) funds, which were substantially inflated because more money was being recorded as MBE expenditures than what was received by MBEs; (2) the regional EDA Office of Civil Rights was not adequately staffed to handle the monitoring requirements for the program; (3) the definitions, regulations, and procedures prescribed for determining eligible MBEs were vague and allowed participation by questionable firms; (4) the absence of financial sanctions eroded the effectiveness of the program; (5) the EDA regional office routinely granted waivers that undermined grantees from making "good faith efforts"; (6) grantees lacked the experience, capacity, and incentive to aggressively enforce and monitor MBE participation; and (7) grantees in Essex County (including Newark) received about $33 million in LPWII funds, while the MBEs received about $11 million. In the end, Newark grantees distributed about $4 million to MBEs, far more than any other municipality.

After completing the LPWII program study, the report was sent to pertinent state and federal agencies. In subsequent years, the report's findings were adopted in many of the newly designed affirmative-action / minority-participation policies for public-sector institutions. Once again, public-policy work completed in Newark ultimately helped create positive outcomes for similar programs throughout the country.

University of Medicine and Dentistry of New Jersey Administrator

In 1980, State Senator Wynona Lipman, Gus Heningburg, and Mayor Ken Gibson sent letters of introduction/recommendation to the president of the College of Medicine and Dentistry, Dr. Stanley S. Bergen, who hired me to be the assistant director of long-range planning for the college, which was subsequently renamed the University of Medicine and Dentistry of New Jersey.

During Ken Gibson's third and fourth terms, I was promoted several times at the UMDNJ until I became a vice president in charge of urban planning and community development, a position that reported directly to the president. One of my primary functions was to direct community-development initiatives for the UMDNJ and the university's host municipalities throughout the state, including New Brunswick, Piscataway, Camden, Stratford, and especially Newark. In that position, time and again, I observed how the economic-development and affirmative-action programs, recommendations, and policies of the Newark-based community advocates of the sixties and seventies were replicated and implemented throughout the UMDNJ and other public institutions. The Newark Agreements and the Board of Concerned Citizens are just two examples of effective policies/programs that were created by those Newark community advocates.

In 1972, another organization, the Council for Higher Education in Newark (CHEN), was created. It was a collaborative initiative among the four public institutions of higher education—the UMDNJ, Rutgers University, the Newark Institute of Technology, and Essex County College. There once was tremendous mistrust among the constituencies in Newark—that is, city government, major corporations, community residents, and the universities. At one point, the city master plan included a provision that limited university land expansion to their existing campuses.

CHEN was created to respond to community/city pressures and concerns. CHEN responded by creating civic-engagement policies that supported neighborhood development, precollege programs, and many other community-based initiatives. Indeed, in emergencies, neighborhood residents often called UMDNJ police because of their rapid response—before calling the city police.

In 1982, as the assistant director of long-range planning for the UMDNJ, I prepared a document titled "The University Heights Master Plan." The report analyzed land-use patterns of a 1.6-square-mile area initially bounded by Springfield Avenue / Market Street, Halsey Street, Orange Street, and Littleton Avenue. There were about seven hundred acres in this area, and about 125 acres were vacant. The report showed how abandonment and dilapidation were commonplace at the time. Between 1970 and 1980, Newark's population had decreased from 382,000 to 329,000—a drop of 53,000 people in just ten years. The percentage of whites had dropped by 14 percent—from 45 percent to 31 percent—while the percentage of blacks had increased by 4 percent. Clearly, people were leaving or, more accurately stated, running away from Newark and especially from the Central and West Wards, the epicenter of the 1967 rebellion. The report proposed calling this area "University Heights." Private developers had been avoiding an area that appeared to them to be abandoned and disinvested. The document's primary point was simple: the anchor organizations—including universities, major corporations, churches, neighborhood community-development organizations, and county and local governmental entities—may have had long-range intentions to grow and expand in the area, but it was apparent that these entities were not sharing or coordinating their plans and that nothing was being done, The report proposed sharing plans to create a "college town," where workers, visitors, students, and residents could come to live, work, play, learn, and worship. The new construction could facilitate job creation that would explode into economic development for the neighborhoods surrounding the universities.

Dr. Bergen sent the report to Dr. Saul Fenster, president of the New Jersey Institute of Technology; Dr. Norman Samuels, provost of Rutgers–Newark; and Dr. Zachary Yamba, president of Essex County College. These four CEOs of the public institutions of higher learning had recently agreed to meet regularly as CHEN. I had no idea that the "master plan" document would cause so much controversy and, a decade later, so much success.

Although the University Heights report was meant to be a draft discussion paper for the universities' CEOs, it quickly resulted in published articles in the Newark newspapers and became the target for a firestorm of protests. The report opened old wounds of mistrust among the community and city elected leadership, and the "urban renewal vs. urban removal" arguments were, once again, being presented by community advocates and being heard at the Newark City Council. The universities were accused of creating new plans for land grabbing, resident displacements, and gentrification.

Led by Junius Williams, Sylvia Jackson, Edna Thomas, the Rev. William Linder of the New Communities Corporation, and city councilmen George Branch and Ronald Rice, the advocates vowed to challenge the universities' plans. The "town vs. gown" animosities and community fears peaked when six hundred riled-up protesters crammed into Essex County College's Mary Burch Auditorium and demanded transparency and clarity about the universities' intentions.

Fortunately, the "town vs. gown" acrimony morphed into community/university cooperation. Newark city government, the community, and businesses joined with the CHEN CEOs in creating the University Heights Community Council, University Heights Neighborhood Development Corporation, University Heights Condominium Association, and the University Heights Science Park project. Subsequently, there has been a critical mass of development in the Heights district. Today, there are more middle-income and educated residents, CHEN and science-park facilities, new neighborhood streetscapes and housing, and a Science Park High

School that stands as a testament to the successful University Heights collaborations.

Some have expressed it this way: "It takes a village." While this saying generally relates to raising a child, I have come to learn that in a village or in a city, when people and institutions work collaboratively, they can raise each other and the place where they live and work to ever greater heights.

NOTES

1. William J. Linder and Gilda Rogers, *Out of the Ashes Came Hope* (Archway, 2016), 116.

2. Julia Rabig, *The Fixers: Devolution, Development, and Civil Society in Newark, 1960–1990* (Chicago: University of Chicago Press, 2016), 233.

CHAPTER 7

FORCES BEYOND
CONTROL

A mayor can have first-rate administrators, sound management skills, and worthy goals, but there will always be factors that influence a city that are well beyond his or her control. Here, we will consider some of those political, economic, and social forces.

Dan O'Flaherty, who grew up in Newark and was an aide to Mayor Gibson, is a professor of economics at Columbia University. He describes and charts socioeconomic forces that were at work during the Gibson era that were too subtle to recognize at the time. These include inflation, stagnating productivity, rising labor-force participation by women, a massive regional slump, and a rising national crime rate.

BRENDAN "DAN" O'FLAHERTY

I was in Newark most of the time between 1970 and 1986 during the Ken Gibson era, but the economic and social environment that I'll concentrate on is not the environment we were conscious of then. Rather, I'll concentrate on changes that were too slow, subtle, and broad for us to recognize at the time but have become apparent to us now. Focusing on them then would have been like "watching grass grow," the popular simile for an incredibly time-consuming and boring activity. We have the benefit of hindsight now, however. The numbers are in, and they reveal a great deal. We don't have to watch grass grow because there's a full lawn to observe. Here's the rundown on what some numbers of yesterday show us today.

Inflation and Growth

Table 7.1 shows the average annual rates of gross domestic product (GDP) growth and inflation for the United States as a whole during the seven Newark mayoralties since the charter change of 1954. Although more separate recessions occurred during Gibson's years than during any other mayoralty, the average rate of growth was not especially slow. What sets Gibson apart is the high inflation rate. First and foremost, Gibson was Newark's "inflation mayor."

TABLE 7.1

GROWTH IN REAL GDP AND INFLATION DURING NEWARK MAYORALTIES, 1954–2016

AVERAGE ANNUAL RATES OF INCREASE

Mayor	Years	Real gross domestic product (%)	Consumer price index (%)
Carlin	1954–1962	3.4	1.4
Addonizio	1962–1970	4.1	3.1
GIBSON	**1970–1986**	**3.3**	**6.7**
James	1986–2006	3.1	3.1
Booker	2006–2013	1.0	2.1
Quintana	2013–2014	2.5	2.0
Baraka	2014–2016	1.0	0.5

Source: U.S. Bureau of Economic Analysis; U.S. Bureau of Labor Statistics. Real GDP growth and inflation are measured at the national level.

What are the implications of inflation? Debtors whose debts are specified in nominal dollars gain from inflation, and creditors lose. To a first approximation, the city of Newark was a large nominal debtor, especially after the Addonizio years and fiscal crisis of the first Gibson years, and so inflation wiped out a good portion of the debt that Gibson would have had to confront. Moreover, because many of the rules of the Newark Employees Retirement System (NERS) were expressed in nominal terms, the real value of pension debt also fell. Inflation freed Gibson from many of the burdens of the fiscal past. Inflation may also have helped Gibson engineer the huge decrease in real property taxes that occurred between

1970 and 1986. Since both the assessments and tax rate were expressed in nominal terms, political pressure to maintain a stable property-tax rate was in fact pressure to cut real property taxes drastically over time, even though each individual year's cut was small. In a regime of constant prices, the same pressure may not have been applied; drastic austerity has never been a popular campaign platform in Newark nor a good way to attract state and federal aid.

Thus inflation allowed Gibson to transfer wealth from Newark's creditors (bondholders and NERS members) to taxpayers. But this transfer had consequences. Inflation raised interest rates on new debt; the steadily falling real property-tax rate made the city's finances shaky, and the New York City fiscal crisis of 1975 made investors more wary of municipal bonds generally. The state's qualified[1] bond act ameliorated some of the problems—at a cost to city sovereignty—but the net effect was probably considerably reduced capital investment. In retrospect, the early 1980s, a period of huge unemployment (the national African American jobless rate topped 20 percent in 1982, higher than it ever reached in the Great Recession), would have been a great time to renew the city's infrastructure (with callable bonds), since it could have used resources that otherwise would have been going to waste, but the opportunity passed untaken and largely unnoticed.

The cuts in the operating budget (the budget that pays for ongoing city activities, as opposed to the capital budget, which pays for long-lived projects) may also have been greater than optimal, since inflation and a political emphasis on nominal dollar targets played a role in determining their size. I will present some evidence later on whether this was the case in the discussion of crime. But if the costs were noticeably too large, one would expect to see the real city payroll bounce back markedly in the three decades since 1986, when other mayors and councils were making the decisions. On a sustained basis, this has not been the case.

Qualifying the Picture of Growth

While U.S. GDP growth was not notably slower during the Gibson mayoralty than it was in other modern Newark mayoralties, several considerations suggest that conventional national measurements may paint too optimistic a picture of Newark's macroenvironment in that period.

Productivity

Table 7.2 shows the rate of increase of labor productivity in the United States since 1947. The 1970s were clearly a break from the immediately preceding decades and the beginning of a long slog. Real GDP could rise in the 1970s while productivity stagnated because many married women and mothers of small children entered the labor force. The value of the work that these women previously did at home was not counted as part of GDP, although it should have been, and so because GDP ignores this work, it overstated the rise in actual output during the 1970s.

TABLE 7.2

PRODUCTIVITY CHANGE IN THE NONFARM BUSINESS SECTOR, 1947–2015

AVERAGE ANNUAL PERCENTAGE CHANGE

1947–1973	2.8
1973–1979	1.2
1979–1990	1.5
1990–2000	2.2
2000–2007	2.6
2007–2015	1.2

Source: U.S. Bureau of Labor Statistics, labor productivity overview, accessed May 16, 2016, http://www.bls.gov/lpc/prodybar.htm.

Regional Stagnation

The 1970s were a particularly bad decade for the New York metropolitan area (of which Newark is a small part) relative to the rest of the country. For instance, from 1969 to 1976, payroll employment in New York City fell about 16 percent.[2]

Table 7.3 follows the population in Newark, New York City, and the Bronx, the only mainland borough, from 1960 to 2000. All three jurisdictions lost population in the 1970s, with the greatest loss being in the Bronx. But New York City and the Bronx turned around sometime in the 1980s, while Newark continued to lose population. The trends don't diverge until late in the Gibson mayoralty or after it.

TABLE 7.3

POPULATION CHANGE IN NEWARK, NEW YORK CITY, AND THE BRONX, 1960–2000

1970 = 100 FOR ALL JURISDICTIONS

	Newark	New York City	Bronx
1960	106	99	97
1970	100	100	100
1980	86	90	79
1990	72	92	82
2000	72	101	91

Source: U.S. Bureau of the Census, decennial censuses.

The same trend is evident in real median household income, as shown in table 7.4. Real median household income declined in the 1970s in the New York metropolitan statistical area (MSA), in New York City, in the Bronx, and in Newark, but recovery in the 1980s in the Bronx and in Newark was not as fast as the recovery in the rest of New York City or the rest of the MSA.

TABLE 7.4

CHANGE IN REAL MEDIAN HOUSEHOLD INCOME,
UNITED STATES AND NEW YORK REGION, 1969–1989

1969 = 100 FOR ALL JURISDICTIONS

	Newark	Bronx	New York City	New York MSA	United States
1969	100	100	100	100	100
1979	77	82	99	85	106
1989	104	98	137	107	113

Source: U.S. Bureau of the Census, decennial censuses. "Median household income in year t in jurisdiction j" refers to the median of year t income for the households residing in jurisdiction j in year $(t + 1)$. Thus, for instance, the median income in 1979 of the households that lived in Newark in 1980 was 77 percent of the median income in 1969 of the households that lived in Newark in 1970.

Thus while measured national GDP showed decent growth during the Gibson mayoralty, the actual experience in the New York area was considerably less salutary.

The loss of population and income has to be considered in light of inflation. Without inflation, losing population and income in a city with property and payroll taxes adds to the losses that the remaining population must bear. A debt of $100 million in a city with three hundred thousand people is considerably more burdensome on each of them than a debt of $100 million in a city with four hundred thousand people. This rising debt burden can cause a spiral, as each increase in burden shrinks the population more and adds to the burden of the remaining population. We may have seen such spirals recently in Detroit and Puerto Rico. But inflation can offset the spiral by reducing the total burden.

Some rough estimates for Newark for 1970 to 1980 can illustrate how much inflation can offset. Population fell 14 percent, and real median (not mean) income fell 23 percent; so real residential aggregate income fell roughly 34 percent. The tax base is not aggregate income but property, and it includes commercial and industrial property as well as residential (a majority of commercial and industrial at this time, especially if you include special taxes and water fees). But commercial and industrial output fell, too, and probably as much as residential income. So roughly speaking, the tax base fell by a third. But inflation between 1970 and 1980 cut the real value of a dollar by 53 percent.

So the real value of a constant nominal amount of debt per dollar of real resources to pay it off actually fell. To be sure, the same effect also cut the real debt of other municipalities, but Newark's nominal debt burden in 1970 was unusually high, and so Newark gained more than alternative locations. Inflation saved Newark from becoming Detroit or Puerto Rico.

Inequality

Income inequality in the United States declined from World War II to around 1973 and has been rising since then. Since most Newarkers were in the bottom half of the income distribution, and the bottom half started getting further from the top, average measures such as GDP growth may overestimate the growth of Newarkers' incomes when inequality is rising (the opposite may have been the case when inequality was falling before 1973). This effect, however, turns out to be small in the period we study.

To see this, we can look at percentiles of the income distribution. In 1969, I estimate that the median Newark household was at the 41st percentile of the U.S. income distribution. If it had stayed at that percentile, its income would have risen to $46,929 in 1979 and $49,969 in 1989 (everything in 2014 dollars). If that had happened, the only effect on Newark would have been the change in the shape of the distribution—that is, the increase in inequality. Instead, Newark median income was $30,640 in 1979 and $41,333 in 1989, far lower than would have been implied by changes in income inequality. The fall of Newarkers' income was much bigger than the increase in inequality would have caused on its own. The direct effects of income inequality were not a major part of the story of the Gibson years.

Crime

The rise in crime was another major national story of this time. I will pay attention to "index crimes"—the seven serious crimes with victims that the FBI has been tracking since the 1960s. Index crime started to rise in the mid-1960s and didn't start falling until the early 1990s. This rise in crime was pervasive, affecting almost all varieties of crime, locations, and demographic groups.

There is no good explanation for this crime rise that we know now (just as there is no good explanation for the subsequent pervasive crime fall). Traditional explanations—police, prisons, poverty, and young men—account for almost nothing in this period (nor does the legalization of abortion, which may account for some of the subsequent fall). Probably the most likely single cause for the crime rise is the large increase in the combustion of leaded gasoline after World War II, which would affect Newark more than most other locations. As Jessica Wolpaw Reyes (2007; 2015) argues, lead in gasoline causes lead in the atmosphere, which causes lead in the blood of young children.[3] Lead exposure in young children lowers IQ and causes aggressivity and attention deficit hyperactivity disorder—which are conditions correlated with criminality. But no serious econometric work has examined this hypothesis for the 1960s and 1970s. See O'Flaherty and Sethi 2015 for more details.

Crime rose in Newark, as it did nationally, and by the 1980s was probably the major source of dissatisfaction among Newarkers. How much of the rise in crime was a part of the national story? Table 7.5 gives a tentative answer. In this table, I compare the ratio of per-capita crime in Newark to per-capita crime in the United States in 1972 with the comparable figure in 1986. (The earliest year for which the FBI published crime statistics for cities is 1972.) If these ratios are the same, then the Newark story is just the national story.

TABLE 7.5

RATIO OF PER-CAPITA NEWARK CRIME TO PER-CAPITA
U.S. CRIME, 1972 AND 1986

	Newark / United States 1972	Newark / United States 1986
Murder	4.49	4.44
Rape	3.93	5.31
Robbery	7.18	8.21
Aggravated assault	3.94	3.90
Theft	2.56	1.31
Burglary	2.64	1.42
Motor-vehicle theft	4.76	8.63

Source: Federal Bureau of Investigation, uniform crime reports. Newark population was interpolated geometrically from the decennial censuses.

Except for motor-vehicle theft and possibly rape, the rise in per-capita U.S. crime accounts for almost all of the rise in Newark crime. (Per-capita murders and per-capita thefts actually fell in Newark between 1972 and 1986, although the latter may be a reporting issue.) Robberies and rapes rose somewhat faster than the national average; assaults, thefts, and bur-glaries somewhat slower. Except for motor vehicle thefts, Newark was not unusual. (Compared with 1986, Newark's murder rate relative to the national rate is much higher in recent years, but Newark's rates for other crimes, especially robbery and assault, are much lower relative to the respective national rates.)

What about the reduction in the police force? Police per capita decreased in Newark over this time span—sworn officers went from 3.9 per thousand residents to 3.5 per thousand—while they increased nationally from 2.0 per thousand to 2.1 per thousand. In those days, the studies that had been done did not generally indicate that police headcounts affected crime, but today, we would not recognize these studies as high quality. High-quality studies of this question started to be published around the turn of the century, and they generally indicate that adding to the size of a police force reduces crime.

Did this matter in Newark? Table 7.6 tries to answer this question. I use the results of Chalfin and McCrary (2013),[4] the most-recent study of this question, and project how much of the crime increase in Newark occurred because police per capita decreased by 9.4 percent instead of increasing at the national rate of 5 percent.

Table 7.6 starts with the actual increase in per-capita crime in Newark between 1972 and 1986. It then parcels this out between three factors: the national crime increase, the part due to the police force's relative shrink-age, and a residual—a portion that can't be explained by either of those two factors.

TABLE 7.6

ATTRIBUTION OF INCREASE IN NEWARK PER-CAPITA CRIME
TO THREE FACTORS, 1972–1986

	Total increase (%)	Due to national increase (%)	Due to police shrinkage (%)	Residual (%)
Murder	−4.3	−3.4	16.3	−14.8
Rape	127.3	68.2	5.7	27.9
Robbery	43.1	25.1	8.9	5.0
Aggravated assault	93.9	95.8	1.3	−2.2
Theft	70.6	231.1	1.8	−49.4
Burglary	−35.8	19.4	5.7	−49.1
Motor-vehicle theft	101.1	11.2	4.8	72.4

Source: See text.

This table shows that for all the crimes that increased in Newark, the national effect was considerably larger than the police effect. The crime increases that would have been caused by the relative fall in police strength alone range from about 15 percent for murder to about 1 percent for assault. For most crimes, the implied changes are in the neighborhood of 5 percent—noticeable but small in comparison with the actual changes. The Newark-specific residuals—the parts of the changes that can't be attributed either to national or police changes—are usually either small or negative (for burglary and theft especially). The exceptions, with large positive residuals, are motor-vehicle theft and rape—the crimes that table 7.5 also highlighted.

Thus by looking at national trends, we can isolate what was different about Newark. The change in rape may be associated with reporting issues, either on the city or national level. Part of the story of motor-vehicle theft may be the increase in the proportion of Newark's households that owned cars—which happened very quickly in this period—and the expansion of the airport, which brought large parking lots filled with unattended cars. The change in the rate of motor-vehicle theft per motor vehicle was less—and probably much less—than the change in the rate of motor-vehicle theft per person.

Conclusion

Ken Gibson was the mayor during a time of inflation, stagnating productivity growth, rising labor-force participation by women, a massive regional slump, and rising national crime. For better or worse, these trends shaped his mayoralty. The changes came so incrementally that they were almost impossible to detect at the time—like the growth of grass—but they turned out to be very powerful.

NOTES

1. The New Jersey Municipal Qualified Bond Act (P.L. 1976, c. 38) allowed the state to guarantee municipal bonds. The bonds that the state guaranteed had to be preapproved by the state. The state pays the principal and interest on these bonds directly but deducts the amount it pays from the state aid that it sends to the city.

2. Samuel Ehrenhalt, "Economic and Demographic Change: The Case of New York City," *Monthly Labor Review* 116, no. 2 (February 1993): 40–51.

3. Jessica Wolpaw Reyes, "Lead Exposure and Behavior: Effects on Aggression and Risky Behavior among Children and Adolescents," *Economic Inquiry* 53, no. 3 (July 2015): 1580–1605; and "Environmental Policy as Social Policy? The Impact of Childhood Lead Exposure on Crime," *B.E. Journal of Economic Analysis and Policy* 7, no. 1 (October 2007). https://www.biologicaldiversity.org/campaigns/get_the _lead_out/pdfs/health/Reyes_2007.pdf.

4. Aaron Chalfin and Justin McCrary, "The Effect of Police on Crime: New Evidence from US Cities, 1960–2010," National Bureau of Economic Research working paper 18815, 2013. I use table 4, column 6, which gives two-stage least squares results for police as measured in the uniform crime reports and uses state-year fixed effects.

BIBLIOGRAPHY

Chalfin, Aaron, and Justin McCrary. "The Effect of Police on Crime: New Evidence from US Cities, 1960–2010." National Bureau of Economic Research working paper 18815, 2013.

Ehrenhalt, Samuel. "Economic and Demographic Change: The Case of New York City." *Monthly Labor Review* 116, no. 2 (1993): 40–51.

O'Flaherty, Brendan, and Rajiv Sethi. "Urban Crime." In *Handbook of Regional and Urban Economics*, edited by Gilles Duranton, J. Vernon Henderson, and William Strange, 1519–1621. Amsterdam: Elsevier, 2015.

Reyes, Jessica Wolpaw. "Environmental Policy as Social Policy? The Impact of Childhood Lead Exposure on Crime." *B.E. Journal of Economic Analysis and Policy* 7, no. 1 (2007). https://www.biologicaldiversity.org/campaigns/get_the_lead _out/pdfs/health/Reyes_2007.pdf.

————. "Lead Exposure and Behavior: Effects on Anti-Social and Risky Behavior among Children and Adolescents." *Economic Inquiry* 53, no. 3 (2015): 1580–1605.

Jon Dubin, who was involved in legal actions to prevent the destruction
of public housing in Newark, is a professor of law at Rutgers in Newark
and dean of the law school's clinical program. He explains that because the
mayor of Newark could only appoint one of seven members to the Newark
Housing Authority, he had little control over critical housing policy.

Jon Dubin, Esq.

My only recollections about Ken Gibson and his sixteen-year tenure as the first African American mayor of Newark are incidental to a major legal matter that I worked on while I was a part of the legal team at the NAACP Legal Defense and Educational Fund Inc. (LDF).[1] My work at the LDF was focused on lawsuits intended to prevent the demolition of public-housing units in various parts of the country. I was involved, for example, in such actions in Jacksonville, Florida. These actions were based on the premise that low-income families in those areas of the country had few, if any, alternatives to public housing, given either a critical shortage of affordable housing or a housing stock that was below acceptable living standards.

The Newark action involved an effort to prevent the Newark Housing Authority (NHA) from demolishing any of the nearly two thousand public-housing apartment units slated for imminent destruction at the Columbus Homes and Kretchmer Homes projects. The legal action also sought to compel the NHA to immediately rent habitable units at these two public-housing locations. Comments about this legal action are relevant to a discussion about the "Gibson years," since the action attacks a public-housing master plan created by the NHA in 1984 while Gibson was serving in his fourth consecutive term in office. The legal action is less relevant to a discussion about Gibson's individual legacy given that the mayor exercised very little control over the policies and activities of the NHA. During Ken Gibson's tenure as mayor, the city's chief executive had the authority to appoint just one among the seven members of the NHA's board of commissioners. Five members were appointed by the city council, and one was appointed by the governor. In his capacity as a state senator, Sharpe James, also Gibson's successor as mayor, spearheaded state legislation to allow the mayor to appoint all seven commissioners.

It is significant in my view for those seeking to understand or assess Ken Gibson's legacy as mayor to recognize that there were significant political, economic, and social forces beyond his control at work during his tenure.

The lawsuit was started as a class action in July in 1988. Legal Services of New Jersey (LSNJ), the lead counsel for the plaintiffs, was represented by Melville D. Miller and Harris David.

Harris David approached me to include the LDF among the plaintiff's counsel. I received an interesting orientation to Newark politics when my boss, Julius Chambers, instructed me to check with Junius Williams and Gus Heningburg before accepting the invitation to join the lawsuit. I did that, checked back with Harris David, and then accepted the invitation on behalf of the LDF. My role in the case was greatly expanded with the sad passing of Harris David.

The plaintiffs, the Newark Coalition for Low Income Housing, together with several organizations, filed a complaint in the Superior Court of New Jersey seeking the relief described earlier. Before the state complaint could be heard, the NHA submitted and the U.S. Department of Housing and Urban Development (HUD) approved an application for the demolition of Columbus Homes (1,506 units) and began activities associated with the proposed demolition of Kretchmer Homes (372 units). Because these actions represented a violation of the U.S. Housing Act, the case was removed from the Superior Court of New Jersey to the U.S. District Court of New Jersey. HUD and its secretary, Jack Kemp, were included as defendants. Between 1985 and the time of the filing of the lawsuit in 1988, the NHA, with HUD's approval, scheduled the demolition of more than five thousand public-housing apartment units without adequate replacement housing. These numbers represent the most massive demolition program in the history of public housing.

At the time of the adoption of its public-housing master plan, the NHA acknowledged that the city's housing-vacancy rate was the highest of any major housing authority in the country and that its level of deterioration was among the most serious in the nation. At that time, against a total population of 316,240 residents, Newark had an estimated homeless population of more than sixteen thousand, among the highest in the nation for any major city. The waiting list for public housing was estimated at the time to include over seven thousand families and had risen to as many as thirteen thousand by 1986.

The negative impact on low-income families associated with the demolition of public-housing units was exacerbated by the lack of affordable housing alternatives in the city. For example, nearly twenty-nine thousand low- and very-low-income tenants were at the time paying unaffordable rents, and the city had 14,055 substandard occupied units. To these grim economic realities can be added the impact of racial discrimination and racial segregation faced by the city's growing black and Hispanic populations. It was documented at the time that racial minority groups comprised a disproportionate share of the homeless and inadequately housed persons in Essex County.

The public-housing master plan called for the abandonment of high-rise buildings for public-housing purposes. During the 1980s, nearly half of the NHA's thirteen thousand public-housing units were in mid-rise and high-rise buildings. This fact together with the NHA's policy to abandon or demolish high-rise buildings made inevitable the fact that scores of very-low-income families would be forced to seek shelter outside of

Newark. Some believe that this was a tacit endorsement of gentrification. This belief is supported by the fact that the NHA had begun to abandon high-rise buildings well before the formal announcement in its master plan, leaving vacant public-housing units that would otherwise have been used to ameliorate a growing waiting list. Those who contend that a desire for gentrification was at the root of the NHA's abandonment and demolition policies can readily point to the NHA's own words. The 1984 master plan recites a finding that the city could not be expected to devote "a major share of its meager resources" to a public-housing system (and its low-income population) already overburdening city services.

In further support of the gentrification theory, it can be noted that both the Columbus Homes site and the Kretchmer Homes site provided at the time a more socially and economically integrated environment than the majority of Newark's public housing, situated in the city's economically and racially impacted Central Ward. The area east and west of the Columbus project, for example, abutted the Colonnade, a private high-rise apartment complex. The elevated Interstate 280 and Lackawanna Railroad tracks pass by the project on its southerly side, creating natural barriers between the city's gentrifying North Ward and its racially impacted Central Ward. The Columbus site had ready access to public transportation, including bus and railroad lines. A major city park, a shopping center, a clinic, and neighborhood schools were located within walking distance of the site. The Kretchmer site was in a quiet tree-lined residential area, bordering the city of Elizabeth. It was within walking distance of grocery and drug stores, a community health center, churches, and a park.

Much of the poor performance of the NHA over the course of its existence occurred during Ken Gibson's tenure as mayor. Examples of such poor performance include major increases in vacancy rates, the lack of essential repairs and maintenance, the slow or lack of completion of construction and modernization projects, and the loss of modernization funds as a result of the lack of timely performance. In 1974 and 1978, the NHA received funding for the construction of approximately 516 units of new housing, of which 372 units eventually became available for occupancy in 1987 and 1988, ten years after HUD first approved and reserved funding for them. During this same period, HUD recaptured 80 units due to delay, and the NHA abandoned 47 units due to inappropriate site selection. In the area of modernization, in 1983, after warnings from HUD, $5 million was recaptured "due to the NHA's failure to make more than minimal use of available modernization funds." In 1979, HUD designated the NHA as an operationally troubled authority. HUD audits of the NHA conducted during the 1980s all sharply criticized the NHA on several grounds. The 1982 audit criticized the NHA for its failure to comply with prescribed time frames for the completion of modernization projects. The 1984 HUD audit again underscored the authority's troubling "lack of urgency in developing an overall planning strategy and timetable for expending available modernization funds totaling $68,641,239." The 1986 audit found that the NHA still had $55 million in unobligated modernization funds and noted that the NHA's failure to submit implementation plans "again calls into question the NHA's modernization capability." This same audit also found the NHA to have the highest vacancy rate of any major public-housing authority in the country despite more than an ample number of applicants to fill all habitable units.

With significant "white flight" from Newark to the surrounding suburbs beginning immediately following the end of World War II and increasing immediately following the 1967 rebellion, by 1970, the city of Newark and its newly elected African American mayor were called upon to respond to the needs of a population that was steadily growing poorer. For a candidate who campaigned on a promise to be "the mayor for all the people," the failures and shortcomings of the Newark Housing Authority made an already near-impossible job even more challenging.

NOTE

1. The NAACP Legal Defense and Educational Fund Inc. is a 501(c)(3) nonprofit civil rights organization that handles legal cases in the areas of criminal justice, economic justice, education, and political participation. The organization, also referred to as LDF or the Inc. Fund, was part of the operations of the NAACP until 1957. My recollections about the legal matter were reinforced by a review of a memorandum of law in support of the plaintiff's motion for a temporary restraining order and preliminary injunction, which I contributed to as cocounsel. The data included in this article can be found in the "Memorandum of Law in Support of Plaintiff's Motion for Temporary Restraining Order and Preliminary Injunction" that was drafted by the author for the U.S. District Court of New Jersey.

CHAPTER 8

MAYOR GIBSON REFLECTS

After so much reflecting on Mayor Gibson and his era, the editors determined to give the mayor a chance to reflect. While he was not provided with any of the earlier reflections, we asked him about some of the things he said, the things he had and hadn't done, the people he knew, the issues of the time, what he had learned, and his approach to his mayoralty.

Mayor Gibson, what, if any, are the personal characteristics, educational credentials, or past experiences that would make a mayoral candidate in a troubled American city more qualified than other candidates?

Anyone with a sincere interest in serving the people would make a viable candidate. I would say that no particular educational credentials are important. In my case, before deciding to seek the office of mayor, I had been actively involved in the civil rights movement. It was my hope and expectation that as mayor, I would be able to continue—and perhaps even advance—my efforts to improve the lives of black Americans. My particular focus was on health disparities, but I was also interested in bringing about improvements in all lifestyle areas, including employment, housing, and education. In my opinion, two other relevant characteristics are a willingness to put in the time and the hard work required to gain the trust of the electorate and a sincere belief that the goal can be achieved. I was the only one among other potential candidates who was willing to attend PTA meetings, Boy Scout meetings, and meetings of black clubs and organizations. I was also the one who sincerely believed that an African American could be elected mayor. The first effort in 1966 was fraught with controversy. The process started but with strong feelings of doubt.

To these limiting factors can be added the fact that we had no money, no organization, and only about six weeks to campaign. While others were unwilling to become candidates in what they perceived to be a demonstration, rather than a real opportunity to win, I believed that a 1966 run for the office of mayor could lay the groundwork for a run in 1970.

I was not always focused on advancing the cause of black people as a politician. As I said, my original approach was to work as an activist in the civil rights movement with people like Bob Curvin.

Mayor, what would you say about the importance of temperament?

Temperament matters! In this regard, we can look at the current Republican candidate (at the time, Donald Trump) for president of the United States. In my case, on the personality spectrum beginning with type A, I would describe myself as being a type Z personality. I tend to take things slow; I am always willing to listen to other points of view before deciding on an action, and I am able to remain calm and effective under stressful conditions. I have told people that I may be slow, but I am persistent. I contrast my approach to leadership with the approach of other officials who speed along like demons and whose voices are the only ones you hear when they are in a group—even in social places like the barber shop. The city of Newark after the riots in 1967 needed a leader with a calm—and calming—demeanor.

Mayor Gibson, some people who knew you as mayor used the word cautious to describe your dealings with them. Does that word fit?

I am definitely cautious by nature, and I consider this (trait) a gift. In business and leadership, it has always served me well. Let me give you just a couple of examples. One of my earliest actions as mayor was to appoint a police captain for the North Ward. Influential people in the North Ward, including Councilman Tony Carrino and former assemblyman Tony

Imperiale, were vehemently opposed to my selection. In response, Carrino and Imperiale led a mob to my office in city hall, forced their way to my office door, and then broke down the door to gain access to me. They didn't know it, but I had a .38-caliber revolver between my legs. The thought went through my mind, Should I shoot these people? A mayor with a different temperament might have done something justifiable but also regretful.

I can recall another occasion when I was informed of an incident in Branch Brook Park. It was reported to me that a young girl had been trampled by a mounted police unit during a Puerto Rican festival. It turned out to be untrue, but the racial tension during those times made the rumor potentially volatile, and the presence of gambling during the festival added to the potential for unrest. I made my way to Branch Brook Park, and I was able to calm the crowd. Leaders in the Puerto Rican community, including Ramon Rivera, insisted that I agree to have a meeting with leaders of the Puerto Rican community to discuss the police-community relations and other issues related to their community's quality of life. As part of my effort to maintain peace, I invited Ramon and others to join me in a walk from Branch Brook Park to city hall. History appears to have missed the fact that the "march" was my idea and that the "march" was not a protest. I can report, however, that Ramon Rivera and Imamu Baraka did lead a demonstration the next day in front of city hall. I can also report that while the rumor regarding a police horse injuring a young woman in the park proved to be false, it turned out that a young man was killed by a police baton during a rock-throwing melee that accompanied the demonstration.

My point is not that I treated these incidents as insignificant but that with my management style, I was able to minimize the damage that might have occurred. I also learned from these incidents that Newark police officers were inclined to accept their responsibility to keep the peace and to protect the mayor, whoever he might be.

Mr. Mayor, has your laid-back style ever been a detriment? Did it make it more difficult for you to command respect?

From day one in office as the first African American mayor—and particularly as an African American man—I did not automatically command respect. I had to demand it. And I was generally able to do that. For example, another of my first actions as mayor was to appoint a police director. To my surprise and disdain, the city clerk at the time sent me a note saying that he did not intend to honor my directive. My response was to let him know that I could and that I would turn the public loose on him if he did not comply. He did, and I did not have any major problems from him after that incident.

Mayor Gibson, you are noted for having said, "Wherever American cities are going, Newark will get there first." Is it true that you borrowed the statement from Donald Malafonte, Hugh Addonizio's chief of staff, and do you believe that it has proven to be true?

Yes, I stole the phrase from Malafonte's application for federal funding of Newark's Model Cities Program. I thought it was a great line. I got a lot of play in national media after I began using it.

I'm not sure whether the phrase still applies, but Newark is certainly a model of urban challenges. The city has not achieved major breakthroughs, but it has also not languished in the dumps. In my view, as is the case for many struggling cities, Newark's reliance on the property tax is at the core of its economic difficulty. The tax is archaic.

On reflection, Mayor, how would you describe your relationship with notable Newarkers such as Robert Curvin, Gus Heningburg, Imamu Baraka, Ramon Rivera, and Steve Adubato Sr.?

All the persons you named were important players in the community, some before my time in office and others during my time in office.

- Robert Curvin (civil rights activist, educator, foundation executive, and author)—I got along very well with Bob. He was a civil rights activist and served as the president of the Newark-Essex chapter of CORE during the Newark Rebellion. Bob led pickets against Bamberger's, White Castle, and other businesses that refused to employ black people as salesclerks. It is hard to imagine how we couldn't get jobs at White Castle. Bob believed in direct action and was not reluctant to use it. He was widely respected, however, in the white liberal community and was instrumental in getting the dean of the Rutgers–Newark Law School, Willard Heckel, to lend his support to my mayoral campaign. Heckel, in turn, was helpful in our fundraising efforts. Bob and I were not only friends; we were neighbors.
- Gustav Heningburg (community leader, civic activist)—Gus was an interesting guy. He was accepted by the white community to an extent that none of the other community activists were; they really liked and respected him. Gus had much talent, but I could never determine whether he worked for us or for the government. Thinking about this reminds me of my experience with the military. When I was sent to Fort Riley, Kansas, I was approached to serve as an informant for the military in predominantly African American communities. If I had accepted the assignment, my commitment would have included preparing a daily report and agreeing to serve an extra year in the army. I declined. Overall, I got along well with Gus. He was no lightweight, and he had access to people who others of us did not.
- Imamu Baraka (author, playwright, and community activist)—Baraka was the spiritual leader of the campaign that led to my election to office as mayor. He was instrumental in getting community volunteers for the campaign. He had status in the community because of his identification with the black arts movement and his black nationalist and Pan-African leanings. I must say, however, that he did some crazy things politically, such as attempting

to build a low-income housing project in the heart of the Italian American neighborhood. We had fights after I assumed office, but overall, we tended to work together. This was possible largely because we shared a commitment to social change and improving the quality of life for black people. Our differences occurred mainly in the area of tactics in pursuit of these objectives.

- Ramon Rivera (Puerto Rican community activist, former member of the Young Lords, and founding executive director of La Casa de Don Pedro, a Hispanic community-development corporation)—Ramon was a bright, dedicated, well-meaning Puerto Rican community leader. Like African American community leaders, he wanted improvements in his community. I liked him, and it was not hard to do so. He, similar to Imamu Baraka, in my view, did some crazy things politically, but often that was because he wanted to make clear that he and his community were not going to be pushed around.

- Steve Adubato—Improving the prospects of the Italian community and protecting their interests in the city were Steve's primary goals. I think that he was successful but primarily because of my help. If truth be told, I made him. I helped him get state and federal funding for his center's programs, but he made the programs work. He insisted on providing quality services, and because his programs were effective, he garnered the deep loyalty of the people the programs served. He used quality service delivery as a basis for building a powerful political organization. For my assessment, he was the only community activist to do so.

Mayor, one phrase often quoted from your inaugural speech was "I am a mayor for all the people." Given the racial divisiveness and competing pressures from the business community and the neighborhoods, did this comment represent a feasible vision?

I firmly believe that every elected official has a sworn duty to respond to the needs of all the people. Having said that, I can also understand the pressure faced by a newly elected African American official in a jurisdiction that has before that time been under an oppressive regime that denied African American residents equal and fair access to a decent lifestyle. We can certainly see this embedded in much of the criticism (that was) leveled at President Obama. And I know that my attitudes and beliefs in this regard caused criticism. Whenever I was asked what I intended to do for the black community, my response was, consistently, "nothing." This, of course, did not mean that I did not intend to address the needs of Newark's African Americans. It did mean that I could not be expected to tailor any of my efforts as mayor specifically to the African American community or to any other particular ethnic group. In my view, an evenhanded approach toward Newark's residents would mean matching the greatest benefit to the greatest need.

Mayor, how was this approach applied when dealing with Newark's business community? And with whom in that community did you have the best relationship?

In the interest of serving Newark's citizens, I subscribed to two basic principles. First, I accepted the principle that real power in any city is not in the hands of city hall but rather in the hands of those who control the economy. Second, I proceeded on the principle that it was imperative that a way be found to fund basic city services, recognizing that property taxation represents an archaic and ineffective approach to this essential task. With all this in mind, in 1969, before I was elected mayor, I visited senior executives in Newark's business community and advised them that I was seeking the office of mayor. They laughed in my face when I said that I would win the election. At that moment, I adopted a third principle: "Don't pick a fight with the guys with the money." Instead, I advised them that I would be back after the election and that I would be looking to them for assistance.

Almost immediately following my election in 1970, I approached the business community again by convening a meeting with the seniormost executives of the major companies doing business in Newark. The meeting included Robert Van Fossen at Mutual Benefit, Malcolm Davis at First Fidelity, Donald McNaughton at Prudential, and Robert Ferguson at First National Bank. While some thought that I might have been out of line to insist that only the seniormost executives attend the meeting, I considered myself to be on par with them as the senior executive over the state's largest municipal corporation. This time, they did not laugh.

Whether as a result of the meeting or a change of heart on the part of senior executives, the business community provided me with extraordinary support in the early months of my administration. For example, senior staff from these companies served as a management team for the first six months, addressing operations, finance, human resources, and budget issues. Prudential provided me with one of the company's senior managers, Bob Smith, to serve on loan as Newark's business administrator. The arrangement was originally for a three-month period but was ultimately extended to six months. And no money was charged to the city.

On the other hand, I had to be careful not to give in to a growing list of self-serving requests put to me by the business community—requests that did not resonate well with the overall needs of the city. These requests included things such as the creation of a special downtown police force, special tax breaks, and a formal separation of the business district from the rest of the city. The interests of the business leaders and the interests of Newark's citizens often overlapped, but when they did not overlap and the business community asked for too much, I paused. Still, I realized that I shouldn't bite the hand that could feed the city's economy.

Mayor Gibson, tell us what it was like working with the Newark City Council.

That landscape was always changing. Over my sixteen years as mayor, I had to deal with various individuals and combinations of individuals. Also keep in mind that there was always someone on the council who wanted to be the mayor. I found the most difficult issue between myself as the chief executive and the council as the legislative branch was a tendency on the part of the council to violate the principle of separation of powers with attempts to encroach upon my executive authority.

My general approach to dealing with the city council was to send staff members to serve as liaisons between the mayor's office and council members. I can recall people such as Harold Hodes, Barbara Sachs, and Dan Blue serving me well in this role. I can also recall having particular respect for Lou Turco, who I considered to be one of the smartest people to ever serve on the city council. Overall, I would describe my relationship with the council as having been sound.

Mayor, how did Newark's role as the largest city in New Jersey change politically during your sixteen-year tenure in office?

The city's relationship with the state varied based on the personality, leadership style, and political motivation of the sitting governor. Gov. Kean, for example, was good. Gov. Cahill showed helpful leadership when, upon his return from a national conference, he pressed for the passage of legislation granting local taxing authority needed to generate revenue for Newark. The need for gubernatorial candidates to get local support in statewide general elections was often an important factor in securing state executive-branch action on what was needed by me as mayor. As an example, following the 1979 election, Gov. Brendan Byrne fulfilled his previously unmet commitment for Newark appointments to boards and commissions of strategic importance to Newark. These included the Passaic Valley Sewer Authority and the North Jersey Water Supply District. Perhaps he had a change of heart when pundits began calling him "One-term Byrne."

You became the first African American to mount a primary campaign for governor of New Jersey. What was your motivation for doing this?

I ran for governor to prove that a black candidate could mount a credible campaign when most people said it could not be done. Then, as now, the county power struggle required building a political organization in each county. Winning a statewide primary election is much different than winning a nonpartisan municipal election for mayor. We were successful in 1981and 1985, finishing in the top three and garnering the same percentage of the total votes cast in both primaries.

Mayor, what do you count among your greatest achievements while serving as Newark's chief executive?

I am very proud of my achievements in the area of health care and the removal of some glaring health disparities that existed in the city before 1970. Again, as I said earlier, to the extent that these health issues and health disparities disproportionately affected African American residents, the benefits of my efforts in these regards were also disproportionately enjoyed by the African American residents. I approached these issues by developing community health care facilities and locating them in the neighborhoods for easy access by neighborhood residents. Through these health centers, we created a policy of comprehensive testing that had been almost totally absent prior to that time. Through these efforts, we were able to dramatically reduce Newark's infant and maternal mortality rates. We also reduced the incidence of tuberculosis by 50 percent and the incidence of venereal disease by 80 percent.

I am also proud of the fact that I was able to balance Newark's budgets during periods of serious shrinkage in the tax base. And during my first two terms in office, Newark fell from first in the nation in the area of serious crime to twenty-third. There can also be little doubt about a correlation between this reduction in crime and a willingness of companies such as Prudential and Public Service to continue to maintain corporate headquarters and further expand their operations in Newark.

I enjoy recalling my success with building first-rate police and fire departments that served as national models, again in the face of a shrinking tax base and the need for layoffs. Also, despite a shrinking tax base, I was able to bring about a steady increase in the city's bond ratings. I created enterprise zones, and I instituted an aggressive demolition program to improve the appearance and overall desirability of Newark as a place to live, work, and visit.

Mayor Gibson, did the use of ancillary nonprofit corporations such as the Housing Development and Redevelopment Corporation (HDRC), Newark Economic Development Corporation (NEDC), and Newark Watershed Conservation and Development Corporation (NWCDC) prove to be helpful in your early years? Was there any legal question about the validity of the approach?

Let me address the second part of the question first. I am aware of the fact that questions have been raised—even in recent times—about the use of nonprofit entities by municipalities to carry out certain ancillary municipal functions. This is different than the question of privatization that is discussed even in the context of primary municipal functions such as police, fire, and sanitation services. With privatization, the city would give up control over these functions. With the use of nonprofit entities, while they may be independent corporations, through board representation, staffing, memoranda of understanding, and other legal devices, the city retains control over their activities. Further, in terms of the letter of the law, there are specific state statutes that set forth the terms and upon which such arrangements can be made. We followed those statutory requirements carefully when we created the entities you named.

As to how helpful they were, I would generally report that they worked very well to the benefit of the city. The key for me was to make sure that each of these entities was staffed with highly competent people, especially the person who headed the operation. I refer to this practice as an objective and studious approach to management, as opposed to a politically motivated approach, which was the approach employed in Newark in the years just prior to my election.

Many of the people I attracted to my administration were involved with teaching or otherwise related to educational institutions. In this regard, the names Terry Moore, Dennis Sullivan, and Paul Ylvisaker come to mind. In the end, whether in city-hall proper or working with one of the ancillary nonprofit entities, I am confident that I assembled one of the best management teams ever.

The creation of the NEDC is not quite the same as the origins of the HDRC or NWCDC. We created the HDRC and NWCDC from scratch. The NEDC has a forerunner that was chamber-of-commerce controlled by Addonizio's people. What I found when I studied the operation was that its focus was strictly limited to the interests of the business community, with virtually no focus at all on regular citizens. With the help of a legal brain trust, I set out to reform the operation by broadening its scope and reach. The legal brain trust was led by Al Faiella and Steve Rother.

Functions of the HDRC were ultimately folded into city-hall operations as part of a department of development. The NWCDC continued for many years after I left office, took over water-supply functions from the engineering department, and was only recently dissolved amid legal controversy. The NEDC, also embroiled in legal controversy, has been reformed at least twice since 1986.

Mayor, what were some of the more difficult aspects of the transition from the Addonizio administration to yours?

The single most difficult aspect of the transition was the lack of communication. Most of Addonizio's people left. And they did not leave behind any form of transition documents to guide me or any of the new people in the various departments of city government. We truly had to start from scratch. The only significant holdover for me was Harold Hodes. I know that there is a general perception that I had the difficult challenge of routing out institutionalized corruption when I took office. This perception might be overblown. What I found was the widespread use of favoritism in the awarding of desirable contracts, a practice that is not particularly rare. My challenge was to reverse that practice and the perception of that practice.

How would you describe the advantages of an appointed as opposed to an elected board of education?

Because it is representative of democratic principles, elected boards are good in theory. They are not good in practice.

When I had the power to appoint members of the board of education, I generally made it a practice to avoid telling my appointees what to do. I relied, instead, on being careful with the appointments, again focusing on my perception of the candidates' commitment to ensuring a quality education. By the same token, I did not hesitate to remove a person from the board who I felt was not pursuing the schoolchildren's best interest. One of my favorite examples is my appointment Larry Hamm. When I appointed Larry, in 1971, it was at the height of the longest teachers' strike in U.S. history. I recall how impressed I was with this schoolboy's ability to rally his fellow students around serious issues related to the quality of public education. I assisted Larry in his efforts to have the teachers' strike negotiations include some of the student demands. I then appointed Larry to the board of education, making him, at that time, the youngest person in the nation to ever serve on a school board. By the end of Larry's first term, I declined reappointing him. I felt at that time that the policies he espoused were not in the best interest of schoolchildren. On the other hand, I continued then—and continue now—to admire Larry for the good that he has done for the city of Newark and for his outstanding academic achievements.

While you were mayor, you seemed to have astutely avoided the "Abscam" sting that ruined a number of New Jersey political careers, and yet you fell prey to an indictment. What can you tell us about these matters?

Abscam was the code name given to an FBI investigation of public corruption. The FBI retained the services of a convicted con man to pose as the negotiator for an Arab company that was supposedly seeking to do business in jurisdictions targeted by the investigation. The con man's assignment was to lure politicians into taking a bribe for political favors intended to advance the bogus company's ambitious development plans.

I recall being approached while I was attending the League of Municipalities Convention in Atlantic City. I was there with Dan Blue, and we were at Resorts. I recall the con man saying to me, "We want to come to Newark, and we have $100 million to invest." I immediately became suspicious and asked the guy to leave. Sometime later, I was in Buffalo giving a speech in support of Jimmy Carter when a reporter approached and asked, "How much did you take?" That was the first time I was made aware that I had been a target of the investigation.

Abscam ruined a number of New Jersey political careers. U.S. senator Harrison Williams was convicted and went to jail; Angelo Errichetti, a state senator and mayor of Camden, went to jail. And Frank Thompson, a Democratic congressman, was convicted and went to jail.

With respect to the indictment, I gave a menial job to a former city councilman, Mickey Bontempo, at the Pequannock Watershed. Mickey had a nephew who was already working there. At that time, management of the watershed was divided between matters affecting the water and matters affecting the land. The department of engineering handled water issues, and the Newark Watershed Conservation and Development Corporation handled matters related to the land. Bontempo's employment was related to the department of engineering.

Unbeknownst to me, Mickey moved to Florida. But his nephew continued to receive his checks. It took some time before the fact of the misdirected checks came to light. By that time, the prosecutor had moved on the matter with an indictment of me and Earl Harris, who was president of the city council at the time. After a trial at which the facts were revealed, both Earl and I were acquitted.

Mayor Gibson, what about regrets or mistakes?

It is obvious to say that everyone makes mistakes by either doing something they wish they had not done or not doing something they now wish they had done. I tried my best to avoid such regrets by surrounding myself with the brightest people I could attract. I learned this approach from the Rockefellers, and overall, I think I applied the practice effectively. In this regard, I would also be pleased to add to my legacy the spawning of some of the remarkable careers that are enjoyed by some of the bright young talent I was able to attract and hopefully in some way inspire.

CONCLUSION

GIBSON'S LEGACY

THE MAN, THE TIME, AND THE PLACE, 1970–1986

Richard W. Roper

Fifty years after the rebellion that began on July 12, 1967, the *New York Times* in a full-page retrospective recalled the tumult of the uprising and gave voice to Newark's incumbent mayor, Ras Baraka, the son of Amiri Baraka,[1] a black cultural nationalist and a leader in the effort to elect Gibson as Newark's mayor, who said this about the city: "Has it recovered? Not completely. . . . There are still some emotional trauma and other things we haven't recovered from and social conditions that led to the rebellion itself . . . the underlying circumstances that create poverty and homelessness have not completely gone or been addressed adequately. That's our job to try to get that done."[2]

The picture the *Times* painted throughout the article spoke of Newark's continuing struggles but failed to discuss any of the progress the city has made in areas such as attracting new private investment, the construction of unsubsidized moderate-income housing, the emergence of a broad-based and thriving cultural community, and the development of a robust higher-education community. Audible Inc., a company that sells digital audiobooks, radio and television programs, and audio versions of magazines and newspapers, located its headquarters in downtown Newark in 2007,[3] and the Panasonic Corporation of North America relocated to

Newark in 2013. Similarly, Prudential Financial, a company that began in Newark, in 2016 constructed a new corporate headquarters in the city. The New Community Corporation, a nonprofit community-based organization took the lead in the 1960s, with Mayor Kenneth Gibson's support, in advancing a massive program of low- and moderate-income housing construction in Newark's Central Ward. Gibson's successor, Sharpe James, presided over the construction of a project initiated by Gibson, Society Hill, a huge housing complex abutting the city's downtown business district that was the first unsubsidized middle-income housing built in Newark in more than forty years. Rutgers University–Newark began its downtown expansion during Gibson's tenure and has continued to extend its reach into the heart of the city. The University of Medicine and Dentistry of New Jersey (UMDNJ), now a component of Rutgers University, also took form during Gibson's time in office and steadily grew into one of the nation's largest academic health centers. Essex County College and the New Jersey Institute of Technology, located adjacent to Rutgers and the UMDNJ and not far from Seton Hall School of Law, rounded out the complex of higher-education institutions that took form and blossomed in Newark. Sadly, these developments have gained little notice in the national press; nor was their recognition of the emergence of a vibrant artistic community that includes the construction of the New Jersey Performing Arts Center, a world-class arts venue that is home to the New Jersey Symphony Orchestra and hosts nationally and internationally renowned performers. Also overlooked was the founding of Newark Public Radio Inc., the licensee for WBGO, the region's premier jazz and public-affairs radio station. There now exists a host of art galleries, including Aljira, a Center for Contemporary Art, which attracts visual artists from throughout the region.

But true to form, the nation's media, led by the *New York Times*, see only what Newark has been unable to address and none of what it has accomplished since the rebellion.

REFLECTIONS AS HISTORICAL TAPESTRY

The reflections presented in the preceding pages provide rich detail about Gibson, his time, and his place in Newark's history. The reflections offer the perspectives of individuals who collaborated with Ken Gibson as he sought and then assumed the mayor's office, of others who worked in his administration, and of still others who were active in the life of the city. They observed Gibson and his administration and formed opinions both positive and negative about the quality of his leadership.

The reflections reveal that Ken Gibson was a man who chose—and was chosen—to lead but who lacked experience as a leader. According to Martin Bierbaum, a member of the faculty at Rutgers University–Newark in the late 1970s, Gibson's professional background may not have been ideal for the challenges he would face as mayor. Bierbaum posits that Gibson's formative experiences were as a government engineer operating within the inherent constraints of state and local government. In his reflections, he writes about the interview he had with Mayor Gibson at city hall as the mayor was preparing to leave office: "As I ascended those city-hall steps, I wondered if Ken Gibson fit the mold that had been cast for the period's African American politicians. Think Jesse Jackson! Think Al Sharpton! Gibson's personal predilections led to dissimilar directions. He seemed to be a different kind of politician, maybe even a nonpolitician, marching to his own drummer. He appeared more modest than flamboyant; he exuded a quiet competence." Barbara Kukla, who had been a reporter at the *Newark Star Ledger*, opines that Gibson's quiet leadership may have been just what the city needed at that time. She writes, "Indeed, he was one of the most unobtrusive persons I had ever met. He also was thoughtful. He approached the city's challenges with an attitude of slow but consistent determination."

Gibson's childhood and lifelong friend, Elton Hill, provides additional context for what was regarded as the mayor's laid-back style. He offers the following: "People ask me what Ken was like as a child and whether there were signs indicating his future. No one among our childhood friends would have doubted that Ken could become the first African American mayor of Newark. The calm, strong demeanor he exhibited as mayor was prominent in him as a child. No one back then confused his reserve for weakness. Ken was hard-headed and at times stubborn when it came to defending important beliefs. He was also academically gifted."

Sharpe James, the man who would succeed Ken as Newark's mayor in 1986, offers a somewhat less sympathetic view of Gibson's style. He writes,

> He was an engineer with a turn-the-other-cheek, nonthreatening personality. Gibson was someone with whom the white establishment could feel comfortable. Ken was inclined to avoid offending people.
>
> This trait was evident throughout the [1970] campaign and into his first term as mayor. For example, during the campaign, Ken conducted himself in such a manner as to not offend anyone supporting other candidates. This included at times appearing to run independent of the team while the rest of us always acted as a team.... Once elected, Ken took a very independent approach to the exercise of his newly gained political power. While key advisors, such as Bob Curvin, believed that the power of the office would be shared in designing plans for running the city, they faced a rude awakening when, once in office, Ken soundly reminded them that he was in charge by saying, "I got elected, not you!"

The reflections also provide a vivid picture of the city. In 1970, Newark was a city of 381,930 people, down from a peak population of 442,337 in 1930.[4] It had become a majority-black city and its white population was declining steadily. And as Grizel Ubarry indicates, the Puerto Rican population was rapidly replacing the Italians, who resided in the city's North Ward and who were abandoning Newark for the suburbs. As Alan Zalkind, Gibson's appointee as director of the Newark High Impact Anti-Crime

Program, points out, Newark was one of eight cities selected by the federal Law Enforcement Assistance Administration to participate in a program designed to reduce stranger-to-stranger crime. Zalkind writes that crime in Newark was increasing: "Newark's 1970 population was 382,417, and that year, there were 48,656 serious offenses, including 374 murders. By 1972, that number rose to 48,915, with 383 murders. Based on criteria selected to assess each city, Newark ranked the worst of the eight cities."

AN OPAQUE PERSONALITY

Al Koeppe, a leader in Newark's diminished but still vibrant business community when Gibson was elected, recalled the mayor as someone who faced challenges in his own way. He posits, "With hindsight, I can also see how Ken's steady, unemotional style could be viewed eventually as a weakness as well as a strength. A careful approach to problem solving is always a good strategy. But it can also be confused with lack of enthusiasm."

In addition to being quiet, Gibson projected a rather unassuming, inaccessible persona. What he was thinking often was a mystery to those with whom he interacted. He was anything but an open book; quite the opposite, he was very hard to read. Shortly after the 1970 election, he was described in an editorial in the *Newark Evening News*, New Jersey's most influential newspaper at the time, as phlegmatic, relaxed, and having a tranquil manner. As Koeppe suggests, while some who dealt with him thought that his quiet demeanor reflected thoughtfulness, others who were not so kind felt that he simply withdrew when complicated issues or difficult decisions had to be navigated.

But his "cool" style could serve him well, as several other reflections indicated, especially when he faced what could have been explosive situations. Harold Hodes, who served as one of Gibson's principal aides, addressed this aspect. Gibson, he said, was faced with maintaining calm during the longest teachers' strike in the nation's history, in 1971. He successfully managed the difficult issues and personalities associated with its resolution. Later, in 1976, as reported in the reflections provided by Sharpe James, a white city councilman kicked in the door to the mayor's office and stormed into the room, followed by a mob of seventy-five screaming, angry North Ward Italians. The issue about which they were enraged was Gibson's refusal to appoint as precinct captain a police officer favored by the Mob. Gibson remained seated at this desk eating grapes as this invasion of his office played out. His quiet reaction diffused what could have been a major racial incident. The use of force in this instance, which many politicians would have thought appropriate, could have resulted in a black-white confrontation with tragic consequences. Coeditor Robert Holmes, who Gibson appointed as head of the Newark Watershed Conservation and Development Corporation, provides a vivid description of Gibson's ability to diffuse a crowd of hostile whites concerned about how Newark's watershed property, located in several suburban communities in which they lived, miles from the city, would be managed. Holmes writes that the mayor displayed his best aspects:

> Arriving on a red-eye from Asia, the mayor met one day with local activists in a hall in Hardyston Township. Reminiscent of a major element of his timely value to the city, Gibson was able to calm an otherwise angry and suspicious group with his unshakable and self-assured demeanor. Through this seemingly simple appearance, Gibson showed me that he was loyal to his managers, that he paid attention to detail, that he was committed to the needs of his city and his constituents over his own personal comfort or gain, and that his calm and reasonable approach could win the day.

Critics suggested that Gibson's demeanor implied a lack of the mental toughness needed to master many of the issues that he had to manage. He did not impress observers as a sharp political operative. Perhaps this view had some validity in Gibson's early days in office, but it was not true after his first four years. His political juices flowed quite nicely as he became

more comfortable in office. Frankly, it may not have been an entirely accu-
rate assessment in the early days either. Koeppe points out that many in
the business community were surprised and impressed early on by Gibson's clear-eyed, direct dealings with them and the issues about which
they cared. He showed them respect and expected them to respect him
in return. He considered the city's business leaders his peers; they were
jointly responsible for the economic health of Newark and needed to work
together. Koeppe says that they quickly determined that he should not
be underestimated. Consequently, business leaders stepped forward and
offered help in areas in which they had expertise. Even so, none of these
leaders felt that they had a solid read of the mayor; rather, they simply saw
the need to help him avoid further decline in the city's economic position.
While Gibson successfully enlisted the business community's support in
fortifying Newark's administrative infrastructure, he never established a
close personal relationship with any of its leaders.

Sometimes the mayor deliberately seemed to set himself apart from
political and stylistic convention. Emblematic of the mayor's perceived
disengagement with the community that had put him in office, according
to some activists, was Gibson's official mode of transportation. As reported
by Camille Savoca Gibson, formerly a secretary in the mayor's office,
who in 2004 became Gibson's third wife, Gibson motored around the
city in a chauffeured 1974 black four-door Checker. Savoca suggests that
this choice of official vehicle reflected the mayor's modest inclinations, as
contrasted with another high-profile mayor during this period. She writes,
"I recall, for example, the extreme contrast between Ken and Mayor John
Lindsay of New York City. Ken was always modestly dressed and rode
around in a checkered cab. Lindsay, on the other hand, had the look of a
Hollywood actor with a flashy air—and he would arrive here and there in
a red Cadillac."

The Checker in which Gibson rode probably amused some and con-
founded other Newark residents but was offensive to those who styled
themselves antiestablishment activists. The car suggested, in the view of

the activists, Gibson's lack of appreciation for black sensibilities. Had he chosen a Cadillac as his official vehicle, a symbol of high capitalism, it might have been appreciated and hailed by some of the city's struggling residents. A Cadillac might have allowed folks the opportunity to experience a degree of vicarious satisfaction. Had he chosen a Ford or a Chevy, another segment of the working-class residents and the poor would have understood the choice as the mayor's attempt to avoid ostentation. The Checker just seemed an odd choice for the black mayor of a struggling American city. To the extent that the car was Gibson's attempt to project a willingness to reject convention, it was successful, but it also appeared a bit cartoonish.

Throughout Gibson's four terms, his personality remained a challenge to most of those with whom he interacted. Like his gait, his approach to the problems that confronted his city was slow, methodical, and deliberate. He frustrated those who would have had him move more quickly in a particular direction.

A Politician Emerges

Yet while his personality remained constant, his political acumen was another matter. It grew. In time, he became a crafty manipulator of the system. As recounted by several reflections, this craftiness was especially evident in his management of school-board appointments. In his first term, for example, Gibson appointed to the school board a young black man, Larry Hamm, who had been a recent high school graduate. Hamm was the youngest person appointed to a local school board in the nation. He also became a big disappointment to Gibson during the mayor's first term in office. In part, it appears that this was because Gibson seemed to feel that Hamm behaved as if he were an independent operative capable of ignoring the mayor's wishes. Hamm writes, "By the end of my first term on the school board, I had fallen out of favor with Mayor Gibson. This resulted in me not being reappointed. While I am uncertain about the specific basis for the mayor's loss of confidence in me, I am certain about his negative feelings in this regard. In an article in the *Star Ledger*, Gibson described my appointment to the board as the worst decision of his administration. I guess that in his view, I did not toe the line, and my close relationship with Amiri Baraka probably didn't help matters."

In his second term, Gibson required all his subsequent appointees to the school board to sign an undated letter of resignation that he could and did use to get rid of uncooperative appointees. It was a somewhat messy form of system management, but it had the effect Gibson wanted. Appointees were uncooperative at their peril.

Indeed, the Newark Board of Education was a constant source of frustration for Mayor Gibson, and he attempted to gain control of it. There was always at least one board member who refused to comply with his wishes on important matters. These matters, however, tended to involve patronage considerations—the awarding of contracts or jobs—not matters of educational philosophy or system improvement. In attempting to gain more control over the system, Gibson decided to put one of his aides on the board and to have that person elected as board president. Carl Sharif, the aide, was assigned this task and seemed to perform it well. The board became much more responsive under Sharif's leadership, and Gibson's frustration subsided. But once in total control of the board, Gibson had to assume responsibility for the system's continuing inability to provide the quality education that Newark's parents so desperately wanted for their children. His failing to turn the system around led to the emergence of a citizens' movement to end the mayoral appointment of school-board members in favor of an elected board. This movement would gain force as Gibson's first term came to a close, and it became a crisis early in his second term.

Gibson's political craftiness also was highlighted in his third term when he was indicted by the federal government and brought to trial for awarding a no-show job to a political supporter. While New Jersey politicians were assumed to behave in this way, it was a surprise and a big disappointment to those who viewed Gibson as above such behavior. He was, after all, someone who had been elected as a reform and good-government nonpolitician, and here he was, charged with corruption. He and his alleged coconspirator, City Council President Earl Harris, however, were acquitted. Unfortunately, this episode tarnished Gibson's reputation as a promoter of governmental integrity.

"A Mayor for All the People"?

Ken Gibson faced cross-cutting sets of expectations once in office. He had no political record that could be evaluated to indicate what his agenda might be, but those he had been elected to serve were clear about what they wanted or what they feared. Expectations were defined by the concerns of the city's various constituent groups. The principal groups whose interests Gibson had to accommodate were the city's black residents, Puerto Ricans, and Italians along with a smattering of Germans and Irish and a growing Portuguese population. Each anticipated a marked change in their life conditions because a black man had been elected mayor. Some, principally blacks and Puerto Ricans, were very hopeful, while others, especially the city's Italians, were horrified about the likely change in their prospects. Still others expected change but were uncertain what the future might hold.

On one hand, the black and Puerto Rican communities anticipated enhanced opportunities to participate in the city's economic, political, educational, and governmental arenas. Indeed, the prospect of improved access to jobs, especially in the public sector and possibly in the private sector, was viewed as one of the most important community benefits the election would produce. Jobs in city government and in the school system were assumed to be logical opportunities for those who felt that they had been excluded from such jobs in the past. Dave Dennison, in his reflections, describes in detail how Gibson attempted to respond to minority residents' expectations that access to public-sector jobs would be ensured. He notes that federal and state grants, which the city was successful in attracting, were critical in this regard. Moreover, residents in the minority community envisioned government becoming much more responsive in general to their concerns and needs.

Improvements in access to health care, more attention given to the educational needs of their children, and governmental support of minority business development were on the list of anticipated changes. Italians, on the other hand, according to Fran and Steve Adubato's reflections, were seriously concerned that Gibson would be hostile to them and show little concern for their interests. Since only a few in that community had supported him, and most had worked hard to secure Addonizio's reelection, the community was anxious about its prospects in the aftermath of the election. The Italians had displaced the Irish and then took control of the political levers in Newark, and now they were fearful that the blacks and Puerto Ricans were about to displace them.

The other, smaller constituent groups—the Germans, Irish, Portuguese, and Brazilians—watched the change in control of the city's political apparatus with a cautious eye but remained relatively quiet. The Portuguese and the Brazilians, who were concentrated in the economically stable and socially cohesive East Ward Ironbound section of the city,[5] focused their energies on maintaining a presence on the city council, protecting their geographic turf, and avoiding too much interaction with the rest of the city. The few Irish and the Germans simply kept their own counsel and went about their business, expecting little from the new administration. Over the course of Gibson's tenure, the Italian, Irish, and German populations declined appreciably in the city while black, Puerto Rican, Portuguese, and Brazilian populations continued to grow.

Clearly, the mayor was not going to make all these groups happy. Yet while Gibson's white critics were plentiful, some of the harshest criticism came from his erstwhile community-activist colleagues, individuals who had been instrumental in getting him elected. In so far as this segment of the Newark community was concerned, the bloom was off the rose early in Gibson's first term. Gibson should have anticipated this loss of support given his early and often-repeated commitment to be the "mayor for all the people." In his interview, Gibson states,

> I firmly believe that every elected official has a sworn duty to respond to the needs of all the people. Having said that, I can also understand the pressure faced by a newly elected African American official in a jurisdiction that has before that time been under an oppressive regime that denied African American residents equal and fair access to a decent lifestyle. We can certainly see this embedded in much of the criticism (that was) leveled at President Obama. And I know that my attitudes and beliefs in this regard caused criticism. Whenever I was asked what I intended to do for the black community, my response was, consistently, "nothing." This, of course, did not mean that I did not intend to address the needs of Newark's African Americans. It did mean that I could not be expected to tailor any of my efforts as mayor specifically to the African American community or to any other particular ethnic group. In my view, an evenhanded approach toward Newark's residents would mean matching the greatest benefit to the greatest need.

This perspective had little support in the long-suffering minority community, as Junius Williams indicates in his reflections and in his highly critical assessment of Gibson's years in office, a book titled *Unfinished Agenda*.[6] It made no sense to Junius and his associates that Gibson couldn't see the urgency of moving first to deal with these concerns. Rather, Gibson's articulated commitment to being the mayor for all the people[7] mystified those who had labored to get him elected. Williams was harsh in his criticism of the Gibson administration's approach to leadership of a majority-minority city. He writes, "Assimilation and accommodation are two words I often think about even now and shake my head in regret for the pain and sense of futility they produced. These people, many of them my friends, wanted to be inside so bad that they were willing to give up all knowledge of recent history, just to achieve a seat at the table of mainstream politics in America."

The mayor's black and Puerto Rican critics maintained, as revealed in several reflections, that he seemed almost dismissive of the concerns that mattered most to the city's black and Puerto Rican political activists. Grizel Ubarry, a young Puerto Rican community activist during the Gibson era, forcefully makes the point in her reflections that Hispanics felt particularly mistreated by the mayor and his administration. Speaking about Puerto Rican community sentiment, she writes, "The Latino community's relationship with Newark's first black mayor was strained at best. . . . In a city where the minority populations—Puerto Ricans and blacks—desperately wanted a change, the two communities had for a brief period united and formed the Black and Puerto Rican Convention (coalition) to agree on issues important to both groups and to elect the city's first black mayor, Ken Gibson."

She states, however, that from the outset, things went awry. The Gibson ticket had a Puerto Rican candidate running for an at-large seat on the city council. That candidate, Ramon Aneses, was unsuccessful. Ubarry states that many in the Hispanic community thought that blacks had voted not for the entire ticket but selectively for blacks running for office, which undercut the spirit of cooperation and support engendered by the convention. Had Gibson, once in office, sought to build an inclusive relationship with the Puerto Rican community, she argues, this early setback could have been overcome. Instead, she posits,

> Dissatisfaction only increased when the mayor appointed just one official in his administration from the Puerto Rican community—to the position of deputy mayor, which many in the community viewed as mostly a weak and ceremonial position. With less than 2 percent of Latinos participating in the city's workforce during the mayor's first term, it was apparent that Puerto Ricans were shut out of jobs,

services, and training opportunities, as well as discriminated against and harassed by an all-white police force.

For most of Gibson's first term and for the most part thereafter, the Latino community remained invisible, voiceless, and powerless.

And according to Ubarry, Gibson seemed to lack an appreciation of the critical nature of the concerns of his Puerto Rican constituents. How could he, Puerto Rican community leaders argued, not realize that his first commitment had to be addressing the wide range of economic, social, and political inequities suffered by an important segment of the voters who had helped put him in office. And while Gibson was hailed for bringing into his administration a diverse group of bright young people, few of these young people were Puerto Ricans. In fact, Puerto Ricans had low visibility in the Gibson administration well into the 1980s.

Unlike Puerto Ricans, Newark's Italian population was not the least bit interested in Gibson's commitment to be the mayor for all the people. They gave him little, if any, credit for what he worked to achieve for all his constituents. Indeed, Italian community leaders, with the exception of political boss Steve Adubato Sr., sought to undermine Gibson's every effort. The heated opposition to Gibson continued throughout the mayor's first term in office and well into his second but began to abate as the second term neared its end. By that time, however, the city's Italian population had shrunk appreciably, and its most outspoken Gibson critics had moved on. As recounted by the Adubatos, Gibson forged a strong working relationship with Steve Adubato Sr., the husband of Fran and father of Steve Adubato Jr. Their relationship, according to Fran and Steve Jr., began when Steve Sr. choose to support Gibson over Addonizio in the 1970 mayoral race and continued thereafter. And Adubato's support of Gibson was met with scorn by his Italian neighbors. He and his family were castigated, called "nigger lovers," and worse. Adubato's wife, Fran, and son, Steve Jr., provide a vivid picture of what Gibson faced in Newark's

Italian community. Fran writes, "After the election, I remember thinking to myself, How will this new mayor ever be able to bring together such a racially divided city? I don't think he ever really captured full admiration or respect from the Italian American North Ward. He certainly never carried the ward in any of his subsequent bids for reelection."

Steve Adubato Jr. discusses how his father was reviled because of his support of Gibson's candidacy. He writes, "I remember death threats against my father that would come in the form of phone calls, pamphlets, and late-night visits from thugs. And it only grew worse over time. My father would rarely travel alone, as it was made clear to him that, as the local Democratic leader in our section of Newark, he was expected to support the Italian American incumbent mayor—even if this mayor was likely to go to jail."

Steve recounts how his father's position as a Gibson supporter impacted the entire family. He states,

> One day, when I was coming home from school and had forgotten my key, I decided to climb into the window of our house. As I approached, I saw a series of holes in the glass. At first, it wasn't clear what I was looking at, but I soon realized they were bullet holes—and they were facing the spot where my father's chair was located when he sat to watch television. I ran to a neighbor's house for help in tracking down my mother. Of course, this alarmed both her and my father, so for the remainder of the 1970 campaign, my two sisters and I were shipped out of our home to live with relatives in a town nearby.

Marie Villani, an at-large member of the city council, one of five white councilpeople and the only female member, reports in her reflections that her votes in support of Gibson's program caused her to suffer the wrath of some in the Italian community. She states that among the nasty things done to her, "the most vicious and hurtful act was the killing of our family dog. The pet was killed and left on our doorstep." While not completely sure, she suspected that Tony Imperiale, a major North Ward Gibson critic, was behind much of the mistreatment she suffered. The Gibson-Adubato relationship also was a constant source of anger to many of Gibson's black critics, Ron Rice and Sharpe James report in their reflections. Adubato, they maintained, accrued substantial benefits over the course of Gibson's tenure because of the support Adubato provided the mayor. Gibson acknowledges as much in his interview. He states that his support helped Steve Sr. achieve the success he enjoyed:

> Improving the prospects of the Italian community and protecting their interests in the city were Steve's primary goals. I think that he was very successful but primarily because of my help. If truth be told, I made him. I helped him get state and federal funding for his [North Ward] center's programs, but he made his programs work. He insisted on providing quality services, and because his programs were effective, he garnered the deep loyalty of the people the programs served. He used quality service delivery as a basis for building a powerful political organization. For my assessment, he was the only community activist to do so.

Despite Steve's support, it's fair to say that Newark's Italian residents, in general, never thought of Gibson as their mayor. In fact, the hostility continued after his first term. In 1974, when Gibson sought reelection, Steve Jr. states in his reflections, he encountered angry pushback after—at the urging of his father—he organized a "Youth for Gibson" campaign at his high school in the North Ward. He writes that he did his best to ignore it: "With little choice, I took up my father's challenge. Our group, with additional recruits from the neighborhood, produced and distributed pamphlets, lawn signs, and other campaign materials. There was still name-calling and threats, but by then I had taken to heart my father's sound advice: 'It's OK to be afraid, but never show it.'"

Perhaps surprisingly, Gibson's failure to respond sufficiently to Puerto Rican leaders' entreaties for inclusion also exacerbated the mayor's difficulty in the North Ward. Charles Auffant's reflections state convincingly how this came to be. He notes that Steve Adubato Sr. interceded on behalf of Puerto Ricans, becoming their strongest advocate in the halls of power. Auffant writes, "Always sensitive to changing demographics, Adubato had little interest in organizing the white/Italian or black community; instead, he concentrated his work and efforts on the burgeoning Puerto Rican community. Adubato used largesse provided by the Gibson administration to build the most powerful political machine in the city of Newark."

Puerto Ricans who gained access to city jobs, appointments to boards and commissions in Newark and Essex County and at the Newark Board of Education did so through Adubato; he was their benefactor. Puerto Ricans rewarded Adubato by giving him control of their vote. Auffant points out that "if you wanted the Puerto Rican vote in Newark, you need not see Puerto Rican politicians—there were none. You had to see Steve."

With Gibson in office, the political landscape, it was assumed, would surely change, and blacks would be ascendant, with an enhanced role for Puerto Ricans. The old order would be upended, blacks and their Puerto Rican colleagues would set the agenda, and the white community would have to cooperate, if its interests were to be protected. That was not to be, due to the failure of black political leadership to respond to the aspirations of the Puerto Rican community.

The now politically successful black community expected that local politics would produce outcomes for it that Irish and Italian politicians in years past had produced for their communities. Gibson, however, while committed to addressing black community concerns about access, economic opportunity, and education improvement, was not wedded to a strictly black agenda. As he settled into office, it appeared he wanted his administration to be viewed as evenhanded in its treatment of those seeking participation in and benefits from city government. Gibson was interested in black political participation but in the traditional sense. He was not, it became clear, into "black politics,"[8] an outgrowth of the black power movement of the 1960s that many of his black critics seemed to crave. Gibson wanted to preside as the mayor who got the garbage picked up and the trees trimmed. Forging a black political movement was the furthest thing from his mind. Indeed, Gibson charted a course that was suited to his quiet, deliberate, go-it-alone personality. Amiri Baraka, who had played a leadership role in the Black and Puerto Rican Convention that selected Gibson as its mayoral candidate, soon became Gibson's biggest critic. Baraka had opined that with Gibson's election, the city's institutions would be "nationalized" in favor of what he saw as the black nation, but four years later, he would label Gibson a "neocolonialist." Baraka complained that Gibson was "for the profit of Prudential, Public Service (Electric and Gas), the Port Authority and other huge corporations that run in and around and through and out of Newark paying little or no taxes" while the residents were ignored.[9]

Gibson maintained a safe distance from county politics, projecting an attitude that suggested he didn't have time to engage in that arena and lacked the desire to do so. It soon became clear that Gibson only intended to pursue peaceful coexistence with county Democratic Party leaders. It appears he felt that if he stayed out of county politics, the party bosses would not interfere with his operations.

Junius Williams offers comments regarding Gibson's lack of engagement with county politics. He writes,

> At one of our Community Development Administration (CDA) / Model Cities dinner meetings (while I was the director of Model Cities), Larry Coggins, a local organizer, came in looking much defeated. He said, "I told Ken he should let me organize the district leaders in Newark and throughout Essex County, to make Ken county Democratic Party chairman." Boom! There it was. Ken, as the "first

mayor," was the highest black elected official in New Jersey history and one of only a handful of black mayors in the country. . . . But Ken told Larry "no," and thus a once-in-an-era opportunity went by.

This arrangement of noninterference in county matters appeared to work. One theory explaining this peaceful coexistence between the mayor and party leaders, posited by some, was that Gibson simply looked the other way whenever county leaders invaded his turf.

While Gibson never embraced what some might call a black political ideology, something Baraka and others would have welcomed, he did attempt to broaden his political reach on two occasions. Eschewing engagement at the county level, he attempted two unsuccessful runs for governor, in 1981 and 1985.

Assessing Sixteen Years in Office

Ken Gibson's place in the history of the city he led should first be viewed in terms of the promises he made to Newark's voters in 1970 and which of those promises he kept during sixteen years in office. Second, it also should be viewed in terms of how effectively he managed the expectations his election raised among the formerly marginalized voters who had worked to put him in office. He set an agenda and made commitments during that first campaign, as I wrote in a 1981 article in the *New Jersey Reporter*, titled "Expectation and Reality: Reflections on the Gibson Decade." That agenda included "honesty and integrity in office, improvement in the delivery of municipal services, quality appointments to the Newark Board of Education, slum housing demolition and new housing construction, better police protection, and active participation by the city's business community in municipal government problem solving."

These policies and programs were not radical, as the article stated. I asserted that had they been, Gibson probably would not have received the endorsement of the *Newark Evening News*, then the most politically

influential newspaper in New Jersey. The agenda, in fact, was like that
of any chief executive of a struggling major city in America, except, perhaps for the racial overlay that colored every attempt to address it. The
expectations his election embodied, however, were a different matter. As
I wrote in the *New Jersey Reporter*, "Whether he knew it or not, Gibson
was considerably more than just a newly elected mayor." The article notes,
"Among Newark's populace and beyond, expectations soared; a Black man
was mayor. Better days were ahead. In a congratulatory telegram to the
new mayor, Senator George McGovern [Democratic candidate for president in 1972] hailed 'a new era of justice.' Coretta Scott King declared that
Gibson's election was a 'victory for justice, human dignity, brotherhood
and equality.'"

   Close examination of the reflections, augmented by other relevant
sources, allows us to discuss further Gibson's legacy as defined both by the
policy agenda he pursued and the extent to which he managed expectations. Moreover, this look will provide important insights about his role in
shaping Newark as we know it today.

PROGRAM INNOVATIONS

The reflections point to several concrete achievements Gibson rightly
claims as his and that were important advances for the city. These
accomplishments include advances in program development, mentoring of young talent, racial pace-setting, and for a while, governmental
integrity. In each of these areas, Gibson's contributions were considerable. The creation of the Office of Newark Studies (ONS), for example, a
policy-research and program-development entity situated as part of the
mayor's office but administered for the city by Rutgers University, was a
conduit for various policy experts to assist the administration without
becoming city employees. The director of the ONS, who functioned as a
member of the mayor's cabinet, managed a team of senior researchers,
policy analysts, and program-development specialists who focused on

issues identified by the mayor while being unencumbered by municipal bureaucracy.

The office was initially headed by Jack Krauskopf, a young Harvard-educated public-policy professional who worked for Carl Stokes, the first black mayor of Cleveland, Ohio, right after getting a master's degree in public affairs from Princeton's Woodrow Wilson School of Public and International Affairs. In his reflections, Krauskopf writes, "The office was a vehicle for foundations to collaborate in assisting the new city administration, and during my five years of experience, Mayor Gibson showed that he appreciated and respected it as a nonpolitical vehicle. I had access to the mayor's office and always felt that my rapport with Ken was strong."

Krauskopf discusses the role that the office played in the design and creation of the Newark Watershed Conservation and Development Corporation, an entity that managed Newark's thirty-five-thousand-acre watershed property in portions of Passaic, Morris, and Sussex Counties. It also initiated the study that ultimately led to the establishment of Newark Public Radio. Later, under my leadership as the second director of the office, it incubated the establishment of a crisis-intervention center called Newark Emergency Services for Families and managed the task force that proposed the establishment of New Jersey's program requiring state government to make payments in lieu of taxes to municipalities hosting state-owned properties.

Indeed, Gibson's first and second terms in office produced several major program innovations that were planned, launched, and successfully executed. These included the Housing Development and Rehabilitation Corporation (HDRC), a nonprofit entity created to develop and administer housing policies and plans for the city. Editor Robert Holmes, a graduate of Cornell and Harvard Law School, was recruited to head the HDRC; he writes in his reflections, "I remember my initial impressions. I was surprised that a position such as the head of housing policy would be entrusted to a recent law-school graduate with little relevant experience. I was further surprised to find that I was given tremendous latitude to hire staff and structure corporate policies. Though this was not at all what I expected to encounter in what I perceived to be a political appointment, here I was."

It also included Planned Variations, a two-year demonstration project testing the feasibility of implementing President Richard Nixon's revenue-sharing program in twenty cities across the nation. David Dennison, who had been recruited from New Jersey state government, where he had served as the director of the Model Cities Program and Community Development Administration, describes Planned Variations in his reflections: "The new two-year program . . . was designed to demonstrate the feasibility of community-development special-revenue sharing within existing Model Cities Programs. The program was designed to help cities better coordinate the use of federal funds in solving critical urban problems, help cities set local priorities, and reduce the red tape that comes with seeking and accepting federal grants."

This period also saw the creation of Gibson's most prized initiative, the network of health care centers that Dennis Cherot helped manage as discussed in his reflections. Each of these initiatives is discussed in the reflections provided by the individuals involved in their design, implementation, or day-to-day operations. Cherot, another young black public-policy professional, played an important role in addressing health and housing issues in the administration. In his reflections, he writes, "The highlight of my professional life was Mayor Gibson's appointment of me as the director of the city's department of health and welfare. It was an awesome responsibility; I was responsible for overseeing all municipal health issues and providing health services to thousands of needy residents. My portfolio included monitoring food safety, addressing communicable-disease issues, operating several health centers, and managing the municipal welfare department."

Some of these initiatives have stood the test of time and continue to provide valued services. The National Public Radio–affiliated WBGO is the New York metropolitan region's premier jazz outlet. Newark Emergency

Services for Families continues to provide crisis-intervention assistance to thousands of city residents daily. Newark's network of health centers also continues to serve as a source of health care for the city's low-income and poor residents. They remain testaments to the creativity and dedication of the men and women who Gibson attracted to his administration and who embraced his determination to meet the challenge of improving Newark's delivery of essential services.

Not all initiatives, however, have survived. The Watershed Conservation and Development Corporation was dissolved in 2013[10] after its executive director, a senior consultant, and one of its vendors were convicted of corruption charges. Its board was disbanded, and the city assumed responsibility for the management of the watershed area. And the HDRC, by the end of Gibson's time in office, had been merged with the city's development office.

Aside from the federally sponsored Planned Variations program, the demonstration that tested the applicability of federal revenue sharing to Model Cities communities, these program innovations during the Gibson era were developed to meet specific needs in Newark and were not replications of efforts under way in other places in the United States. And as such, they demonstrated the amazing capacity of individuals working to address myriad problems faced by an old, industrial, declining Northeastern rust-belt city. Just some of the programs mentioned in the reflections attest to this.

At the same time, these programs managed to shine a bright light on Newark's desperate need for massive financial assistance to address its challenges. Gibson might argue that he could have done more innovative things had the federal and state governments been more responsive to his request for funds. He does, however, acknowledge that the federal government did provide more funds to Newark after his election than had been the case in the years before he assumed office. Dave Dennison asserts that state and federal financial support provided valuable fiscal relief as Gibson sought to improve conditions for residents of his city. He writes, "We had flexibility in terms of how to spend large sums of state and federal funds but soon found that represented both a blessing and a curse. On the one hand, the administration could hire with considerable freedom, which meant that we could find work for many more people. On the other hand, that meant more people looking for a reward for their political support of the mayor than could possibly be accommodated."

One principal source of federal funds, in those early days, was the Economic Opportunity Act of 1964, the centerpiece of President Lyndon Johnson's "War on Poverty."[11] The war, however, began to lose support in the late 1960s and ended in 1974. Another War on Poverty initiative, the Model Cities Program,[12] and the Comprehensive Employment and Training Act (CETA)[13] were of considerable benefit to Newark, but they fell short both in terms of the amount of funds provided and in their duration. Later would come Nixon's revenue-sharing program—the no-strings, simple oversight federal program through which states and localities shared a portion of the tax receipts collected by the federal government—and the assistance programs of the Carter administration. Newark's fiscal plight was lessened but still looms large.

COORDINATING STATE, LOCAL, AND COUNTY RESOURCES

As Newark mayor, Gibson had to recognize which issues could be dealt with on a strictly local basis and which required working with the county, state, and other local governments. The relative success or failure of particular efforts was often seen differently depending on the vantage point of the evaluator. Diane Johnson, who was a field director in the Newark office of the U.S. Department of Housing and Urban Development during Gibson's time in office, suggests that his administration missed many opportunities to meet the needs of the city's residents. She states,

> I am of the mind that the city did not take anything close to full advantage of the financial and other opportunities available to it at the time.

In some ways, it is also a challenge for me to identify any particular person, including Mayor Gibson; department of city government; or ancillary city agency to blame for this underutilization of
programs. Overall, I would attribute the city's failure to fully utilize
available funding to three primary factors: (1) the proverbial "too
many cooks in the kitchen," (2) a general lack of sound planning,
and (3) a general lack of understanding of the value of certain programs and how they worked.

Johnson's perspective, it should be noted, is that of a federal bureau-
crat. David Dennison, the director of the Mayor's Policy and Development
Office (MPDO) offers a contrasting view:

> Early on, we concluded that jobs, the education and training of
> employees, and service delivery would be necessary for the sustain-
> ability of the Gibson administration. Providing services to all the
> people was Gibson's stated goal. We knew, however, that he wanted
> us to place a special emphasis on enhancing the living conditions
> for black and Puerto Rican residents of the city. . . . We created a
> living, dynamic organization to create policy, planning, and imple-
> mentation programs, being adaptable as the environment we lived
> in changed. The results or outcomes over the years were highlighted
> by our ability to attract millions of dollars to the city that greatly as-
> sisted city departments and agencies in spite of the turbulence those
> flexible funds seemed to create.

Rufus Miles, former assistant secretary for administration of the U.S.
Department of Health, Education, and Welfare, in 1975, while teaching at
Princeton University, penned an essay titled "The Origin and Meaning of
Miles' Law," stating that "where you stand depends on where you sit."[14]
This law of the bureaucracy, which is intended to describe the changes
in point of view and behavior of public officials as they move from one

position to another, also helps us understand the different perspectives offered by Johnson and Dennison in describing Newark's utilization of the federal funds it received.

CULTIVATING DIVERSE YOUNG PUBLIC ADMINISTRATORS AMID ENTRENCHED RACIAL POLITICS

Gibson attracted a substantial cadre of talented, progressive young men and women who wanted to participate in helping revitalize one of the nation's oldest and most troubled cities. These people, who ranged in age from their early twenties to midthirties, were also excited by the fact that they were involved in a history-making experiment. Clearly, this was an experiment in black municipal leadership. Thus black and white, they came to the city from some of the nation's prestigious colleges and universities—Harvard, Princeton, Cornell, Rutgers, Yale, and Penn—and from federal and state government agencies. Others were drawn from community-based organizations where they had labored as community organizers, social-service providers, and social-justice advocates.[15] They populated the mayor's office and headed traditional municipal agencies and newly created offices and authorities. They worked long hours and reveled in the opportunity afforded them to put their skills to use in a place that valued what they had to offer. In his reflections, coeditor Holmes aptly refers to the mayor's early administration as "Gibson University"—a nod to the range of opportunities and experiences to which young public policy–oriented professionals were exposed.

When addressing Gibson's role as a mentor of young talent, several reflections, including those of Holmes and myself, highlight Gibson's efforts in this regard, especially in his first and second terms. Krauskopf, Cherot, and George Hampton also echo the sentiment that Gibson sought to surround himself with talented young people and supported them in their work. Krauskopf mentions several who worked with him at the Office of Newark Studies; among them were Terrence Moore, Mildred Barry

Garvin, Donald Harris, Bob Ottenhoff, Marty Klepper, and me. Dennis Sullivan, who served as Gibson's chief of staff during his first term, had a special relationship with the mayor. Sullivan worked as one of Gibson's aides in the 1970 campaign while completing his senior year at Princeton. During that period, he lived in Gibson's home.

The mayor's embrace of these young professionals was rewarded by their strong job performances. The track record established in program development and implementation was surely a source of satisfaction as Gibson attempted to navigate the maze of challenges his city faced. But as many of the reflections reveal, both significant victories and major defeats were met with the same stoic, reserved persona that was Gibson's trademark.

These young professionals helped the mayor tackle challenges in the areas of economic development, the delivery of basic services, school-district governance, police-department management, and minority hiring in Gibson's early years as Newark's chief executive.

PURSUING ECONOMIC PROGRESS: THE STARS WERE NOT WELL ALIGNED

It was clear from the outset of the Gibson administration that quality-of-life conditions in the city would not improve until economic development and job creation were given front-and-center attention. Early in his first term, Gibson and the business community reconstituted the Newark Industrial Development Corporation (NIDC), a public/private partnership formed during the Addonizio administration, and they jointly created the Newark Economic Development Corporation (NEDC). The new entity, like its predecessor, was charged with assisting local businesses and prospective new businesses by cutting government red tape, identifying vacant buildings that could be recycled for relocation or expansion purposes, and working with local financial institutions to secure capital needed by businesses for these purposes. Not until his second term, however, did the entity begin to show promise. By 1977, the NEDC had helped businesses secure 655,800 square feet of new or recycled space and stimulated the creation of 1,117 new jobs. And in the next two years, the agency went on to assist commercial and industrial projects worth $100 million, providing 2,435 new jobs. Yet Newark's unemployment statistics remained grim. In 1980, unemployment in the city hovered between 16 and 22 percent. When Gibson left office in 1986, unemployment statistics had not improved.

The city's manufacturing base had been eroding for decades when Gibson assumed office, and local government's efforts to stanch the outflow and attract replacement businesses were comparable to plugging holes in a badly damaged dam. Suburban office parks were attracting Newark's commercial businesses, and suburban malls with free parking were pulling retail establishments from the city. Besides their impact on jobs, these major shifts in business locations had a big impact on Newark's tax base, which in turn further limited the city's resource options. The attempts by the mayor and others to reverse the economic decline were not enough to overcome Newark's obvious difficulties.

But as Daniel O'Flaherty, a former aide to the mayor and now a professor of economics at Columbia University, points out, there were developments that were shaping the economic environment that local leaders in both the public and private sectors did not and, in some cases, probably could not grasp. O'Flaherty suggests that several of the more important factors in play included the opportunity that inflation afforded Gibson to wipe out the debt he inherited. At the same time, however, inflation made it more difficult to manage the cost of new debt, thereby constraining capital investment. He also argues that stagnating productivity growth, a massive regional economic slump, rising labor-force participation by women, and rising national crime were notable influences that shaped the Gibson era in Newark. O'Flaherty concludes, "For better or worse, these trends shaped his mayoralty. The changes came so incrementally that they were almost impossible to detect at the time—like the growth of grass—but they turned out to be very powerful."

O'Flaherty's reflections and historical evidence suggest that Gibson's efforts to halt Newark's economic-decline trajectory were doomed; they were overwhelmed by forces over which he had no control. Try as he might, the inexorable economic downward spiral of his city could not be reversed by the levers available to the mayor. He could tinker on the margins by helping local businesses and supporting job-creation activities, but he lacked the ability to do more. After sixteen years under Gibson, the city's unemployment rate had risen nearly 50 percent, its population had continued dropping, and it had no movie theaters and only one supermarket.

A Case in Point: Providing Basic Municipal Services—
Dealing with Limited Resources

The black community expected the provision of municipal services to improve substantially once Gibson was in charge. The city's predominantly black wards, residents felt, had been underserved by the Addonizio administration and those that preceded it. Gibson had campaigned to end the perceived mistreatment by upgrading the services provided to these wards. But the demand for city services was becoming more and more difficult to meet as municipal resources shrank and the city's tax base eroded. The contraction of the manufacturing, commercial, retail, and financial sectors put downward pressures on the city's ability to provide the services residents thought they deserved. Public safety, health services, garbage collection, street cleaning, tree trimming, and water and sewer services impacted the average resident's daily life and were the things they were quickest to complain about if they were not provided promptly. Gibson's commitment to improve municipal service delivery was sincere, but his ability to respond in a way that met the expectations of his constituents was constrained by limited resources. When he took office, he found himself saddled with a $65-million budget deficit. The federal and state funds he attracted to Newark could not help him address that problem inherited from the scandal-ridden Addonizio administration.[16]

Perhaps unfairly, some of Gibson's critics maintained that he tended to be more concerned about serving the residents of the city's North and East Wards, which were predominantly white, than in addressing the needs of South and Central Ward residents, who were predominantly black. This criticism was particularly strong with respect to the provision of municipal services but not so regarding the allocation of federal resources, which heavily favored the more distressed black wards of the city. Black community dissatisfaction with the provision of municipal services—in one instance, trash removal—was dramatized in the late summer of 1973 by a black Central Ward councilman, Dennis Westbrooks, who led a group of his constituents to city hall and dumped garbage on the steps of the municipal building. Gibson's commitment, as stated by him, to be the mayor for all the people, was belied, Westbrooks felt, by the favored treatment being given to the city's white residents.

As Dennison points out in his reflections, federal programs that brought money to Newark such as the Urban Development Action Grant (UDAG), Planned Variations, and the Comprehensive Employment and Training Act (CETA) helped the city address a wide range of needs, but until the enactment of the Community Development Block Grant (CDBG) program in 1974, basic municipal services were not the main activities the funds could be used to support. The CDBG program, which is still in operation today, is the longest-running program of the U.S. Department of Housing and Urban Development (HUD), providing funds that support activities such as affordable housing construction, antipoverty programs, and infrastructure development. Block-grant funds are subject to less federal oversight and are used at the discretion of the state and local governments and their subgrantees receiving the funds. The Model Cities Program, which preceded the CDBG program, also provided funding for a wide range of municipal services, but the services were available only in city neighborhoods that met certain federal eligibility requirements. By the end of Gibson's first term, however, Newark, in its entirety, was determined eligible for support under the program.

SCHOOL-BOARD APPOINTMENTS: DISAPPOINTMENTS GALORE

Gibson kept his promise to appoint blacks and Puerto Ricans to the Newark Board of Education. But the number of blacks appointed far outnumbered his Puerto Rican appointments. In fact, Franando Zambrana and Dr. Hilda Hidalgo[17] were Gibson's only Puerto Rican appointees in the years he exercised appointing authority.

Black school-board appointments notwithstanding, community leaders across the city became increasingly impatient with the school system's inability to provide students a quality education. The mayor had promised in his 1970 campaign that improving Newark's public schools, which once were considered among the best in the nation, would be one of his highest priorities. Shortly after assuming office, however, Gibson had to contend with two teachers' strikes. The first of the two, which was of short duration, occurred in 1970; the second, in 1971, lasted almost three months, then the longest teachers' strike in the nation's history. Once the strike ended, Gibson established an education task force with members drawn from Newark's key public-school stakeholders. He asked the group to recommend steps that he, in collaboration with other stakeholders, should take to achieve the city's educational improvement goals. The task force's value was principally that it provided a forum in which those involved in the system and those impacted by its failure could discuss their concerns about educational quality without shouting at each other.

Reverend Dr. James A. Scott, the pastor of Newark's second-oldest black church and one of its largest such churches, whom Gibson asked to chair an education task force, mentions two miscalculations:

> As I look back, I realize that the task force could do little to change the infrastructure of schools. Our optimism began to pale as we tackled our job. We examined reading programs and asked ourselves what could be done on a short-term basis to improve achievement. We were hampered by two decisions: first, we feared being caught

up in hostility—and losing focus—if we interacted too closely with school personnel, administrators, and teachers; second, we thought that we understood what community residents, especially parents, wanted schools to do.

The short timeline and incessant demands on schools (teacher strikes, charges against key administrators, threats of state takeover, and ploys to reform that fizzled) shifted the ground of our investigation and left us looking helpless.

Dr. Scott suggests that in attempting to structure innovative solutions to Newark's public-school failures, the task force may have overlooked important assets present in the system. He posits:

Perhaps our most serious failure was not examining the effective or successful programs that actually existed in Newark's schools. We were aware that some schools, including a few in what were considered ghettoes, performed at or above standards set for Newark schools and, in some cases, surpassed national averages. We didn't examine the role of school leadership, for, if done poorly, we worried that could have been too easily misinterpreted, hardening judgments about why schools fail. I don't mean that the task force overlooked school leadership, but we didn't examine it closely enough to isolate some desirable variables that could be considered while evaluating and helping other schools.

Gibson and others who pushed for urban education reform argued that the mayor's inability to achieve improvement in the system's performance had more to do with inadequate resources to do the job than with the quality of mayoral oversight. Perhaps that view has some merit given that subsequent efforts—first by an elected Newark school board and then by a state takeover of school systems in Jersey City, Paterson, and Newark—did not produce appreciable positive change.

Gibson's appointees to the Newark school board were unable to provide the leadership required to produce the mayor's promised turnaround.
Vickie Donaldson, then a twenty-three-year-old recent Rutgers–Newark
graduate, whom Gibson appointed to the school board, in her reflections offers insight into some of the challenges the system confronted:
"The school board was the largest employer in the city, with more than
one hundred school buildings and several thousand employees, serving a
population that was increasingly African American. A school system once
known as one of the best in the nation became the focus of attention as the
transition from white control to black control began."

Donaldson also points out that school-board meetings were chaotic,
often hotbeds of political protest, community controversy, and cries for
economic parity and empowerment. What Donaldson does not state
explicitly but alludes to is the fact that board members were much more
concerned with and focused on matters of resource allocation—how
the spoils of being in control were allotted—that is, who got jobs and
contracts—than they were with education policy and pedagogy. She
makes clear, however, that she did not participate in the patronage arena
and operated in the area of policy but that she was in the minority. She
states that in her six years of service on the board, the mayor advanced
many issues that she could not support—mostly personnel issues.

Larry Hamm's experience on the board highlights the extent to which
the cultural and political issues Donaldson mentioned impacted board
member participation. In his reflections, Hamm, the board member who
Gibson appointed right out of high school, suggests that he and the mayor
were unable to get on the same page regarding the system's educational
priorities and how its challenges should be addressed. Hamm states that
his close association with Amiri Baraka probably contributed to the may-
or's dissatisfaction with his school-board service.[18] Gibson did not reap-
point Hamm to a second term and, as stated in his reflections, Hamm was
aware that the mayor considered his appointment to the board the worst
decision of his time in office.

Gibson's appointees made little, if any, progress in meeting black community expectations of marked improvement in the delivery of education services to their children. It had been assumed that with blacks in charge of the schools, the problems that had plagued the system and prevented it from meeting the educational needs of black children would be swiftly corrected. But change did not come. The board was unable to craft and implement educational reforms that would transform the schools. After several years of no measurable improvement, parents and community leaders began to conclude that the problem was Gibson's selection of individuals to lead the system. The board-member selection process became a major issue when Gibson sought reelection in 1974. The control he exercised through his appointive power was questioned, and a push for the election of school-board members by Newark voters took shape. Despite this, Gibson was easily reelected to office because his opponent was the black community's nemesis, Anthony Imperiale. In 1975, in a referendum the year after his reelection, the city's voters chose to end mayoral appointment of school-board members and place their selection in their own hands.[19] The change did not, however, produce a change for the better—when Gibson left office in 1986, the system was still failing. High school dropout rates were among the highest in the state, and student test scores were among the lowest.

POLITICS OF POLICING IN A RACIALIZED ENVIRONMENT

Relations between the city's black and Puerto Rican communities and the Newark Police Department were extremely bad when Gibson assumed office. It had been just three years since the city's 1967 rebellion, an event that was precipitated by the police arrest and beating of John Smith, a black cab driver. The root cause of the rebellion, however, went much deeper than a reaction to a single police action. Complaints about police treatment of minorities were common, but little attention had been given the outcry. The July 12 uprising that lasted five days, during which twenty-six

lives were lost, 750 individuals were injured, and more than one thousand
were jailed and in which property damage exceeded $10 million,[20] was
an expression of anguish, an indication that the black community had
reached its limit with respect to police mistreatment.

Once Gibson took over as the city's chief executive, his first major
appointment was of a police director, an appointment that broadly stirred
strong emotions. Indeed, Gibson's selection of John L. Redden, the deputy
police chief, a white officer with twenty-three years of service in the department, who had been the commander of a special gambling enforcement
unit, enraged both blacks and whites. Blacks were upset because Redden
was white; whites were upset because his record, as reported by Fred Cook
of the *New York Times*, "seemed to say he was the kind of man no politician could control."[21] On the day Gibson was to be inaugurated, the city
council, in a nine-to-zero vote, refused to confirm Redden. The mayor, as
reported by Robert Curvin, thereupon, threatened to tell the thousands
of people standing in front of city hall awaiting his inauguration what the
council had done. Fearing an adverse reaction from the crowd, the council
backed down and approved Redden's appointment by a vote of seven to
two.[22]

Gibson has said that he never regretted his appointment of Redden
and that he had complete faith in his honesty and ability. Moreover, the
mayor said that he felt a black police director would have been sabotaged
by a white police department.[23] Redden lasted as police director until overwhelmed by the turmoil surrounding the construction of Kawaida Towers,
a low-income housing complex sponsored by Amiri Baraka in the city's
predominantly Italian North Ward. The episode led him to resign.[24] Redden assigned blame for the turmoil to Baraka because of his insistence
that the project be built in the heart of the Italian community, but he
also criticized Gibson and the political leadership of the city for creating
the situation.[25] Gibson then appointed Edward Kerr, a black lieutenant in the
department, to the director's position, but he too had a short term. As
recounted in the reflections provided by Hubert Williams, who succeeded

Kerr as the police director, Kerr's leadership of the department was constrained by police officers who previously had authority over him and who
would again have authority over him when he returned to his civil-service
position as a lieutenant. Williams's appointment in 1974, however, lasted
until 1985, when he resigned to assume the presidency of the Washington,
DC–based Police Foundation.

During Williams's tenure, according to his reflections, the department made concerted efforts to address the issue of corruption, which
had been alluded to by the New Jersey Governor's Select Commission on
Civil Disorders following the 1967 rebellion. He also implemented policies
that reduced the use of deadly force and abuse of authority and strengthened polices that advanced accountability and the effective use of police
resources. Williams made the department the laboratory for early studies key to the evolution of community policing through a national nonprofit think tank he eventually headed called the Police Foundation—for
example, *The Newark Foot Patrol Experiment* and a federally funded fear-
reduction experiment.[26]

Gibson's appointment of Williams as police director was probably one
of his best. Williams's eleven-year tenure was marked by a commitment
to evidence-based policing and the promotion of community policing.
While tension between the police department and Newark's minority
communities did not disappear, it did subside. Citizen complaints about
police abuse or mistreatment were substantially lessened during this
period, something for which Williams takes pride.

Still, there were complaints about the department's inability to get
Newark's crime rate under control. Paula Span, in a 1983 *New York Times
Magazine* article, wrote that the department had been stripped by layoffs
of a third of its 1974 strength, but at the same time, the arrest rate per officer had increased. Yet the number of major crimes, reduced from record
highs in 1980 and 1981, was roughly the same in 1982 as it was in 1970, when
Newark's population was higher.[27] Under Williams's leadership, solid gains
were made by the department in police-community relations, but efforts

to put a dent in the crime rate were largely unsuccessful. In Williams's view, crime-reduction efforts were undercut by the city's twin demons: poverty and unemployment. What, Williams asked, can the police do about poverty, about unemployment? The answer is nothing, and Williams says that police have stopped lying about being able to reduce crime if only given more dollars and more manpower.[28]

PUBLIC-SECTOR MINORITY EMPLOYMENT

Residents of the city's black and Puerto Rican neighborhoods expected that once Gibson became mayor, municipal and school-district employment opportunities would be substantial. It was assumed that jobs in city agencies and with the school system would finally be open to those who, for reasons of race or ethnicity alone, had been excluded. But Gibson faced two major obstacles that made his ability to meet those expectations, insofar as municipal government jobs were concerned, difficult if not impossible. In the first instance, Gibson was confronted with a $60-million budget deficit when he entered office in 1970.[29] The city's finances were in shambles, and raising taxes was not an option, as Fred Cook points out in his July 25, 1971, New York Times article, since property taxes were already at a virtually confiscatory level. Taxes, he said, on a small $15,000 home ran to $1,000 or more a year. And the city lacked other sources of revenue.[30] Under such fiscal constraints, it simply was not in the cards for Gibson to launch a massive hiring program. There was no money to bring on additional employees. At best, Gibson could address the expectation of enhanced job opportunities for his minority supporters by laying off holdover staff from the previous administration and replacing them with his supporters. But because of the municipal budget deficit, Gibson already faced the prospect of having to lay off four hundred city employees. To help the city raise additional revenue, the New Jersey Legislature allowed Newark to impose a payroll tax, and that, along with a surplus available in the separate water department, closed the deficit.

Moreover, replacing Addonizio staff with Gibson appointments was constrained by the second obstacle limiting the employment of sizable numbers of black and Puerto Rican Newarkers: state civil-service regulations that governed the hiring and firing of municipal employees were rigid and strictly enforced. Applicants for most municipal jobs had to take an exam that assessed the extent to which the applicant met the requirements needed to perform the job. The applicant's score on the exam determined the individual's rank among all applicants for the job. The higher the individual ranked, the more likely that person would be offered employment. Blacks and Puerto Ricans, who, in most cases, were unfamiliar with the civil-service process and were the products of the failing Newark public schools, tended not to do well on the exams and, therefore, were not competitive. Moreover, civil-service rules specified the conditions under which city employees could be terminated, rules that mandated a series of steps documenting an unsatisfactory job performance.

Constraints were less severe in securing jobs for minorities in the school system, but they existed there as well. In the first instance, the mayor had to work through his appointees on the school board to hire people. Gibson's track record in obtaining the support of board members on personnel matters in the early years was uneven. He battled his appointees often, as Vickie Donaldson and Fred Means explain in their reflections. The pushbacks the mayor received when some of his appointees were asked to approve particular board agenda items, which tended to be personnel or contract requests, were frequent. Indeed, in some instances, the mayor's patronage requests competed with the interests of individual board members. The way forward in providing jobs for the city's expectant minority population, in view of these obstacles, appeared quite bleak, but a way forward was identified, thanks to the War on Poverty.

While President Lyndon Johnson's War on Poverty began to wane after the 1960s, enough energy remained during Gibson's first term to allow Newark to get its share of federal funding under the program. The Model Cities and other antipoverty funds flowing from the federal government could not be commingled with the city's tax revenue; they had to be managed separately. The Addonizio administration had established a parallel city bureaucracy, the Community Development Administration (CDA), whose director reported directly to the mayor to administer the federal money coming to the city. Gibson and his team maintained this arrangement, much to the chagrin of the city's business administrator.[31] Dave Dennison, who was the deputy director of the CDA from 1970 to 1972 and headed the agency from 1972 to 1978, describes, in his reflections, the comprehensive nature of the CDA's role in city operations. The agency had as its purview city planning, manpower development, economic development, and the Model Cities Program. And through the CDA and the federal funds it managed, the mayor was able to respond to some of his supporters' requests for city jobs. Dennison, who had been a state government official prior to joining the Gibson administration, persuaded civil-service officials to allow the administration some flexibility in its hiring practices. State officials desirous of being of some assistance to the Gibson administration acquiesced. Most of the positions that Gibson's supporters filled had their civil-service examinations delayed or postponed for extended periods. In the interim, the CDA put proposed new hires who required civil-service certification through training programs that equipped them with the information and skills necessary to pass the exams when taken.

CDA-managed antipoverty and community-development funds, which were primarily federal but also included some state grants, provided Gibson with the means to deliver on his promise to make employment opportunities available in city government for Newark's minorities. However, blacks were the principal beneficiaries of these jobs; Puerto Ricans were much less likely to obtain employment. By the time Gibson's tenure in office had come to an end, though, opportunities for both blacks and Puerto Ricans to secure jobs in all city agencies had become common. But in the early days of the administration, federal funds were key to the mayor's keeping of his political promise.

MANAGEMENT OF EXPECTATIONS

While Gibson's policy and program agenda were daunting, addressing his supporters' expectation that his election heralded the beginning of a major change in the social, economic, and political order in the nation was even more daunting. Much like Barack Obama, America's first African American President,[32] the challenge of managing those expectations was both exhilarating and frustrating. Gibson's early proclamation that "wherever American cities are going, Newark will get there first" was probably an expression of his belief that he was, indeed, in the vanguard of reordering urban American possibilities. But the reflections suggest that although the mayor achieved some success in advancing his policy agenda in his first term, Gibson quickly abandoned any interest in meeting expectations that were beyond what the typical mayor should be expected to address.

A PLACE IN NEWARK'S HISTORY

New Jersey's largest city, located in the shadows of New York City, has in recent years begun to show signs of rejuvenation. Among the developments that suggest improvement include a sizable increase in the construction of unsubsidized middle-income and even some luxury housing, a booming arts and culture industry, enhanced private investment in the central business district, and an ever-expanding higher-education and health care infrastructure. Each of these developments may make an important contribution to Newark's sense of renewal. But progress comes slowly.

The past fifty years have not been easy for this city of 275,000 people. Ken Gibson's election as its first black mayor in 1970, three years after the calamitous Newark Rebellion, was viewed by many as possibly the beginning of a revival. But was it? Unfortunately, Newark's difficulties continued for years. But perhaps Mayor Gibson laid a foundation for change or at least gave hope for a while to a city regarded as hopeless.

If Newark, in fact, does have a brighter future, is Gibson to be recognized for the contribution he made to it a half-century ago?

In the introduction, Robert Holmes asked several questions about how we should evaluate Gibson's sixteen years as mayor. To what extent did the mayor fulfill his election promise? How might we view Gibson's historical significance? What is a historic figure? The reflections in this book indicate that Gibson was able, in his early days, to effectuate a number of important initiatives dealing with personnel, programs, and policies.

For a troubled city like Newark, his success in attracting talented, young black and white public-minded professionals was impressive. The talent he assembled was extraordinary and made working for city government exciting and productive. Many of these talented young people remained to serve in his second term, moving on to make their marks with bigger jobs in the public and private sectors. The reflections also have noted a host of significant innovations, including the creation of the Newark Watershed Conservation and Development Corporation (NWDC), the Housing Development and Redevelopment Corporation (HDRC), Newark Emergency Services for Families (NESF), the network of health centers, Newark Public Radio Inc. (WBGO), the New Jersey Payment in Lieu of Taxes program, and the Mayor's Planning and Development Office (MPDO). These initiatives enabled the administration to provide a wide range of critical services to Newark residents using federal and state government resources.

Gibson also achieved success in responding to his campaign promise to improve police services. After a couple false starts, he found a capable leader for the police department. Once Hubert Williams, a young police officer with a law degree, was installed as the police director, police productivity, effectiveness, and efficiency improved, as did police-community relations. The mayor also can be credited with fulfilling another campaign promise—finding jobs in city government for his supporters, which he did with funding from federal programs, He pushed the state to moderate its strict civil-service rules, which in turn allowed the employment of more minorities in city government. This was all to the good.

All these accomplishments allowed Gibson to rightly claim that he was working to fulfill as many promises as conditions would allow. And conditions were daunting. Facing a substantial budget deficit as he entered office, he struggled to make ends meet. He closed the deficit with the help of the state legislature, however, when lawmakers granted the city the authority to impose a local tax. But adding an additional tax on an already heavily taxed municipality eventually proved to be counterproductive.

Consequently, Gibson struggled to meet the municipal service needs of his city as its tax base continued shrinking. Abandoned houses dotted the city's landscape, and virtually no new housing was being constructed. With respect to education- and government-reform promises, Gibson ultimately fell short. His appointments to the Newark Board of Education were unable to turn the school system around. Board members spent too much time securing school-system jobs and contracts for their supporters. Gibson's status as someone committed to clean government faded over time and was seriously tarnished at the end of his second term when he was indicted for political corruption. Gibson was acquitted, but the damage was done. Perhaps what was expected of Ken Gibson was unreasonable.

Clearly, he tried to assume the mantle of municipal leadership at a time when Newark was at its nadir. He was an untested nonpolitician whose stoic demeanor served him well in some instances but not in others. He brought hope to some, at least for a while. An activist segment of the black population hoped to ascend under Gibson's leadership. Newark's civic life, this group believed, could be shaped by tenets of the black power movement. And the Puerto Rican community expected to participate in the changed political environment and see conditions improved for its members. But both groups were disappointed; neither saw their dreams fulfilled. In fact, Gibson was accused by erstwhile supporters of paying too much attention to white interests while ignoring black community needs and Puerto Rican aspirations.

Despite the mixed grades, we suspect that history will be kind to Kenneth Gibson. He will likely be regarded as a man who strove to make a difference but was limited, if not overwhelmed, by near-impossible challenges. He is, rightly, a historic figure because he achieved a major political milestone when he became Newark's first black mayor. Newark may have a better future now, and Kenneth Gibson's role in its attainment will likely be hotly debated.

NOTES

1. Amiri Baraka (1934–2014), known as Imamu Amiri Baraka in 1970, was an African American writer of poetry, drama, fiction, essays, and music criticism. His career, which addressed themes that ranged from black nationalism to white racism, spanned fifty years. After founding the Black Arts Repertory Theater/School, Baraka, in 1965, left Harlem and returned to Newark, where he was born and raised. Describing himself as a "black cultural nationalist," he broke away from the predominantly white Beat movement and became critical of the pacifist and integrationist civil rights movement. In opposition to the peaceful protests inspired by Dr. Martin Luther King Jr., Baraka believed that a physical uprising must follow the literary one.

2. Rick Rojas and Khorri Atkinson, "Five Days of Unrest That Shaped, and Haunted, Newark," *New York Times*, July 12, 2017, A20.

3. Donald Katz, Audible's founder, explained the Newark location when he said, "The vision behind the move was to try to combine a missionary, disruptive, technology-driven company with Newark's transformation. I consider the Newark move one of the best decisions we've made as a company."

4. "Newark, NJ Population History: 1840–2017," Usbiggestcities.com, accessed June 31, 2019, http://www.usbiggestcities.com/city/Newark-nj.

5. Newark's Ironbound section is located between the Pennsylvania Train Station and Newark Liberty International Airport and abuts Port Newark, the marine terminal operated by the Port Authority of New York and New Jersey. While economically stable, it is quite congested and environmentally challenged.

6. Junius Williams, *Unfinished Agenda: Urban Politics in the Era of Black Power* (Berkeley, Calif.: North Atlantic, 2014), 248.

7. Gibson would suffer considerable criticism from some blacks for stressing his oft-repeated commitment to serving as the "mayor for all the people." The critics maintained that the phrase implied that he cared more about being perceived as evenhanded in addressing the concerns of black and white Newarkers than advancing the interests of the black and Puerto Rican voters who had elected him to office.

8. The term *black politics* refers to political behavior informed by the black power movement of the 1960s. The movement promoted achieving self-determination for people of African descent. It emphasized racial pride and the creation of black political and cultural institutions to promote black collective interests and advance black values. In the political sphere, it advocated people coming together to form a political force and either electing representatives or forcing their representatives to speak to their needs. "Stokely Carmichael," *King Encyclopedia*, Martin Luther King Jr. Research and Education Institute, Stanford University, California, accessed June 30, 2019, https://kinginstitute.stanford.edu/encyclopedia/carmichael-stokely.

9. Thomas Dolan, "Newark and its Gateway Complex, Part 3: A Weakened City," *Newark Metro*, 2008, https://www.newarkmetro.rutgers.edu/reports/display.php ?id=17&page=3.

10. David Giambusso, "Newark Watershed Dissolves, Leaving City to Manage Water for 500,000 Customers," *Star Ledger*, March 26, 2013.

11. The War on Poverty is the unofficial name for legislation first introduced by U.S. president Lyndon B. Johnson during his State of the Union Address on January 8, 1964. This legislation was proposed by Johnson in response to a national poverty rate of 19 percent. The speech led the U.S. Congress to pass the Economic Opportunity Act, which established the Office of Economic Opportunity to administer the local application of federal funds targeted against poverty. The War on Poverty waned after the 1960s.

12. The Model Cities Program was another element of Johnson's Great Society and War on Poverty. Legislation in 1966 resulted in the creation of more than 150 five-year-long Model Cities experiments to develop new antipoverty programs and alternative forms of municipal government. The federal urban aid program succeeded in fostering a new generation of mostly black urban leaders. The nation, however, moved to the right after the riots of the late 1960s, which led to a shift in goals to brick-and-mortar housing and building projects. The Model Cities Program ended in 1974.

13. The Comprehensive Employment and Training Act was enacted by Congress and signed into law by President Richard Nixon on December 28, 1973. The program provided funds to local governments to train workers and provide them with jobs in the public services. It offered work to those with low incomes and to the long-term unemployed as well summer jobs to low-income high school students. The act was intended to decentralize control of federally controlled job-training programs, giving more power to the individual state governments. It was replaced by the Job Training Partnership Act nine years later.

14. Michael McKinney, "Miles' Law and Six Other Maxims of Management," Leadershipnow.com, https://www.leadershipnow.com/leadingblog/2008/02/miles _law_and_six_other_maxims.html.

15. Among the young talent Gibson recruited were: Dennis Sullivan, a white Princeton undergraduate alum who lived in Gibson's home while working in the 1970 mayoral campaign; Samuel Shepard, a black Oberlin undergraduate and Princeton University's Woodrow Wilson School of Public and International Affairs graduate school alum; George Hampton, a black Rutgers University–Newark alum; Jerome Harris, a black Rutgers University–New Brunswick undergraduate alum; Thomas Massaro, a white Harvard undergraduate alum; Ira Jackson, a white Harvard undergraduate alum; Jack Krauskopf, a white Harvard undergraduate and Princeton Woodrow Wilson School graduate school alum; Junius Williams, an Amherst undergraduate and Yale Law School alum; Robert Holmes, a black Cornell undergraduate and Harvard Law School alum; Richard W. Roper, a black Rutgers University–Newark undergraduate and Princeton's Woodrow Wilson School graduate school alum; Hubert Williams, a black graduate of the John Jay College of Criminal Justice and Rutgers Law School; Sheila Oliver, a black graduate of Lincoln University and Columbia University's graduate school; Dave Dennison, a former federal government and New Jersey State government official; Dennis Cherot, a black Fordham undergraduate alum; and Carl Sharif, a community activist and prominent member of Newark's Muslim community.

16. Fred Cook, "Mayor Gibson Says—'Wherever the Central Cities Are Going, Newark Is Going to Get There First,'" *New York Times*, July 25, 1971.

17. Franando Zambrana was a Puerto Rican community activist, and Hilda Hidalgo, PhD, was a member of the Rutgers University–Newark faculty. Zambrana's tenure as a board member was uneventful, but Hidalgo was a constant, vocal critic of the Newark school system's inability to adequately address the needs of Puerto Rican students.

18. Indeed, Baraka's influence on Hamm probably shaped his decision to change his name to Adimu Chunga.

19. Direct election of school-board members by the voters did not produce the desired improvement in the performance of Newark's schools. The state, which provided hundreds of millions of dollars in education aid to Newark's schools, took control of the school system in 1995. Local control of the system was restored in 2018. Board member are still elected by the voters.

20. Tabitha Wang, "Newark Riot (1967)," June 17, 2008, https://www.blackpast .org/african-american-history/newark-riot-1967/.

21. Fred Cook, "Mayor Gibson Says."

22. Robert Curvin, *Inside Newark: Decline, Rebellion, and the Search for Transformation* (New Brunswick, N.J.: Rutgers University Press, 2014), 161.

23. Curvin, *Inside Newark*, 161.

24. Williams, *Unfinished Agenda*, 303.

25. Curvin, *Inside Newark*, 161.

26. "Hubert Williams to Retire as Police Foundation President," *Crime Report*, March 27, 2012, https://thecrimereport.org/2012/03/27/2012-03-hubert-williams-to-retire-as-police-foundation-presi/.

27. Paula Span, "Newark's Failing Dream," *New York Times Magazine*, October 2, 1983.

28. Span, "Newark's Failing Dream."

29. Mark Krasovic, *The Newark Frontier: Community Action in the Great Society* (Chicago: University of Chicago Press, 2016), 283.

30. Cook, "Mayor Gibson Says."

31. All city operating departments and agency heads reported through the business administrator to the mayor. The city ordinance that created the Community Development Administration (CDA) exempted it from this reporting relationship. This arrangement was a major factor in the resignation of Gibson's first business administrator, Cornelius Bodine, in 1973 (Sandra King, "Bodine Quits, 'Untenable' Position," *Newark Star Ledger*, October 31, 1973).

32. By 2008, when Barack Obama was elected president, the accepted term in use to describe individuals of his racial/ethnic background was no longer black but was instead African American.

AFTERWORD

Robert C. Holmes

As we set out to explore Mayor Kenneth Gibson's legacy in Newark, we were put in mind of Spanish American philosopher George Santayana's famous warning: "Those who cannot remember the past are condemned to repeat it." We are not historians, and so we determined to add to the memory of the past, the Gibson era, by having the important people who were there at the time give us their reflections. Our approach is informed by the West African griot tradition. Among other official duties, griots, who were often known for their exceptional memories, would transmit the story of their people to future generations. While we make no such claims for our own memories, the collective memories of the key figures at that historical moment, when combined, present a broad picture of the Kenneth Gibson era. Our timing was both deliberate and fortuitous. We felt that due to the age of many of our contributors, these past three years might present the last best chance to record their voices. So many of those who were there at the time contributed enthusiastically and gave us their remarkably clear recollections. Sadly, several of these same individuals have since passed on, and others are no longer able to articulate their thoughts: Al Koeppe, Monsignor William Linder, and Kenneth Gibson are gone, and several others gave us their last memories of Newark during this critical moment in its past—the election and tenure of its first African American mayor.

Through his mayoralty, Kenneth Gibson changed society's perception of African American politicians and, along with some of his contemporaries, paved the way for the vital participation of African Americans in city, state, and national politics. New York City mayor Fiorello Laguardia, an Italian American with a Jewish mother, ranked first in a Penn State study (cited in the introduction) rating the best mayors of all time. Laguardia was seen as "a symbol of ethnic probity and honesty" and an "antidote to the widespread public view that ethnic politicians and crooked politicians were one and the same and part of the problem of big cities."[1] While each American ethnic group seems to need to prove its own worthiness of political representation, it seems unarguable that prior to the Gibson era, African American politicians faced greater challenges in convincing the voting populace that they were capable of good governance.

To see the impact of Mayor Kenneth Gibson, we hear from the three mayors, all African Americans, that followed him in Newark. In his reflections, Sharpe James put it this way: "Ken Gibson mixed the mortar for sixteen years, and I followed by laying the bricks for a better and more prosperous Newark." On the WBGO Newark radio program, *Newark Now*, former mayor Cory Booker said of Ken Gibson's era in Newark that "he was able to make a way out of no way." Booker went on to say that Gibson believed things (about what could be accomplished in Newark) that other people could not believe were even possible and that Gibson had to fight battles that "I did not have to face." On the same program, current mayor Ras Baraka echoed now Senator Booker's comments when he said with respect to evidence of a Newark renaissance that "Gibson set the groundwork" and we have now come "full circle." Beyond New Jersey, it seems likely that a young Barack Obama, on seeing examples like Kenneth Gibson, gained fuel for the "audacity of hope" that led to his two-term presidency.

While Gibson was an inspiration to young African American politicians, we wonder if he positively affected other political aspirants and citizens. Was he, as he famously claimed to be, "a mayor for all the people?"

In our recent interview, former New Jersey governor and Dutch American Tom Kean said of Mayor Gibson that "he was one of the giants" and that "we younger politicians looked up to him." Yet while Gibson surely did have some crossover appeal among both politicians and the electorate, in a racially divided city like Newark, could he possibly have believed that he could—to paraphrase President Lincoln—please all of the people all of the time? The simple answer is probably not. While there is plenty of documentation within this volume concerning Mayor Gibson's nonpolitical, sometimes awkward, nature and approach to political power, he clearly understood his—and any politician's—ultimate limitations. As the Greek fabulist Aesop put it, "If you try to please all, you please none." So maybe Mayor Gibson's famous declaration was more about his goodwill and willingness to work hard and faithfully for all the people of the city he loved.

Governor Kean says of Mayor Gibson simply that "he was one of the good people." This book contains copious examples, both in the reflections and in editor Richard Roper's conclusion, that such a brief and benign assessment might need to be qualified. Yet Mayor Kenneth A. Gibson does stand as an example, like Laguardia, of a politician who changed public perception about the ability of his ethnic group to govern and, probably, about its perception in general. And as former mayor of New York David Dinkins noted in chapter 1, in contrast to his own mayoralty, Gibson did this in a place that was engulfed in despair and on the brink of ruin.

History will continue to write and rewrite both its evaluation of Mayor Gibson's era in Newark and of the city itself. Probably, his reputation will wax and wane in some complicated relationship to the struggles that his city inevitably will face. That he will have a place in that history is certain. So we have added to the historical record from which future historians, griots, students, and other readers can continue to make and refine their own assessments.

Newark, New Jersey
January 2019

NOTE

1. "America's Big-City Mayors: The Experts Name the Best and the Worst," *New York Times*, accessed November 7, 2016, http://www.nytimes.com/books/first/h/holli-mayor.html.

NOTES ON
CONTRIBUTORS

DAVID NORMAN DINKINS, born in Trenton, New Jersey, in 1927, served the City of New York as its first African American mayor from January 1, 1990, until December 31, 1993. There has not since his term in office been another African American mayor in New York City. From 1986 to 1989, Dinkins served as the twenty-third borough president of Manhattan, and he earlier served as a member of the New York State Assembly. He also served as the president of the Board of Elections and as the city clerk for the City of New York. He was elected Manhattan borough president in 1985. Following his term as mayor, Dinkins was named a professor of public affairs at Columbia University's School of International and Public Affairs. He was a member of the board of directors of the U.S. Tennis Association and a member of the Jazz Foundation of America. Dinkins has served on the boards of the New York City Global Partners, the Children's Health Fund, the Association to Benefit Children, and the Nelson Mandela Children's Fund. He is also associated with the Black Leadership Forum and the Council on Foreign Relations and is chairman emeritus of the board of directors of the National Black Leadership Commission on AIDS. Dinkins earned a bachelor's degree cum laude from Howard University and a law degree from Brooklyn Law School.

FRED MEANS, EdD, was an early and active member of the Newark/Essex chapter of the Congress of Racial Equality (CORE) and was the founding president of the Organization of Negro Educators (ONE), an organization dedicated to pursuing educational change in the Newark school system and enhanced opportunities for African American school teachers. He was appointed by Ken Gibson to the Newark Board of Education in 1973 and struggled with the school system's inability—and in his view, unwillingness—to address the need for systemic change in the delivery of educational services to Newark's children and particularly its African American children. Means was denied admission to Rutgers, the State University of New Jersey, in 1951 but was admitted to New York University, where he received a bachelor's degree after serving in the army and returning to complete his education thanks to the GI Bill. He earned an Ed. from Rutgers in 1975 and began a teaching career at Jersey City State College, now New Jersey City University, where he taught courses related to the black experience in urban schools and was the dean of the School of Professional Studies. He retired in 1994.

ELTON HILL and Ken Gibson have been friends since they first met in 1940 at the Monmouth Street School, the first Newark school Gibson attended following his arrival in Newark at the age of eight. Hill was a key figure in the creation of the Ken Gibson Civic Association, the organization behind each of Gibson's mayoral—and other—campaigns for elective office. Following his election in 1970, Gibson appointed Hill to the position of assistant business administrator and later to the position of business administrator. Hill has a master's degree from Fairleigh Dickinson University.

HAROLD GIBSON is Ken Gibson's younger brother. He holds a JD degree from Seton Hall University and a BA degree from Rutgers University. Gibson served twenty-four years as a member of the Newark Police Department, from 1961 to 1985, rising to the rank of lieutenant. He became the public safety director for the City of Plainfield, New Jersey, in 1986 and, in the last two years of his five-year tenure in that position, also served as city administrator. He later spent five years as Union County's deputy manager and county public safety director. He subsequently served as chief of detectives in Essex County before returning to Union County as public safety director and then chief sheriff's officer. He is currently the supervisor of security for the Plainfield Municipal Utility Authority.

WILLIAM J. LINDER, PhD, has been a Catholic priest for fifty-four years. Monsignor Linder is the founder of the New Community Corporation (NCC), one of the nation's largest and most successful community-development corporations. Created in response to the aftermath of the 1967 Newark Rebellion, the NCC encompasses a network of housing, employment, day care, education, social services, job training, health care, economic development, and banking services to urban residents. Now known globally, the efforts of Monsignor Linder and the NCC are a model for successful grassroots community development across the nation and the world as documented in his doctoral dissertation "An Urban Community Development Model" (May 1988) at Fordham University. Through his many other academic endeavors, Monsignor Linder continues to consult internationally to community groups, bankers, and community development aficionados.

MARTIN A. BIERBAUM has a PhD in planning and public policy and a law degree, both from Rutgers University. In the 1970s and 1980s, Marty was a lecturer in urban studies and the director of an urban-studies program at Rutgers University–Newark. During that period, he also served as a policy advisor to the Essex County executive Peter Shapiro. Between 1987 and 2004, he served in policy-making posts in New Jersey State government, including as an assistant director of state planning in the treasury department, the director of environmental planning in the department of environmental planning, a quality-management coordinator, a special assistant to the commissioner for state plan implementation in the department of community affairs, and the deputy director of the governor's policy office.

He has taught courses in public policy, urban and environmental planning; public administration, and law at Rutgers University, the New Jersey Institute of Technology, the College of New Jersey, and the University of Maryland. He continues to be affiliated with the National Center for Smart Growth at the University of Maryland and the Bloustein School for Planning and Public Policy at Rutgers University.

ELIZABETH DEL TUFO has served Newark in many different capacities: as an activist, educator, preservationist, historian, and hostess. In 1974, Liz and a small group of people founded the Newark Preservation and Landmarks Committee with the goal of preserving and protecting one of Newark's greatest assets—its architecture. In 1976, she started the successful "Newark Tours" program to show those outside Newark that the city was worth saving. She was appointed the first Essex County director of cultural affairs in 1980. In 1986, Liz was appointed the first executive director of the Newark Boys Chorus School. Upon her retirement, the chorus had traveled to six foreign nations, establishing its role as "Newark's Finest Ambassadors." In 1990, Liz convinced the Newark city administration to create the Newark Landmarks and Historic Preservation Commission, which would by state and municipal ordinance protect all Newark sites on the historic registers. She served as commission chair for sixteen years.

ROBERT PICKETT received his law degree from the University of Michigan School of Law in 1972. Bob began his legal career in Newark at the firm of McCarter and English, one of New Jersey's largest and most prominent law firms. After leaving the firm in the mid-1970s, he became the general counsel to the Newark Board of Education and served in that capacity for several years.

Bob has served as an aide to U.S. vice president Hubert Humphrey and an assistant general counsel for education to Governor James Florio. He also was appointed as an administrative-law judge with the Administrative Court of New Jersey. While still active as a civil and criminal lawyer, Bob also is an on-air personality and cohost for New York City radio station WBLS's Sunday morning public-affairs program, *Open Line.*

GRIZEL UBARRY is a consultant in nonprofit management and community development. She is a 1971 graduate of Douglas College at Rutgers University. During the early years of the Gibson administration, she served as the director of ASPIRA of New Jersey, headquartered in Newark. ASPIRA, an organization founded in 1961, seeks to empower the Puerto Rican and Latino community through advocacy and leadership development of its youth. She subsequently worked for Essex County government before establishing in 1985 a consulting film that works with nonprofit organizations, community-development corporations, businesses, and financial institutions in the development of successful community revitalization projects. Her clients extend along the Route 95 interstate corridor from New York City to Miami, Florida. Grizel serves on the board of the Newark-based Victoria Foundation; on the board of the Fund for New Jersey, a public-policy-focused philanthropy; and on the board of the New Jersey Institute for Social Justice.

RICHARD W. ROPER is a public-policy consultant who has held senior-level positions in local, state, regional, and federal government agencies and has had experience in nonprofit organizations, private consulting, academic research, teaching, and administration. He served as the director of the Office of Newark Metropolitan Studies for the City of Newark, as a special assistant to U.S. Department of Commerce secretary Juanita Kreps, and as the director of the department's office of state and local government assistance in the Carter administration. For twelve years following his work with the federal government, Roper served as the director of the Program for New Jersey Affairs, the director of the Council on New Jersey Affairs, and a lecturer in public and international affairs at Princeton University's Woodrow Wilson School of Public and International Affairs. During his last four years at Princeton, he also served as an assistant dean at the Woodrow Wilson School. Following his years at Princeton, he served as a senior executive at the Port Authority of New York and New Jersey, from which he retired as the planning department director in 2010. Roper is a member of the Rutgers University Board of Governors; a trustee of the Fund for New Jersey; a trustee of La Casa de Don Pedro, a Newark-based community-development corporation; and a visiting associate at the Eagleton Institute of Politics at Rutgers University–New Brunswick.

DIANE JOHNSON began work for the New Jersey Office of Housing and Urban Development (HUD) in 1972. There she served as the director of the housing management division, deputy office manager, and acting office manager, and in 1994, she was appointed the director of HUD's Newark field office. In this latter capacity, she oversaw a staff of 126 and administered HUD funds in excess of $300 million. Following a thirty-year career at HUD, in retirement she became the chief of staff to the acting mayor of Newark, Luis Quintana, in 2014. She now serves as a housing consultant to several community-development organizations.

RICHARD CAMMARIERI began his community activism in Newark after graduating from Rutgers–Newark in 1973 and has remained active since then. He is the director for special projects with a focus on resident organizing, civic engagement, and public-policy awareness and advocacy at the New Community Corporation. His extensive experience in Newark grassroots community organizing and neighborhood policy development has included serving as executive director for the Newark Coalition for Neighborhoods and associate director for Economic Initiatives, Newark Fighting Back Partnership. He serves as the chairperson for the Newark Community Development Network, comprising all the major community-development corporations in the city. He is an executive committee member of the Newark branch of the NAACP and a former two-term member of the Newark Public Schools Advisory Board.

JAMES ARTHUR SCOTT, PhD, is a pastor emeritus at Bethany Baptist Church in Newark, New Jersey, where he served as pastor from 1963 to 2000. Rev. Scott was the eleventh pastor of the church, the oldest black Baptist church, founded in 1871, and the second-oldest black congregation in Newark. He also retired from the Rutgers University–Newark Education Department faculty in 2000. He now resides in Windham, Vermont, and serves as a guest preacher and guest lecturer at churches and universities throughout the country.

RONALD RICE, a Marine Corps veteran of the Vietnam War, has represented New Jersey's Twenty-Sixth Legislative District in the state senate since 1986. Ron is currently the state's fourth-most senior senator. Senator Rice has held a variety of significant leadership positions, including associate minority leader, assistant deputy minority leader, and assistant minority leader. He has also served as the chair of the Community and Urban Affairs Committee and as a member of the Joint Committee on the Public Schools and the Health, Human Services, and Senior Citizen Committee. Senator Rice served for sixteen years as a member of the Newark Municipal Council from 1982 to 1998 and also served the City of Newark as deputy mayor from 2002 to 2006. Senator Rice held the positons of state senator and municipal council member simultaneously, a practice that has since been banned. Senator Rice relinquished his position as deputy mayor in order to make a run for the office of mayor of the City of Newark in 1998. Sharpe James, Ken Gibson's successor as mayor in the 1986 election, was reelected for a fourth term in 1998. Senator Rice lost a second bid to be the mayor of Newark in 2006, this time losing to Cory Booker. Senator Rice received an AS degree in police science from Essex County College, a BS from John Jay College of Criminal Justice in administration and planning, and an MA from Rutgers University in criminal justice.

BARBARA KUKLA retired from her position with the *Star Ledger* in 2004. Overall, Ms. Kukla spent forty-three years as a journalist. While with the

Star Ledger, Ms. Kukla served as a general assignment reporter and as the Sunday city editor. In 1979, she created and was named editor of *Newark This Week*, a section of the newspaper focused solely on news of interest to the residents of the city of Newark. Over the years, Ms. Kukla has served on numerous boards, including The Leaguers Inc., the North Jersey Philharmonic Glee Club, and the Newark Public Schools Historical Preservation Committee. Barbara Kukla has written and published five books. She holds a BA degree in English from Bloomfield College, an MA in sociology from Rutgers University, and an honorary degree in humanities from Essex County College.

GEORGE HAMPTON spent the bulk of his youth in the city of Newark. He attended Newark public schools and obtained a degree from Rutgers University-Newark. Most of his working career has been in Newark, and he has been a continuous resident of Newark. Following graduation from college, Mr. Hampton was hired by the City of Newark to be the deputy director of the Interim Assistance Program, a program designed to duplicate in the South Ward the citywide goals of the larger Model Cities Program. In 1974, Mr. Hampton was hired by the Office of Newark Studies as the project director of a "redlining" study. His work in this regard resulted in the creation of a mortgage pool in Newark and was a forerunner to the federal Community Reinvestment Act. Mr. Hampton went on to numerous executive positions, including executive assistant to the commissioner of the New Jersey Department of Environmental Protection, director of research at the Greater Newark Urban Coalition, assistant director of long-range planning for the University of Medicine and Dentistry (UMDNJ), and vice president at the UMDNJ in charge of planning and community development.

ZACHARY "ZACK" YAMBA. When Zack Yamba stepped down as the president of Essex County College in March 2010, he had earned the distinction of being the longest-serving college president in the history of New Jersey.

Before his retirement, Dr. Yamba had been affiliated with the college for four decades, originally joining the humanities faculty when the college first opened in 1968. He served as the dean of faculty prior to his appointment as president in 1980. In March 2016, Dr. Yamba was asked by the college's board of trustees to exchange the title of president emeritus for the title of acting president. He accepted the challenge. Dr. Yamba served for more than a decade as a commissioner of the Middle States Association of Colleges and Schools, and he is a founding member of the President's Round Table, an affiliate of the National Council of Black American Affairs of the American Association of Community Colleges. He serves on the board of trustees of the Victoria Foundation, Newark Downtown Core Redevelopment Corp., and the American Conference on Diversity. Dr. Yamba earned a bachelor's degree from Seton Hall University, where he also holds the title of regent emeritus on the board of regents. Seton Hall University inducted Dr. Yamba into the university's hall of fame and awarded him an honorary degree. He also holds honorary degrees from Rutgers University and the University for Development Studies in Ghana.

LAWRENCE "LARRY" HAMM, a civil rights activist, humanitarian, and lecturer, currently serves as the chairman of the People's Organization for Progress (POP). POP is an independent grassroots political organization that is active in Newark and in northern New Jersey. Under Mr. Hamm's leadership, POP addresses issues confronting the African American community, including the struggle for quality education and employment opportunities, access to health care, and protection against racial profiling. Mr. Hamm has been a relentless advocate for African American people and the cause of human rights for more than thirty-five years. Raised in Newark, Mr. Hamm attended Newark public schools and emerged at the age of seventeen as a forceful, articulate spokesman for the educational needs and aspirations of Newark students and the community. Recognizing his unique understanding of educational needs at the time of the country's longest teachers' strike, in 1971, Mayor Ken Gibson appointed

Larry Hamm to the Newark Board of Education, making him the youngest school-board member in the United States. Mr. Hamm received a
bachelor's degree cum laude from Princeton University in 1978.

Sharpe James was elected the thirty-fifth mayor of the city of Newark in
1986, denying Ken Gibson a fifth term. James's political career began in a
similar manner to Gibson's—they were both selected to a slate of candidates endorsed by the Black and Puerto Rican Convention in 1970. Gibson
went on to be elected mayor; James went on to be elected councilman
of Newark's South Ward. James served an unprecedented five four-year
terms, including running unopposed in 1990. He declined to seek reelection for a sixth term. From June 1999 until July 2006, James simultaneously
served as the mayor of Newark and as a state senator. He declined to run
for reelection to the state senate in 2007. In 2002, James was named "Mayor
of the Year" by the New Jersey Conference of Mayors. Sharpe James earned
a BA degree in education from Montclair State University and an MA
degree in physical education from Springfield College. James completed
postgraduate studies at Washington State University, Columbia University,
and Rutgers University. He was also awarded an honorary doctor of laws
degree from Montclair State University and an honorary doctorate from
Drew University.

Alfred C. "Al" Koeppe, son of a longshoreman and the first in his family
to attend college, began his professional career as a lawyer for New Jersey
Bell in the 1970s. He earned his law degree from Seton Hall Law School and
an undergraduate degree from Rutgers University. Al spent four years in
Washington, DC, as a trial attorney in the department of justice at the time
of the famous MCI Communications Corp. and Southern Pacific anti-
trust cases. Upon his return to Newark in 1982, he became the president
and chief executive officer of New Jersey Bell, and in 2000, he became the
president and chief executive officer of PSE&G. Al also served as a director
of Horizon / Blue Shield of New Jersey, the chair of the New Jersey Higher

Education Commission and the New Jersey Chamber of Commerce, the chairman of the New Jersey Economic Development Authority, a trustee of the New Jersey Institute for Social Justice and St. Benedict's Prep School, the founding executive director of the Newark Alliance, and the cochairman, with Ken Gibson, of Mayor Ras Baraka's transition team.

SAUL FENSTER was the president of the New Jersey Institute of Technology (NJIT) from 1978 to 2002. Dr. Fenster set NJIT on a course of steady growth when, in 1979, he orchestrated the opening of NJIT's first dormitory, making NJIT a residential campus. Under Dr. Fenster's leadership, four new schools were established at NJIT: the College of Science and Liberal Arts in 1982, the School of Management in 1988, the Albert Dorman Honors College in 1994, and the Ying Wu College of Computing Sciences in 2001. Dr. Fenster received a BS from the City College of New York, an MS from Columbia University, and a PhD in mechanical engineering from the University of Michigan. Dr. Fenster is a fellow of the American Society of Mechanical Engineers and the American Society for Engineering Education.

STEVE ADUBATO JR., an Emmy Award–winning television broadcaster, author, motivational speaker, syndicated columnist, university lecturer, and native of Newark, was just thirteen years old in 1970, when Ken Gibson was elected as the first African American mayor of the city of Newark. Despite his age, Steve Jr. was keenly aware of the change signaled by Gibson's candidacy and subsequent election. Steve Jr.'s father had done the unthinkable—particularly in the eyes of his North Ward Italian neighbors. He refused to support the reelection of incumbent mayor Hugh Addonizio—a favorite son of the Italian community—in favor of supporting the African American candidate, Kenneth Gibson. Adubato Jr. is the president of Stand and Deliver, a professional development and executive coaching program he created to help professionals improve as leaders. He is also a Rutgers University visiting lecturer and a "distinguished visiting professor" at Montclair State University. Adubato Jr., the author of five books, has also been named a "distinguished visiting professor" at NYU, NJIT, and West Point. Adubato Jr. was the youngest member of the New Jersey General Assembly when elected in 1984 at the age of twenty-six. He served in that position until 1986. Adubato Jr. earned a master's degree from Rutgers University's Eagleton Institute of Politics and a doctor of philosophy degree in mass communication, also from Rutgers.

HUBERT WILLIAMS was appointed the director of the City of Newark's police department by Mayor Kenneth Gibson in 1974, having previously served on the city's police force for twelve years. He held the position of director of the police department for eleven years. Under Williams's leadership, the Newark Police Department served as the laboratory for two police-foundation studies seminal to the evolution of community policing—the Newark foot-patrol experiment and the NIJ-funded fear-reduction experiment. He later became the president of the Police Foundation. Dr. Williams is the founding president of the National Organization of Black Law Enforcement Executives (NOBLE). NOBLE's goal is to be recognized as a highly competent public-service organization that is at the forefront of providing solutions to law enforcement issues and concerns as well to the ever-changing needs of our communities. He has also served as president of the National Association of Police Relations Officers. Williams has been a leading advocate for professional standards and uniform practices in policing and has presided over the design and implementation of scientific field experiments that are the leading edge of the development of modern police policy and procedure. Williams earned a B. degree from John Jay College of Criminal Justice and a juris doctorate from Rutgers University School of Law. Williams was also a research fellow at Harvard Law School's Center for Criminal Justice, and he is a graduate of the FBI National Academy.

DAVID DENNISON served in the Gibson administration as the executive director of the Mayor's Office of Policy and Development, director of the Mayor's Office of Policy and Review, and deputy director of New-ark's combined Model Cities Program and Community Development Administration. All the foregoing operations were funded by federal dollars, providing Newark with what some have characterized as a "shadow government" operating within the confines of city hall. Dennison has also served as an urban-renewal representative for the Philadelphia Regional Office of HUD, as director of the Model Cities and Community Development Programs for the New Jersey Department of Community Affairs, as vice president and director of community investment and corporate services for the Federal Home Loan Bank of New York, as director of Washington, DC's Department of Housing and Community Development, and as manager of Tonya Inc., HUD's contracting division. From 1991 to the present day, Dennison has been the president of Dennison Associates Inc., a company he created to provide executive management and project management services to both public and private entities. Dave Dennison earned a PhD in organizational behavior from Union Institute and University, an MPA in public administration from Temple University, a BS in education from Temple University, and an AS in police science and administration from Temple University.

ROBERT C. HOLMES is currently a clinical professor of law at Rutgers Law School. He is also the deputy director of the overall clinical program and director of the Community and Transactional Lawyering Clinic. Following graduation from law school, Professor Holmes joined the Gibson administration as executive director of the Newark Housing Development and Rehabilitation Corporation (HDRC). HDRC was one of three nonprofit entities created at the behest of the city upon the recommendation of the Office of Newark Studies to supplement and expand the scope of the city's reach in meeting the needs of Newark residents. Holmes later served as executive director of the Newark Watershed Conservation and Development Corporation, another among the three nonprofit quasi-city agencies. Other positions held by Professor Holmes include assistant commissioner and interim commissioner of the New Jersey Department of Community Affairs and partner in the law firm Wilentz, Goldman and Spitzer, P.A. Professor Holmes earned a BA degree from Cornell University in 1967 and a JD degree from Harvard Law School in 1971.

HAROLD HODES, a Newark native, served on the Newark Human Rights Commission in the 1960s. He later served as an aide to Mayor Hugh Addonizio, Ken Gibson's predecessor in office. After a stint as a staff member in the New Jersey Department of Community Affairs, Harold was offered a position by Mayor Gibson as deputy director of a federally funded community-development initiative created during the Nixon administration. Harold's position in Newark under Ken Gibson quickly expanded to that of executive assistant to the mayor in charge of managing the relationship between the mayor's office and the city council. Harold later went on to become the chief of staff in Governor Brendan Byrne's administration. He also served as a senior political advisor for the Clinton/Gore presidential campaign. He has served as a visiting professor at the Eagleton Institute of Politics and at Rutgers University. He has served on the New Jersey Turnpike Authority and as a member of the Board of Trustees of Monmouth University. He has been included on the PolitickerNJ Power List and New Jersey Monthly's Top 25 Most Powerful People in New Jersey. Harold is a founding member of Public Strategies Impact LLC, one of the largest legislative advocacy organizations in New Jersey. Harold received a bachelor's degree in political science from Monmouth University.

JAMES "JACK" KRAUSKOPF has been a distinguished lecturer and director of the Center for Nonprofit Strategy and Management at Baruch College since 2004. Jack teaches and writes in the areas of public and nonprofit management, policy and administration of human services, and emergency preparedness and recovery. Before joining the faculty at Baruch, Jack was the chief program officer for the 9/11 United Services Group, administrator/commissioner of the New York City Human Resources

Administration; deputy secretary of the Wisconsin Department of Health and Social Services, deputy and acting director of the Cleveland Department of Human Resources and Economic Development, and director of a Rutgers University–based research office called the Office of Newark Studies to assist in the structuring of Mayor Kenneth Gibson's inaugural administration. Jack has also served as dean of the New School's Robert J. Milano Graduate School of Management and Urban Policy, senior vice president for administration and finance for the New School, and president of the Corporation for Supportive Housing and has been a senior fellow at the Aspen Institute in New York. Jack has a BA in government from Harvard University and an MA in public affairs from the Woodrow Wilson School of Public and International Affairs.

JON DUBIN is a tenured professor of law and associate dean for clinical education at Rutgers Law School. He has published over a dozen law-review articles, coauthored several books, and won national awards for his scholarship, public-interest lawyering, and contributions to clinical legal education. Professor Dubin received his AB degree from Dartmouth College and his JD from NYU. Professor Dubin has served as a law clerk to U.S. district judge John L. Kane Jr.; assistant counsel for the NAACP Legal Defense and Educational Fund; director of litigation for the Harlem Neighborhood Office of the Legal Aid Society, Civil Division; director of clinical programs at St. Mary's Law School; and the Marvin M. Karpatkin Fellow on the American Civil Liberties Union's national staff. In his role as assistant counsel at the NAACP Legal Defense Fund, Jon was cocounsel on a case seeking to prevent the demolition of public housing in the city of Newark called for in a 1984 public-housing master plan promulgated by the Newark Housing Authority.

FRANK ASKIN retired in 2016 after serving for fifty years as a professor of law at Rutgers Law School. A nationally known constitutional-law expert, Professor Askin founded the Rutgers Law School Constitutional Rights

Clinic and was instrumental in the creation of the overall clinical program at Rutgers Law School, one of the earliest law-school clinical programs in the nation. Professor Askin received his undergraduate degree from the City College of New York and his JD from Rutgers Law School. Professor Askin was the longest-serving General Counsel for the ACLU, and he was a member of the National Board of the ACLU for forty years. Upon his retirement, he was awarded the Rutgers Medal, and the clinical wing of the law school was renamed after him and his wife, Marilyn.

GENE VINCENTI. Before retiring in 2010, Gene Vincenti served as assistant provost and executive vice chancellor at the Newark campus of Rutgers University. In these roles, Vincenti was closely involved with the university's development plans in the city of Newark. In this regard, Vincenti interacted with city officials with the understanding that the university's expansion plans should resonate in a positive way with the city's vision for its future. Mr. Vincenti received his undergraduate degree from Rutgers University and an MBA from the Rutgers Business School. His first job following his degree work was with Rutgers University in New Brunswick, The next thirty-four years of his career were all spent working for Rutgers at the university's Newark location.

VICKIE DONALDSON, a product of the Newark public schools, was a student activist at Rutgers University–Newark and participated in the 1969 occupation of a campus building, Conklin Hall, that is today commemorated as a seminal event in the history of the university and a major expression of black student disenchantment during that period with life on a predominantly white university campus. After graduating in 1971, she worked in Newark city government for several years before obtaining a law degree from Rutgers Law School in Newark. Mayor Gibson appointed her to the Newark Board of Education in 1973, where she served one four-year term. After practicing law in Newark and the surrounding county of Essex for several years, she moved to Los Angeles, California, in early 2011 and began working in the field of community development. Donaldson returned to Newark in 2016 and is again working for city government, in the Newark Department of Health and Community Wellness as a homeless-program manager.

BRENDAN "DAN" O'FLAHERTY was born and raised in Newark. He was a teenager in the 1960s, when the city was engulfed by racially charged political battles and violence. Today, Dan is a professor of economics at Columbia University and explains his interest in issues surrounding race by saying, "I'm from Newark." O'Flaherty holds a PhD from Harvard, where he studied after working for the Gibson administration in the early 1970s. He served as an assistant to the director of the Comprehensive Employment and Training Act (CETA) program for several years. He subsequently taught at the New Jersey Institute of Technology, whose campus is in Newark, before joining the Columbia University faculty. Dan studies a wide range of urban issues, including homelessness, crime, and most recently, panhandling.

PHILIP ELBERG received his law degree from Rutgers Law School in Newark in 1970 and immediately thereafter began working in Newark. He first served as an assistant corporation counsel in the Gibson administration briefly and a few years later established a two-person partnership, Medvin and Elberg, with Alan Medvin, another Rutgers–Newark law-school graduate. Phil's entire legal career has been spent in Newark specializing in commercial law, litigation, municipal tax appeals, and medical malpractice law. Once his firm began operations, he provided legal assistance to several municipal government agencies and helped launch several major city programs and institutions. He continues to be an active participant in the life of the city.

SHEILA OLIVER joined the Gibson administration in the early days as one of the well-trained, talented young people with whom the mayor surrounded himself. After college in 1970, she interned in the mayor's office before attending Columbia University, where she earned a master's degree in planning and public affairs. She returned to Newark City Hall and joined the staff of the Mayor's Office of Employment and Training, where she remained until 1980, when she left to head a Newark community-based organization. Oliver served as a member of the Essex County Board of Chosen Freeholders from 1996 to 1999 and was elected to the New Jersey General Assembly in 2004. In 2010, she became the first African American woman chosen as assembly speaker and served until 2014. In 2017, she was elected the state's lieutenant governor, the second person to hold the position and the first African American. Governor Phil Murphy also appointed her the commissioner of the New Jersey Department of Community Affairs.

FRAN ADUBATO, a lifelong resident of Newark, has served in various community, civic, and charitable activities for many years, including as director of senior citizen services at the North Ward Center, first woman chair of the North Ward Democratic County Committee, commissioner with the Newark Housing Authority, and commissioner with the Essex County Board of Elections.

SHELDON BROSS was born and raised in Newark. He is a graduate of Weequahic High School, Rutgers University–Newark, and Rutgers Law School, where he is presently serving as an adjunct professor teaching civil trial practice. Attorney Bross has spent most of his legal career as a civil trial lawyer and was one of a small group of attorneys in New Jersey to first be recognized as a certified civil trial attorney.

VINCENTE PEREZ relocated from Puerto Rico to Newark with his family in 1982. He had been earlier exposed to Newark by way of visits with his sister, who had moved to Newark in 1968. Within a year following his arrival in Newark, Mr. Perez was engaged in civic activities, initially serving on the board of directors of the United Community Corporation, Newark's oldest community action program. He later served on the board of the Newark Arts Council, the Mayor's Commission on the Homeless, and University Heights Science Park among others. Mr. Perez earned an MPA degree from Rutgers University in 1998.

MARIE VILLANI served five terms on the Newark City Council from 1973 to 1993. She had previously completed the final year of her husband Ralph Villani's third term on the council when he became too ill to continue. Mrs. Villani was born in Newark in 1921 to first-generation Italian immigrants. For part of her youth and throughout her time on the Newark City Council, she lived in Newark's predominantly Italian North Ward. During her tenure on the Newark City Council, the council was racially divided—five white councilmen (including Mrs. Villani as the only female) and four black councilmen. Mrs. Villani's legacy on the council includes her frequent departure from voting strictly along racial lines and providing the deciding fifth vote for the black minority that often reflected the policies and vision of Ken Gibson, the city's first African American mayor.

DENNIS CHEROT came to Newark in 1965 after graduating college. He worked for the Addonizio administration and was retained by the Gibson administration. He served as an assistant business administrator during Gibson's first term and subsequently was the director of Newark's health and welfare department in the latter part of the administration's third term and throughout its fourth and final term.

CAMILLE SAVOCA GIBSON and Ken Gibson married in 2003. Camille was born and raised in Newark and attended its public schools. She worked as a secretary in Newark City Hall and became Ken's secretary after he became mayor. She was a vice president of Gibson Associates, the engineering consulting firm Ken established when he left office in 1986. In 1996, she returned to Newark City Hall as a secretary during the administration of Ken's successor, Sharpe James. When James left office in 2006, she joined the staff at city hall in Orange, New Jersey, and retired in 2009. She and Ken reside in Newark's South Ward.

JUNIUS WILLIAMS, a nationally recognized activist, attorney, musician, and educator, recently chronicled his life, including his historic work in the city of Newark in a book, *Unfinished Agenda: Urban Politics in the Era of Black Power*. Mr. Williams's impactful involvement in Newark has a number of facets:

- Before attending law school, he joined Tom Hayden and other members of Students for a Democratic Society's urban organizing project to mobilize black residents around a number of issues affecting the quality of life for black residents at the time.
- At age nineteen, he was selected to be the campaign manager for Ken Gibson's historic and successful run for mayor.
- At age twenty-six, Mayor Gibson appointed him to the position of director of the Model Cities Program.
- Following the 1967 rebellion, he formed the Newark Area Planning Association (NAPA), an organization created to develop an alternative plan for the 150 acres eyed by the New Jersey College of Medicine and Dentistry for its planned expansion.
- He unsuccessfully ran for mayor—against Ken Gibson—in 1992.
- He was the youngest president of the National Bar Association, the oldest and largest organization of black attorneys in the United States.
- He was listed as one of the "100 Most Influential Blacks in America" in *Ebony* magazine.
- He now teaches leadership and community organization at Rutgers University.

Mr. Williams received a BA degree from Amherst College and a law degree from Yale Law School.

ALAN ZALKIND currently serves as the director for the Rutgers Center for Government Services, providing training and professional development services to employees of local jurisdictions. He has also served as the executive director for the New Jersey Municipal Management Association, the professional association for municipal managers in New Jersey, since 2009. In addition, he has been the principal of Cambridge Management Associates LLC since 1998, a firm that provides management training and grant writing to nonprofit agencies. He has over thirty years of experience as a manager in the public sector and has managed the state's largest local human service agency serving thousands of children and families. He has also managed a county-level government budget office. Prior to his employment experiences with a county, he served as the director of constituent services for the City of Newark within the mayor's office. He was the former director of Newark's executive MPA and MPA programs and has taught in each of those programs. He has extensive teaching experience, having taught public administration courses at Montclair State University, Seton Hall University, and the New School. He currently teaches in the EMPA Program offered by Rutgers through its Camden campus. He has an MA, an MPA, and a MPhil, all obtained at New York University.

PATRICIA "PAT" SHEEHAN was the first woman to serve as mayor of the city of New Brunswick when she was elected in 1967. She was elected for a second term in 1970 (the same year Ken Gibson was elected mayor of the city of Newark). Pat was also the first woman to serve as commissioner of the New Jersey Department of Community Affairs when she was appointed to that position by Governor Brendan Byrne. Pat was employed by Johnson and Johnson as a compensation analyst from 1963 to 1972 and then as a corporation relations administrator from 1972 to 1974. She received her bachelor's degree in history and government from Trinity College in 1955 and later attended the Rutgers Graduate School of Education. Pat received honorary doctor of law degrees from the College of St. Elizabeth (1974), Rider College (1975), and St. Peter's College (1977).

CHARLES I. AUFFANT, ESQ., is currently a clinical professor of law at Rutgers Law School. He is also a supervising attorney in the law school's Community and Transactional Lawyering Clinic. During his illustrious career, Charlie has worked as counsel with Essex-Newark Legal Services (where he currently serves as chairman of the board of directors), and he has served as director of housing for the Urban League of Essex County, as associate counsel with the Newark Board of Education (where he was appointed commissioner of school board elections), and as part of the legal team of the University of Medicine and Dentistry of New Jersey. He currently serves as chairman of the zoning board of the City of Newark. Charlie earned an undergraduate degree from Herbert Lehman College and a law degree from Rutgers Law School–Newark.

JEROME "JERRY" C. HARRIS is the managing director of the Harris Organization LLC. He is also the vice chairman of the New Jersey Institute for Social Justice and cofounder and chairman emeritus of the New Jersey Black Issues Convention (NJBIC). Jerry is the former COO of the Shiloh Community Development Corporation, former director of the Department and Economic Development for the City of Trenton, former executive director of the Urban and Public Policy Institute at Rowan University, and former assistant secretary of state and former assistant state treasurer for the state of New Jersey. In addition, Jerry has served as the administrator for Essex County, New Jersey; city administrator for the City of Plainfield; and vice president for government affairs for the Metro Newark Chamber of Commerce. Jerry earned a BA degree and an MS degree in urban planning and policy analysis from Rutgers University.

INDEX

Page numbers in *italics* refer to tables.

Abscam sting operation, 238
Accountability and Productivity Program, 155–156
ACLU. *See* American Civil Liberties Union
Addonizio, Hugh, 6, 15–16, 34, 53, *209*; administration of, 28–29, 236–237, 278; corruption and, 24–25, 55, 152–153, 185–186; watershed and, 121, 126; white opposition to, 86, 100
Adubato, Fran, 73–75, 253–254
Adubato, Mike, 58
Adubato, Steve, Jr., 85–88, 253–254
Adubato, Steve, Sr., 71, 72, 79, 86–88, 100, 253–256; Gibson on, 230; largesse provided to, 101–102; Puerto Ricans and, 95, 102–103, 256; relationship with Gibson, 58, 73–75
affordable housing. *See* housing: affordable
African Americans: criticism of leaders, 231; health disparities and, 234; leadership by, 83, 131, 251; mobilization of, 193; political base, 16, 72–73; political class, 29, 96; stereotypes of, 197; threats against, 132

Allen, Wilbert, 174–175
American Civil Liberties Union (ACLU), 193
anchor institutions, 26–27, 79, 178, 205. *See also individual institutions*
Aneses, Ramon, 92, 252
antipoverty programs, 44, 277–278, 283n12
Aprea, Robert, 176
Armet, Daniel, 67
arson, 78, 127, 132
Arts High School, Newark, New Jersey, 144, 145
Askin, Frank, 192–196
ASPIRA Inc., 90
assimilation, 96, 251
Atlanta, Georgia, 61, 68
Atlantic, 2, 6–7
Audible Inc., 240, 282n3
Auffant, Charles, 98–99, 256

Bakke, Robert, 176
Balz, John, 39–40n80
Bamberger, Louis, 4
Bamberger Broadcasting Service, 4
Bamberger's department store, 4, 229

Baraka, Amiri (Imamu), 4, 16, 145, 187,
    192, 282n1; black nationalism and, 28,
    61, 65; Gibson on, 229–230; Kawaida
    Towers and, 43, 68, 79, 274; opposition
    to Gibson, 30, 257; political activities,
    13, 34, 105, 227; Puerto Ricans and, 23;
    school board and, 146, 272; support
    for Gibson, 33, 67, 139–140, 183
Baraka, Ras, 209, 240, 288
Barringer High School, Newark, New
    Jersey, 53
basketball, 55, 172
Bateman, Alma, 184
BCC. See Board of Concerned Citizens
Beatty, Pearl, 164
Bell, Charlie, 149
Bergen, Stanley S., 204, 206
Bierbaum, Martin, 59, 242
Bilingual Education Act of 1968, 101
Black and Puerto Rican Convention
    (1970), 35, 67, 92, 252, 257; endorse-
    ment of Gibson, 16, 70, 82, 99, 105;
    Gibson seen as betraying, 102, 103;
    goals of, 33, 99, 101
Black Liberation Army, 16
Black Lives Matter, 54
Black Muslims, 77, 284n15
black nationalism, 54, 61, 65, 187, 282n1
Black Organization of Students (BOS),
    Rutgers University–Newark, 134, 139,
    200–201
black politics, 257, 258, 283n8
black power, 38n34, 43, 53–54, 96, 98,
    114–115; movement, 13, 30, 257; at
    universities, 199
Black Power Conference (1967), 13, 99
black rage, 115
Black Student Unity Movement
    (BSUM), Rutgers University–Camden,
    139
Black United Front, 13
Bloustein, Edward, 120
Blue, Daniel, 69, 71, 233, 238
Blumrosen, Alfred, 195
Board of Concerned Citizens (BCC),
    199, 204
Bodine, Cornelius, 285n31
Bohannon, Rod, 139, 140
Boiardo, Richie "the Boot," 4, 24
Bontempo, Michael, 69, 238–239

Booker, Cory, 143, 209, 288
BOS. See Black Organization of
    Students
Bottone, Michael P. "Mickey," 71
Bowers, Arthur, 139
Boyden, Seth, 3
Bradley, Tom, 61
Branch, George, 57, 149–150, 206
Branch Brook Park, Newark, New Jersey,
    22, 64, 93, 227
Bressler, Barbara, 109
Bronx, New York City, New York, 212,
    212
Bronze Shields, 55
Bross, Sheldon, 75–77
Brown, H. Rap, 61
Brown, Joe, 199–200
Brown, Paulette, 140
Brown, Raymond A., 67
Brown, Willie, 43
Brummell, Jeanette, 130
BSUM. See Black Student Unity
    Movement
Burch, Mary, 45, 189
business administrators, 105–106, 117,
    123, 167–168, 169, 232, 278, 285n31
Business and Industrial Coordinating
    Committee, 53
business community, 137, 236, 240–241,
    246, 266–268; Newark Rebellion and,
    61; relationship with Gibson, 176–177,
    179–180, 231–232
Byrne, Brendan, 31, 61–62, 90, 130–131,
    233

cable-television franchises, 122
Cahill, William, 31, 61, 233
Callahan, James, 55
Cammarieri, Richard, 183
Campisi Family, 4, 24, 25
CAP agencies. See Community Action
    Programs
Carmichael, Stokely, 53, 61
Carrino, Anthony, 68–69, 136, 152, 226
Carrion, Sigfredo, 23
Carter, Jimmy, 31, 89, 107, 110
Cary, Dennis, 97
Casa de Don Pedro, La, 91, 181, 230
Catholic Community Services, 44
Caufield, John, 105

CDA. *See* Community Development Administration

CDBG. *See* Community Development Block Grant

CDCs. *See* Community Development Corporations

Center for Urban Policy Research, Rutgers University–Newark, 120

Central High School, Newark, New Jersey, 5, 63, 127, 172

Central Ward, Newark, New Jersey, 5, 24, 146, 192, 222; clearance of, 16; demographics of, 14, 205; housing and, 18, 241; MCP and, 201; perceived neglect of, 71–72, 269

Central Ward Democratic Committee, 43

CERC. *See* Chief Executive Review and Comment Component

CETA. *See* Comprehensive Employment and Training Act

CFUN. *See* Committee for a Unified Newark

Chambers, Julius, 220

Chambers, Walter, 53

Chaneyfield, Joseph, 184

Checker cab, 110, 246–247

CHEN. *See* Council for Higher Education in Newark

Cherot, Dennis, 122–125, 170, 261, 284n15

Chicago, Illinois, 8

Chief Executive Review and Comment Component (CERC), 173

Chunga, Adimu. *See* Hamm, Lawrence "Larry"

City Planning Division, 174–175

Civil Rights Act of 1964, 81

civil rights movement, 10–13, 282n1; activism and, 6, 18–19; black mayors and, 61; federal law and, 194; history of, 37n29; strikes and, 20; student involvement, 134, 139

civil-service rules, 51, 71, 277, 278, 280

Clark, Kenneth, 113, 135

clergy, 112, 116

Cleveland, Ohio, 11, 12–13, 30, 61, 68

Coggins, Clarence "Larry," 43, 97, 141, 170, 257–258

Columbus Homes, Newark, New Jersey, 219–221, 222

Committee Against Negro and Puerto Rican Removal, 34

Committee for a Unified Newark (CFUN), 16, 139

Community Action Programs (CAP agencies), 181

Community Choice Team, 68

community development, 88, 182, 183–185, 204, 278

Community Development Administration (CDA), 97, 98, 117, 166–168, 169–170, 278, 285n31

Community Development Block Grant (CDBG), 118, 141, 181, 269

Community Development Corporations (CDCs), 26

community organizations, 6, 55, 172, 174

Community Reinvestment Act, 202

Comprehensive Employment and Training Act (CETA), 44, 263, 269, 283n13

Congress of Racial Equality (CORE), 16, 51–54, 184, 229

Conklin Hall, Rutgers University–Newark, 139

Cook, Fred, 9, 31, 274, 276

CORE. *See* Congress of Racial Equality

Corporation for Public Broadcasting, 128

corruption, 8, 18, 24–25, 262, 281; as cause of flight, 12; factors in, 65

Council for Higher Education in Newark (CHEN), 204–205, 206

county politics, 97–98, 257

crime, 4, 267, 275–276; as cause of flight, 12; increase in, 159–161, 214–217, *215*, 244; reduction of, 234–235. *See also* arson; corruption; Mob

cronyism, 24, 55

Curtin, Pete, 145

Curvin, Robert, 16, 28–29, 51–52, 67–68, 76, 105, 243; Gibson on, 229; as mentor, 200; NCC and, 184; on Newark, 10; ONS and, 120, 134

Danzig, Lou, 15, 18, 80

Darden, Mary, 44, 45

David, Harris, 220

Davis, Malcolm, 232

DCA. *See* Department of Community
  Affairs
Del Tufo, Elizabeth, 78–81, 191
Del Tufo, Raymond, 78
Democratic Party, 74, 86, 96–97, 143–
  144, 257
Dennison, David, 140, 166–177, 249–
  250, 261, 262–263, 264, 269, 278;
  education, 284n15
Department of Community Affairs
  (DCA), 47, 131
DePodwin, Horace, 120, 136
Detroit, Michigan, 11, 12, 30
development: housing, 127, 175, 185;
  urban, 130, 175, 187; watershed and,
  120–121, 126–127, 131–133
Dinkins, David, 41–42, 289
discrimination, 49–50, 52, 195; employ-
  ment, 51, 54, 252–253, 276
Division of Youth and Family Services.
  See New Jersey Division of Youth and
  Family Services
Donaldson, Vicki, 57, 139, 147–150, 200,
  272
Douglass, Frederick, 57
dropout rate. *See under* schools
Dryden, John Fairfield, 3
Dubin, Jon, 219
Dungan, Ralph, 134
DYFS. *See* New Jersey Division of Youth
  and Family Services

East Ward, Newark, New Jersey, 71,
  269; Ironbound section, 110, 250,
  282n5
Economic Development Administration
  (EDA), 203
Economic Opportunity Act of 1964, 181,
  263, 283n11
EDA. *See* Economic Development
  Administration
Edison, Thomas, 3
education, 19–21, 270; corruption
  and, 24; higher, 27, 204, 206, 241;
  Hispanics and, 94; reform, 115–116,
  122, 135–136, 271–273, 281. *See also*
  Newark Board of Education; schools;
  universities
Educational Opportunity Fund (EOF),
  134

Education Task Force, 111, 112–114,
  115–116, 122, 135, 270–271
EEOC. See Equal Employment Opportunity Commission
Elberg, Philip, 121, 125–126
Elizabeth Avenue Community Center,
  181
employment: decline in, 211; discrimination, 51, 54, 276; of minorities,
  276–278, 280. *See also* jobs;
  unemployment
engineering, 5, 63–64, 81–82, 104, 118,
  184
Enterprise, Alabama, 5
EOF. *See* Educational Opportunity Fund
Episcopal Community Development
  Inc., 181
Equal Employment Opportunity Commission (EEOC), 195
Essex County College, Newark, New
  Jersey, 27, 189–190, 204, 206, 241
ethnic groups, 13–14, 100, 249–250, 288,
  289; commitments to, 16; favoritism
  and, 21. *See also* politicians, ethnic;
  individual ethnic groups

Faiella, Al, 176, 236
Farber, Zulima, 140
Farmer, James, 52, 53
Farrakhan, Louis, 77
Federal Housing Administration (FHA),
  11
Fenster, Saul, 188, 206
Ferguson, Clarence Clyde, 76
Ferguson, Robert, 232
FHA. *See* Federal Housing
  Administration
Fitzpatrick, Ellen, 7
Florence and John Schumann Founda-
  tion, 120
FOCUS Hispanic Center for Commu-
  nity Development, 181
Ford, Gerald, 173
Ford, Mary Mathis, 199
Ford Foundation, 75, 120, 126, 131
fraternities, 43
Friday Group, 142
Frisina, Joseph, 32
Fullilove, Helen, 57, 149–150
Fund for New Jersey, 120

funding: applications for, 171–172; federal, 15, 31–32, 89, 117, 173, 202–203,
262–263, 269, 277–278; inefficient use
of, 117–119, 165, 222–223, 263–264;
procurement of, 167; restrictions on,
44–45; state, 31–32, 117, 262–263, 278
fund-raising, 25, 54, 67, 164, 171–172

Garvin, Mildred Barry, 119, 265–266
Gary, Indiana, 11, 12, 30, 61
Gateway Center, Newark, New Jersey, 4,
36n10
GDP. *See* gross domestic product
Geller, Willard, 51
gentrification, 79, 222
ghettos, 11, 114, 198, 271
GI Bill, 11, 51
Gibson, Ann Mason, 5
Gibson, Camille Savoca, 77, 108–110,
246
Gibson, Daisy, 5
Gibson, Harold, 5, 106
Gibson, Kenneth: biography, 5–6, 81–82,
106–107; campaign promises, 28, 68,
175, 258, 280–281; challenges facing,
9–10, 17–21, 47–48, 56–59, 118–119,
150–152, 187, 218, 242; education,
5, 63; election of (1970), 16–17, 57,
139–140; election of (1974), 141;
expectations for, 33, 59, 115, 249–250,
273, 276, 279, 281; gubernatorial campaigns, 73, 142–143, 234; indictment
of, 24, 32, 69, 238–239, 248–249, 281;
influence of, 33–35, 46–47, 138, 150,
265–266; as inspiration, 41–42, 45,
60–61, 66, 288–289; leadership style,
45, 58, 79, 80–81, 82, 89, 158, 160–161,
179–180, 242–243, 244–246; legacy of,
48, 190, 239, 281–282, 287; management style, 29, 227–228, 236, 247;
negotiation and, 23, 93, 133, 245; personal qualities, 48, 62–63, 66–67, 105,
108–109, 119, 147, 158, 226, 242–243,
244–247, 289; self-assessment, 64, 125,
146, 225–239; threats against, 68–69,
152, 227, 245
Gibson, Muriel Cook, 5
Gibson, Willie, 5
Gibson administration: Addonizio appointees and, 28–29, 88–89, 122–123,

169, 237; appointments to, 62,
105–106, 115, 123, 129–130, 148–149,
161–162, 200; diversity of, 111; young
professionals in, 265–266, 280, 284n15
"Gibson for Governor" campaigns,
142–143
"Gibson University," 128, 133, 138, 140,
142, 265
Ginsburg, Ruth Bader, 195
Giuliani, Rudy, 2–3, 17
Gladys Dickinson Health Center, 130
Glenville Shootout, 13
GNUC. *See* Greater Newark Urban
Coalition
Goodwin, Doris Kearns, 7
Governor's Select Commission on Civil
Disorder (Lilley Commission), 33, 53
Great Depression, 12
Greater Newark Urban Coalition
(GNUC), 68, 202–203
Great Migration, 49, 81, 83
Great Recession, 210
Great Society, 157–158, 283n12
gross domestic product (GDP), 209, *209*,
211, 213, 214
growth, economic, 209, *209*, 211, *211*,
213, 214

Hague, Frank, 8
Hale, Mamie, 167
Hamm, Lawrence "Larry," 42, 144, 148–
149, 237–238, 247–248, 272, 284n18
Hampton, George, 196–207, 284n15
Handler, Charlie, 162
Harper's Magazine, 29, 69
Harris, Donald, 119, 122, 135, 266
Harris, Earl, 32, 68, 69, 124, 239, 249
Harris, Jerome, 138–144, 284n15
Harris, Joseph, 220
Harris, Patricia, 89, 187–188
Hatcher, Richard, 11, 30, 61
Hayden, Tom, 161, 163, 190, 192, 194
HDRC. *See* Newark Housing Develop-
ment and Rehabilitation Corporation
health services, 34, 64, 82, 123–125, 130
health system, 234, 250, 261, 262, 280
Heckel, Willard, 120, 193, 194, 229
Heningburg, Gustav, 29, 68, 105, 202,
204; Gibson on, 229; as mentor, 200
Hidalgo, Hilda, 270, 284n17

Hill, Bessie, 199, 200
Hill, Elton E., 71, 104–106, 141, 169, 242–243
Hispanic Emergency Council, 93–94
Hispanics, 18, 34–35, 64; demographics of, 90–91; after Gibson years, 182; leadership groups, 91–92, 93–94; relations with Gibson, 65, 92–93. *See also* Puerto Ricans
historic preservation, 79–80, 191
Hodes, Bill, 163
Hodes, Harold, 28–29, 88–90, 109, 233, 237, 244
Holmes, Robert, 125–126, 128–133, 245, 260–261, 284n15
Hough Riots, 13
housing, 118, 281; affordable, 22, 185; availability of, 19, 186–187; construction of, 185, 241; demolition of, 219, 220–221; Hispanics and, 94; low-income, 19, 43, 187, 221; modernization of, 222–223; police and, 108; public, 15, 18–19, 80, 183–184, 219–222; rehabilitation of, 102, 130, 175, 185; vacancy rate, 221, 222; violations, 124, 220–221
Housing and Community Development Act of 1974, 173
Housing and Urban Development. *See* U.S. Department of Housing and Urban Development
Housing Development and Rehabilitation Corporation. *See* Newark Housing Development and Rehabilitation Corporation
Housing Redevelopment Program, 187
HUD. *See* U.S. Department of Housing and Urban Development
Hughes, Richard, 34, 47, 134, 192
Humphrey, Hubert H., 81
Hutchings, Phil, 16
Hyatt, John Wesley, 3

IAP. *See* Interim Assistance Program
Imperiale, Anthony, 58, 65, 68–69, 72, 87, 141, 152, 226–227, 255, 273
income: decline in, 212–213, *212–213*, 214; inequality, 14, 214
industrialization, 3, 13
industry, as leaving cities, 11, 12, 83

infant mortality, 9; reduction of, 64, 82, 234
inflation, *209*, 209–210, 213, 267
inner cities, 11, 22, 201
Innis, Roy, 54
Inside Newark: Decline, Rebellion, and the Search for Transformation (Curvin), 52–53, 120
Interim Assistance Program (IAP), 201
International Youth Organization (IYO), 181
Italian Americans, 15, 84, 99–100, 230, 243; opinion of Gibson, 65, 74, 249, 250, 253–255; in politics, 8, 32, 33, 58, 192, 288, 289; stereotypes of, 33
IYO. *See* International Youth Organization

Jackson, Ira, 284n15
Jackson, Jesse, 143
Jackson, Maynard, 61
Jackson, Sylvia, 206
James, Sharpe, 29–30, 63, 66, 71, 109, 163, 220, 241; election of, 70, 180; opinion of Gibson, 34, 243,·255, 288
Jersey City, New Jersey, 8
Jessie, Waymon, 71
Jewish Americans, 75–76, 77, 161
jobs: equal opportunities for, 6, 52; loss of, 12; relocation to suburbs, 12, 32, 58, 267. *See also* employment
Job Training Partnership Act, 283n13
Johnson, Diane, 116–119, 263–264
Johnson, Jim, 143–144
Johnson, Lyndon B., 81, 193, 263, 277, 283nn11–12
Jones, Carol, 167
Jones, Delora, 51
Jones, LeRoi. *See* Baraka, Amiri

KAGCA. *See* Kenneth Allen Gibson Civic Association
Kaptur, Marcy, 188
Kawaida Towers, 43, 68, 79, 127, 230, 274
Kean, Thomas, 233, 289
Kearny, New Jersey, 5
Kemp, Jack, 221
Kennedy, David, 2
Kenneth Allen Gibson Civic Association (KAGCA), 71, 105

Kerr, Edward, 153, 274–275
King, Coretta Scott, 259
King, Martin Luther, Jr., 2, 52, 282n1;
  assassination of, 61, 139
King, Vivian Sanks, 139
Kinoy, Arthur, 194
Klein, Ann, 46
Klepper, Marty, 119, 266
Koch, Ed, 3
Koeppe, Al, 178–180, 244, 246
Kornegay, Mary, 164
Kramer, Pat, 88
Krauskopf, James "Jack," 119, 136;
  education, 284n15; ONS and, 125, 135,
  201, 260, 265
Kresge, Sebastian S., 4
Kretchmer Homes, Newark, New Jersey,
  219–221, 222
Kukla, Barbara, 57, 242
Ku Klux Klan, 108

labor productivity, 211, *211*
labor strikes. *See* strikes: labor
La Guardia, Fiorello, 8, 33, 288, 289
land acquisition, 21, 198
"land banking," 130
land use: patterns, 205; plans, 43, 127,
  131; regulations, 27
Latinos. *See* Hispanics; Puerto Ricans
Law Enforcement Assistance Adminis-
  tration (LEAA), 159–160, 244
LDF. *See* NAACP Legal Defense and
  Educational Fund Inc.
LEAA. *See* Law Enforcement Assistance
  Administration
lead-based paint, 124
Leaguers, 45, 189
Lefcourt, Samuel, 4
Legal Services of New Jersey (LSNJ), 220
Lester, Al, 162
Levy, Carroll, 199
Lilley Commission. *See* Governor's Se-
  lect Commission on Civil Disorder
Linder, William, 184–188, 189, 206
Lindsay, John, 109–110, 246
Lipman, Wynona, 200, 204
Lissex, Gail, 51
Local Public Works Program II (LPWII),
  202–203
Lofton, Oliver, 33, 105

Long, Lester, 53
Lordi, Joseph, 154
Los Angeles, California, 61
Lowenstein, Roger, 161–165
LPWII. *See* Local Public Works Program
  II
LSNJ. *See* Legal Services of New Jersey

MacInnes, Gordon, 120
Madison Junior High School, Newark,
  New Jersey, 76
Mafia. *See* Mob
Malafonte, Donald, 29, 89, 228
manufacturing, 12, 13; decline in, 17,
  267
Massaro, Thomas, 175, 186, 187, 284n15
mayors: African American, first genera-
  tion, 11, 28, 30–31, 37–38n32; African
  American, first-generation, 135;
  qualifications for, 225; rating of, 6, 8;
  responsibility of, 25–26; social prog-
  ress and, 61; women as, 45
Mayor's Development Team, 175–176
Mayor's High School Invitational Holi-
  day Classic basketball tournament, 172
Mayor's Office of Employment and
  Training (MOET), 44
Mayor's Planning and Development Of-
  fice (MPDO), 117, 141, 174–176, 177,
  264, 280
Mayor's Policy and Review Office
  (MPRO), 117, 173–174
MBE. *See* Minority Business Enterprise
McCall, Carl, 120
McGovern, George, 259
McGraw, Marvin, 200
McKissick, Floyd, 54
McNaughton, Donald, 232
MCP. *See* Model Cities Program
Means, Fred, 49–57, 53, 149–150
Mercer, Bill, 105
middle class: black, 44, 58, 112; flight of,
  11, 12, 32
Miles, Rufus, 264
Miller, Melville D., 220
Minority Business Enterprise (MBE),
  203
Minority Student Program (MSP), 194,
  195, 196
Mob, 74, 86, 187, 245

Model Cities Program (MCP), 29, 97, 117, 166–170; in Addonizio administration, 123; funding for, 228, 263, 269, 277–278; goals of, 173, 201, 261, 283n12; leadership of, 129, 174; youth and, 172

MOET. See Mayor's Office of Employment and Training

Moore, Bernie, 181

Moore, Terrence, 119, 121, 125, 236, 265

Morgan, Douglas, 199, 200

mortgage pool programs, 201–202

Mount Laurel doctrine, 22, 126, 132

MPDO. See Mayor's Planning and Development Office

MPRO. See Mayor's Policy and Review Office

MSA. See New York metropolitan statistical area

MSP. See Minority Student Program

Mt. Zion Baptist Church, Newark, New Jersey, 51–52

MUAs. See municipal utilities authorities

municipal council, 25–26, 151–152

municipal services, 268–269, 281

municipal utilities authorities (MUAs), 126

Murphy, Phil, 143–144

NAACP. See National Association for the Advancement of Colored People

NAACP Legal Defense and Educational Fund Inc. (LDF), 219, 224n1

NAPA. See Newark Area Planning Association

National Association for the Advancement of Colored People (NAACP), 6, 134

National Democratic Council, 97

National Teacher Examination, 51

NCC. See New Community Corporation

NCE. See New Jersey Institute of Technology

NCUP. See Newark Community Union Project

NEDC. See Newark Economic Development Corporation

Neighborhood Improvement Program, 187

neocolonialism, label of, 30, 65, 257

NERS. See Newark Employees Retirement System

NESF. See Newark Emergency Services for Families

Newark, New Jersey: assets of, 171; budget, 69, 210, 234, 268, 276, 281; demographics of, 90–91, 95, 205; depiction in press, 9–10, 17, 240, 241, 275; forms of government, 25–26; history of, 3–5, 9, 13–16; negative characterizations of, 9, 29, 197–198, 240, 241; progress of, 240–241, 279–280; public opinion of, 9, 17, 24; socioeconomics and, 208–218, 212, 267–268; state government and, 202, 204

Newark Agreements, 198–199, 204

Newark Area Planning Association (NAPA), 16

Newark Arts Council, 80

Newark Board of Education, 19–20, 56–57, 82, 145–146, 149, 247–248, 277; as appointed by mayor, 59, 138, 237; appointments to, 24, 270, 272, 273, 284n19; discrimination and, 51, 270–273; as Newark's largest employer, 148; patronage and, 57, 281; radio station, 128, 137

Newark City Council, 32, 83–85, 109, 232–233; ethnic representation, lack of, 22; opposition to Gibson, 69; racial division and, 68, 84; role of, 69

Newark Coalition for Low Income Housing, 220

Newark College of Engineering (NCE). See New Jersey Institute of Technology

Newark Community Union Project (NCUP), 192, 194

Newark Economic Development Corporation (NEDC), 177, 235, 236, 266–267

Newark Emergency Services for Families (NESF), 138, 260, 261–262, 280

Newark Employees Retirement System (NERS), 209

Newark Evening News, 55, 244, 258–259

Newark Federation of High School Student Councils, 144–145

Newark Foot Patrol Experiment, 275

New Ark Fund, 67

Newark High Impact Anti-Crime Program, 153, 157, 158–161, 243–244

Newark Housing Authority (NHA), 69, 105, 117–118, 219–223; Addonizio administration and, 187; appointments to, 220; Gibson's role in, 5, 183–184, 186; public housing and, 18, 19, 183–184; urban renewal and, 15

Newark Housing Development and Rehabilitation Corporation (HDRC), 117, 129, 175, 235, 236, 260–261, 262, 280

Newark Human Rights Commission, 71, 88, 94

Newark Industrial Corporation (NIDC), 266

Newark International Airport, 121, 176

Newark Junior Chamber of Commerce, 6

"Newark Law Commune," 161

Newark Law Department, 161–165

Newark Legal Services Corporation, 193

Newark mayoral election (1966), 6, 34, 183, 223–226

Newark mayoral election (1970), 16, 34, 67, 82, 139–140, 183, 243; campaign workers, 200, 266, 284n15; candidates, 44; corruption and, 25; optimism and, 184; threats to Gibson supporters, 78–79, 86–87, 88

Newark mayoral election (1974), 141

Newark mayoral election (1978), 32

Newark mayoral election (1982), 32

Newark mayoral election (1986), 29, 34, 70, 73, 180; negative campaigning and, 109

Newark Municipal Council, 76, 106, 146

Newark-Pequannock Watershed, 16, 21–22, 120–121, 125–127, 131–133, 238–239; management of, 18, 260, 262

Newark Police Department, 70–71, 150–157; abuses of, 192–193; African Americans in, 14, 55, 84, 107–108, 153, 157, 274–275, 280; directors of, 84, 153, 157, 274–276, 280. See also police

Newark Pre-School Council, 181

Newark Preservation and Landmarks Committee, 79

Newark Public Radio Inc., 127–128, 137–138, 241, 260, 280. See also WBGO radio station

Newark Rebellion (1967), 10, 13, 25, 98–99, 229; aftermath of, 78–79, 81, 151, 273–274; business community and, 61; causes of, 34, 192, 198, 273–274; fiscal results of, 96, 117; government response to, 134; longterm effects of, 240; political results of, 183; population loss and, 58

Newark Star Ledger, 55, 57

Newark Teachers Union (NTU), 19–20, 56

Newark Urban Coalition, 135

Newark Urban Institute, 140

Newark Watershed Conservation and Development Corporation (NWCDC), 121, 126–127, 131–132, 235, 236, 238–239, 245, 260, 262, 280

Newark YMCA, 43

New Brunswick, New Jersey, 45, 46–47

New Community Associates, Newark, New Jersey, 186

New Community Corporation (NCC), Newark, New Jersey, 26, 181, 184–185, 186–188, 206, 241

New Jersey Advisory Committee, 18

New Jersey Assembly, 42, 72

New Jersey Bell Telephone, 53

New Jersey Black Issues Convention (NJBIC), 142

New Jersey Civil Service Division, 174

New Jersey College of Medicine and Dentistry. See University of Medicine and Dentistry of New Jersey

New Jersey Department of Community Affairs, 46, 166

New Jersey Department of Environmental Protection (NJDEP), 202

New Jersey Department of Institutions and Agencies, 46

New Jersey Division of Youth and Family Services (DYFS), 135

New Jersey Education Association (NJEA), 56

New Jersey Education Reform Project, 135–136

New Jersey Institute of Technology (NJIT), Newark, New Jersey, 5, 6, 27, 63, 188, 204, 206, 241

New Jersey League of Municipalities, 46

New Jersey Performing Arts Center, Newark, New Jersey, 241

New Jersey Public Policy Research Insti-
tute (NJPPRI), 142
New Jersey Reporter, 258–259
New Jersey Supreme Court, 22, 132, 162
Newsweek, 11
New York City, New York, 8, 41, 210,
211–212, *212*
New York City Housing Authority, 98
New York metropolitan statistical area
(MSA), 211–213
New York / New Jersey Federal Regional
Council, 170–171
New York Times, 125, 274, 276; assess-
ment of Gibson, 17; depiction of
Newark, 9, 240, 241; Newark mayoral
endorsements, 32
New York Times Magazine, 275
NGOs. *See* nongovernmental
organizations
NHA. *See* Newark Housing Authority
NIDC. *See* Newark Industrial
Corporation
1967 rebellion. *See* Newark Rebellion
(1967)
Nixon, Richard, 31, 173, 261, 283n13
Nixon administration, 61, 88
NJBIC. *See* New Jersey Black Issues
Convention
NJDEP. *See* New Jersey Department of
Environmental Protection
NJEA. *See* New Jersey Education
Association
NJIT. *See* New Jersey Institute of
Technology
NJPPRI. *See* New Jersey Public Policy
Research Institute
Noll, Mark, 36–37n17
nongovernmental organizations
(NGOs), 26
nonviolence, 52, 53, 282n1
North Ward, Newark, New Jersey, 24,
73–75, 99–100; demographics of, 86,
243; gentrification of, 222; Hispanics
in, 91, 101, 181; Italian American con-
trol of, 58, 91; Kawaida Towers and, 43,
68, 79, 274; perceived favoritism, 71,
72, 269; police and, 152, 226–227, 245;
political machine, 101–103
North Ward Center, Newark, New Jersey,
75, 102

Notte, Robert, 176
NTU. *See* Newark Teachers Union
NWCDC. *See* Newark Watershed
Conservation and Development
Corporation

Obama, Barack, 231, 251, 279, 288
Office of Economic Opportunity,
283n11
Office of Newark Studies (ONS), 119–
122, 127–128, 136–138, 175; creation
of, 120, 259–260; leadership of, 119,
125, 134, 201, 259–260, 265–266;
watershed and, 126, 260
Office of Youth Services, 44
O'Flaherty, Brendan "Dan," 45, 141, 208,
267–268
Old Third Ward, Newark, New Jersey.
See Central Ward, Newark, New Jersey
Oliver, Alvin, 43
Oliver, Sheila, 42, 284n15
ONE. *See* Organization of Negro
Educators
ONS. *See* Office of Newark Studies
Organization of Negro Educators
(ONE), 51, 54–56
Osborne, Albert, 16
Ossery, Wilfred, 54
Ottenhoff, Robert, 119, 121–122, 125,
128, 137, 266
Out of the Ashes Came Hope (Linder),
184

Parker, Wilbur, 55
patronage, 29, 57, 69, 114, 149, 169, 248,
272, 277
Payment in Lieu of Taxes (PILOT), 136,
280
Payne, Donald, 42–43, 76
Payne, William, 51
Penn State University, State College,
Pennsylvania, 6, 8
Pennsylvania State Civil Service Com-
mission, 71
People's Council, 189
Pequannock Watershed. *See* Newark-
Pequannock Watershed
Perez, Vincente, 180–182
Pickett, Robert, 81–83
PILOT. *See* payment in lieu of taxes

Planned Variations Demonstration Program, 117, 173, 261, 262, 269

police: accountability of, 152, 153, 155–156; community relations and, 152, 156, 227, 273, 275, 280; corruption and, 18, 24–25, 152–154, 275; excessive force by, 150–151, 152, 154–155; excluded from events, 172; mistreatment of minorities, 22–23, 93, 150–151, 192, 253, 273–274; per capita, 216–217, *217*; at UMDNJ, 205. *See also* Newark Police Department

police brutality, 25, 53, 93–94

Police Foundation, 275

politicians, ethnic, 8, 33, 62, 96, 288, 289

population: African American, 14, 19, 43; decline in, 33, 205, 212, *212*, 213, 243; growth of, 13–14, 19; Puerto Rican, 90–91. *See also* Newark, New Jersey: demographics of

Pop Warner Citywide Football League, 72

Port Authority of New York and New Jersey, 121

Port Newark, 121

Pray, Wayne "Akbar," 4, 24

privatization, 69, 235

Proctor, Richard, 51

professional organizations, 46

"Project Rehab," 130

protests, 43, 52–53, 139, 206, 229

Prudential Insurance Company, 3, 58, 232, 235, 241

public housing. *See* housing: public

public-housing master plan, 220, 221–222

Puerto Rican Riots (1974), 18, 22–23, 93, 103, 227

Puerto Ricans, 16, 22–23, 230, 243, 249–250, 256, 284n17; demographics of, 90–91; perceived neglect by Gibson, 35, 100–103, 252–253, 270, 278, 281; political power of, 102–103. *See also* Hispanics

Puerto Rican Socialist Party, 23

Queen of Angels Catholic Church, 184, 185

Quintana, Luis, 103

Quirk, Howard, 120

racial tension, 14, 15, 17; between blacks and Hispanics, 92, 252; at government level, 182; public education and, 20; urban renewal and, 198

racism, 75–76; housing and, 18; institutional, 147; overt, 14; threats and, 78–79, 84–85, 86–87, 88, 110, 132, 254–255

Raymond Commerce Building, Newark, New Jersey, 4

rebellions, 12–13, 46, 162; claimed prevention of, 16. *See also* riots; *individual rebellions*

Redden, John, 153, 274

redlining, 11, 137, 201

Redlining Project, 201–202

Reichenstein, Harry, 163

Republican Party, 97

Reservoir Site, Newark, New Jersey, 130

revitalization, 15, 118, 134, 137, 186

Reyes, Jessica Wolpaw, 215

Rice, Ronald, 70–73, 206, 255

Richardson, George, 33, 34, 105

Rinsky, David, 176

riots, 22–23, 93, 283n12; damage claims, 162; after Gibson's 1970 election, 74. *See also* rebellions; *individual riots*

Rivera, Ramon, 23, 91, 227, 230

Roberts, Tom, 199, 200

Rodino, Peter, 177

Rodriguez, Miguel, 105

Roper, Richard, 119, 122, 125, 133–138, 139, 199, 200, 284n15

Rother, Steve, 236

Rutgers Law School, Newark, New Jersey, 193–196, *194*, *196*

Rutgers University Board of Governors, 139, 199

Rutgers University–Camden, 139

Rutgers University–Newark, 27, 76, 120, 190–192, 206; expansion of, 241; student activism, 139–140, 147, 199–201

Rutgers University–New Brunswick, 120, 139–140

Rutherford, Shirley, 43

Sachs, Barbara, 233

Samuels, Norman, 191, 206

Sanks-King, Vivian, 200

SAS. *See* Student Afro-American Society

Saunders, Don, 145
Schenck, Fred, 135
school board. *See* Newark Board of Education
schools, 113–114, 135, 148; demographics of, 54; dropout rate, 22, 33, 94, 273; funding for, 136; public, 31, 270–271. *See also* education; universities
Science Park High School, Newark, New Jersey, 206–207
Scott, James A., 111, 112, 270–271
SDS. *See* Students for a Democratic Society
Seattle, Washington, 68
Section 8 Rent Subsidy Program, 119
Section 108 Loan Guarantee Program, 118
segregation, 14, 49–50; housing and, 18, 221
Selma, Alabama, 60, 66
Senator John Heinz Award, 83
Seton Hall University School of Law, Newark, New Jersey, 27, 241
Shabazz, Kaleem, 140
Shapiro, Al, 130
Sharif, Carl, 137, 248, 284n15
Sheehan, Pat, 45
Shepherd, Samuel, 140, 284n15
Singleton, Claude, 199, 200
Sixty-Fifth Engineer Battalion, 5
Skidmore, Owings, and Merrill, 130
slums, 11; clearance of, 15, 16
Smith, Bob, 232
Smith, John, 192, 273
Smith, Zinnerford, 170
SNCC. *See* Student Nonviolent Coordinating Committee
Snell, Harrison, 139
Soaries, Deforest "Buster," 140
social services, 34, 44–45, 89, 102, 181, 182, 184
sororities, 43
Southern Rural Research Project, 60
South Side High School, Newark, New Jersey, 197
South Ward, Newark, New Jersey, 71, 201, 269
Span, Paula, 275
Spina, Dominick, 25, 153
Stavis, Morton, 193

Stella Wright Rent Strike, 18–19
Sternlieb, George, 120
Stevens, Susan, 130
Still, Timothy, 184
Stokes, Carl, 11, 30–31, 61, 62, 135, 260
Strickland, Maurice, 77
strikes: labor, 12; rent, 17, 18–19, 118; student walkouts and, 144–145; teachers', 17, 19–21, 56, 89, 135, 144–145, 237, 244–245, 270
Student Afro-American Society (SAS), Rutgers University–New Brunswick, 139
Student Nonviolent Coordinating Committee (SNCC), 16
Students for a Democratic Society (SDS), 161, 192
suburbs: flight to, 243; political power and, 96; racial makeup of, 18; relations with city, 20, 22; relocation to, 11–12, 58, 267; taxes and, 21–22; watershed and, 21–22, 127
Sullivan, Dennis, 29, 236, 266, 284n15
Sullivan, Sue, 125
Superior Court of New Jersey, 220–221
Supreme Court of New Jersey, 27

Tager, Richard "Dick," 130
Talbott, Malcolm, 120
Tapper, George, 120
tax base, 17, 213, 281; shrinking of, 234, 235
taxes, 11, 31–32, 96, 168, 281; decrease in, 209–210; payroll, 213, 276; property, 21–22, 69, 209–210, 228, 231, 276; watershed and, 121, 127, 131–132
tax-exempt properties, 21–22, 131–132, 136
teachers' strikes. *See* strikes: teachers'
Tea Party, 54
Third Ward, Newark, New Jersey. *See* Central Ward, Newark, New Jersey
Thomas, Edna, 206
Thompson, William H. "Big Bill," 8
Time, 6, 7, 8, 37n20
Tobin, Austin, 121
Treat, Robert, 3
tuberculosis, reduction of, 64, 82, 234
Tucker, Donald, 123, 142, 170, 174, 200
Tucker, Homer J., 51

Tuller, Charles, 51
Turco, Lou, 233
Turner, Irvine, 76
Twelfth Street Riot (1967), 12

Ubarry, Grizel, 90, 243, 252–253
UCC. *See* United Community Corporation
UDAG. *See* Urban Development Action Grant
UMDNJ. *See* University of Medicine and Dentistry of New Jersey
unemployment: Hispanics and, 22, 94; increase in, 83, 180, 268; rate of, 9, 14, 33, 210, 267, 268
Unfinished Agenda (Williams), 251
unions, 14, 56, 187; blacks excluded from, 20; teachers', 19–20
"United Brothers," 34
United Community Corporation (UCC), 181–182
universities, 27, 204–205, 206, 241. *See also* education: higher; *individual universities*
University Heights, 205, 206–207
University Heights Master Plan, 205–206
University of Medicine and Dentistry of New Jersey (UMDNJ), Newark, New Jersey, 27, 90, 200, 204–205, 241; conflict over, 16, 34
uprisings. *See* rebellions; riots
Urban Development Action Grant (UDAG), 187, 269
Urban League, 6
"urban removal," 141, 198, 206
urban renewal, 15, 18, 198, 206
U.S. Conference of Mayors, 171; Gibson as president of, 32, 41, 63, 89, 97; support from, 46
U.S. Department of Commerce, 176–177, 203
U.S. Department of Housing and Urban Development (HUD), 117–118, 130, 140, 186, 220–221, 223, 269
U.S. District Court of New Jersey, 221
U.S. Housing Act, 220

van der Rohe, Mies, 4
Van Fossen, Robert, 232
Victoria Foundation, 120

Villani, Marie, 83–85, 109, 254–255
Villani, Ralph, 83
Vincenti, Gene, 190–192

Wallace El Jabar Foundation. *See* Fund for New Jersey
Walls, William, 125, 161–162, 164, 175
Ward, Honey, 43, 72
War on Poverty, 193, 263, 277, 283nn11–12
Washington, Barry, 174
watershed. *See* Newark-Pequannock Watershed
WBGO radio station, 119, 121–122, 125, 127, 261–262. *See also* Newark Public Radio Inc.
Weequahic High School, Newark, New Jersey, 76
Weequahic section, Newark, New Jersey, 75
Weinglass, Len, 78, 163
Westbrooks, Dennis, 146, 269
West Milford Township, New Jersey, 132
Weston, Edward, 3
West Ward, Newark, New Jersey, 24, 71–72, 205
Wheeler, Harry, 33–34, 44, 45, 70, 105, 141
White Castle, 52, 229
"white flight," 11, 17, 62, 86, 223; effect on demographics, 91
whites: banned from CORE, 54; concerns about black mayors, 58; fear of uprisings, 14; in Gibson campaigns, 67; 266, 284n15; opposition to Gibson, 65, 86–87, 245; support for black politicians, 10–11; support for Gibson, 86–88, 100, 161, 230, 253
Williams, Hubert, 150–152, 274–276, 280, 284n15
Williams, Junius, 16, 29, 95–98, 129, 190, 200, 206; CDA and, 166–167, 170, 174, 175; criticism of Gibson, 251–252, 257–258; education, 284n15; as mayoral candidate, 32
Willis, Mary, 44
Wood, Gordon S., 2
Woodson, S. Howard, 72
WOR radio station, 4
Wright, Nathan, 13, 38n34

Wright, Willie, 184

Yamba, Zachary, 189–190, 206
Ylvisaker, Paul, 47, 120, 170, 236
Young, Coleman, 11, 30
Young, James, 191
Young Lords, 23, 91, 230

"Youth for Gibson" campaign, 87, 255
youth programs, 45, 55–56, 72, 172

Zach, Al, 176, 177
Zalkind, Alan, 157–161, 243–244
Zambrana, Franando, 270, 284n17
Zwillman, Abner "Longie," 4, 24